MODERNITY AND THE GREAT DEPRESSION

CultureAmerica

Erika Doss
Philip J. Deloria
Series Editors

Karal Ann Marling
Editor Emerita

MODERNITY AND THE GREAT DEPRESSION

THE TRANSFORMATION OF AMERICAN SOCIETY, 1930–1941

KENNETH J. BINDAS

UNIVERSITY PRESS OF KANSAS

An earlier version of parts of chapter 3 appeared in *The Civilian Conservation Corps and the Construction of the Virginia Kendall Reserve, 1933–1939* (Kent State University Press, 2013), and is used with permission.

Published by the University Press of Kansas (Lawrence, Kansas 66045), which was organized by the Kansas Board of Regents and is operated and funded by Emporia State University, Fort Hays State University, Kansas State University, Pittsburg State University, the University of Kansas, and Wichita State University.

Library of Congress Cataloging-in-Publication Data
Names: Bindas, Kenneth J.
Title: Modernity and the Great Depression : the transformation of American society, 1930–1941 / Kenneth J. Bindas.
Description: Lawrence, Kansas : University Press of Kansas, 2017. | Series: CultureAmerica | Includes bibliographical references and index.
Identifiers: LCCN 2016047591 | ISBN 9780700624003 (cloth : alk. paper) | ISBN 9780700624010 (ebook)
Subjects: LCSH: United States—Civilization—1918–1945. | Social change—United States—History—20th century. | Depressions—1929—United States. | New Deal, 1933–1939. | Civilization, Modern.
Classification: LCC E169.1 .B4974 2017 | DDC 973.916—dc23
LC record available at https://lccn.loc.gov/2016047591.

British Library Cataloguing-in-Publication Data is available.

10 9 8 7 6 5 4 3 2 1

The paper used in this publication is acid free and meets the minimum requirements of the American National Standard for Permanence of Paper for Printed Library Materials Z39.48-1992.

For Marina

CONTENTS

MODERNITY AND THE GREAT DEPRESSION

INTRODUCTION

ORDER, PLANNING, AND REASON

When Franklin D. Roosevelt became president in 1933, the country was teetering on the brink of collapse. Many people saw hope in the new president, even though he had not yet done anything. For several weeks after his March inauguration, people wrote letters and sent telegrams to the White House expressing their admiration and respect, sometimes comparing his election to a second coming of sorts.[1] Of course they knew he wasn't really the Son of God, nor did they associate his time in office as the arrival of the millennium, yet given the depth of the crisis that was the Great Depression, many people resorted to metaphors rooted in religious meaning to acknowledge the seriousness to the situation. There was in their appropriation and dissemination of this language, where terms such as faith, salvation, conversion, and a host of many more held secular meanings, a recognition that a new era and new way of thinking was necessary to confront the immediacy of the crisis and to build a better future.

Much of their usage of this language was rooted in their understanding of modernity, which held that through reason, order, and planning, a foundation for a better world could be built—a better world that was as much a feeling as a way of being. In many ways these were inseparable. Modernity offered a new way of being, and with that promise came a variety of practices and belief structures that provided hope for the future. The salvation modernists espoused was not eternal but temporal, tangible, and—for a generation with little to hold on to—practical. Oftentimes this version of modernism manifested itself in organizational structures, but in other times it came through utilizing rhetorical connections to religious understandings and ideals. In the end, modernity's emphasis on order, planning, and reason became part of the way in which people experienced the Depression era and spoke to their commitment and belief that a better world could be built upon the ruin to which they were witnesses. This does not imply that modernity substituted or replaced religion, but that the times demanded new language, new solutions, and new meanings for terms that reflected back on America's religious traditions.

Pare Lorentz's classic documentary on the Resettlement Administration, *The Plow That Broke the Plains* (1936), opens with the sounds of Virgil Thomson's religious (or at least spiritual) musical score as the film visually outlines how the country had, in a jeremiad version of the frontier thesis, sinned against the bounty provided by God in the pursuit of wealth. Once the narration begins, spoken in the fashion of a homily, the documentary details how unplanned growth and the relentless rape of natural resources had reduced the country to a shambles, challenging the very meaning of democracy and America's exceptionalism. Even the traditional symbols of American mythology—cowboy, plowman, and citizen soldier—are transformed into symbols of vanity whose mindless exploitation of the country's bounty brought about what came to be called the Great Depression, a label that is in itself an important signifier. Although the documentary dealt specifically with the ravages of the Great Plains and the ensuing Dust Bowl, to the millions of Americans who viewed the film, the connection to their own situation was clear—something had gone terribly wrong and the only solution lay in the faith that through more reasoned planning and organization, a secure future could be expected.[2]

The narrative of *The Plow* underscores the search during the Depression era for credible answers that would place human agency over that of the supernatural, while at the same time relying on the power of faith to unify ideological divisions. This required a shift in consciousness. John Dewey pointed to this change in 1934, writing how the new secular way comes with its own set of rites, communion, and collective identity, where the "temple [is] a public institution." The social modes of education, politics, economics, and culture, he argued, opened the mind to new possibilities that would benefit many while shifting consciousness away from the superstitious nature of organized religion and into the realm of a new way of being—modernism. "Here are all the elements for a religious faith that shall not be confined to sect, class, or race," he concluded, but one that "has always been implicitly the common faith of mankind. It remains to make it explicit and militant."[3]

The transition of the 1930s involved the acceptance and appropriation of modern solutions and ideas to the issues facing the nation. This process involved making modernity approachable, understandable, and nonthreatening. These three aspects came in diverse manifestations, some organized, most not, but all orbiting the belief that the present situation and the future lay firmly in the hands of human choice, and whatever world lay ahead would come from the application of reason and logic, and the belief that through planning by appropriate experts, salvation in the here and now could be achieved. *Modernity and the Great Depression* examines several significant symbolic and representational manifestations of this process to reveal an ideological shift and its larger implications for US society.

Numerous studies have explored the meaning and context of modernity during the 1930s, in everything from eugenics to literature to architecture. Coming up with a unified definition or set of terms to define modernism and modernity is a task beset with detours, dead ends, and frustration, especially when one tries to locate its meaning after the years following World War II, when scholars tried to lock down definitions for these terms and in doing so lost themselves in the ambiguity of time and space, which, of course, meant more discussion of its meaning and impact. Recent discussions among leaders in the field concerning the terms have done little to clarify the debate, but they do provide a context for understanding the meaning, application, and significance of the terms. Susan Friedman argues that as scholars continue to try to solidify a definition of the terms, the process becomes, like modernism itself, both liberating and enslaving and reflects more who is doing the defining than what is being discussed.

The disagreement between the social sciences and the humanities over what constitutes modernism imagines a sharp divide between a "specific set of historical conditions" that unite liberal social theory of the nation-state with industrial advance and individual liberation, and the "loosely affiliated movements and individuals" who in their artistic expressions break from the past in creating a new consciousness. Yet these are different ways of saying the same thing, she argues, and she lays bare "both the formation of hegemonies and their dissolution . . . [for] modernity is a term at war with itself."[4]

Daniel Singal, who has spent his career analyzing the meaning of the terms "modernity" and "modernism," suggests that "exact answers remain elusive." Oftentimes the terms are connected to modernization, which ignores the ambiguity that is at the heart of modernity, namely, the fear that the same rational designs and ideas applied to technology would somehow lead to the demise of the human spirit. To him and many others, then, modernism reflects a "pattern of beliefs and values" and "comprises a culture." Within this consciousness, which reaches its apogee during the crisis of the Depression era, those adhering to modernity were forced to recognize the "paradox" of living in a world where things may appear "chaotic" while at the same time attempting to create "order."[5] Accepting this ambiguity as part of the meaning of modernity helps better explain how critics of modernization were at the same time adherents to modernity, or how nostalgia worked as a reflective action to reconcile the past (and its failures) with the present. This allows for the interrogation of modernist manifestations during the Depression decade that accepts both the conscious break from the past and search for authenticity, and the recognition of the personal limitations imposed through rational planning, organization, and scientific methodology.

Modernity and the Great Depression places modernism in this context and also suggests that it drew, consciously or not, on American religious traditions. Modernity came to be accepted in large part due to its metaphoric, symbolic, and sometimes functional connection to existing ideologies that can be traced back to the revivalist tradition that was so prevalent in earlier times of crisis and was often connected to the Great Awakenings. The examples discussed here signal the willingness of American society to hear a call to arms for a new way of being, seeing, and discussing the possibility of solving the problems that plague the human condition. Salvation lies at the center of the promise of modernity, and its potential was espoused, accepted, and celebrated. Modernism, with its calls for a new world while retaining many of the traditional exceptionalist ideals that make it uniquely American, is at the heart of *Modernity and the Great Depression* and outlines the desire for a new road to salvation, yet another Eden.

Central to understanding this concept is the placement of the discussions concerning the definition of modernity/modernism within the specific time and space of the Depression, when the idea was governed by a unique set of circumstances that indicated a clear break from what had been "modern" before. The modernism of the 1930s in many ways developed out of the antimodernist movement of the early part of the twentieth century. The people absorbed many of the issues and critiques, especially regarding the issue of authenticity, which manifested itself in the 1930s version of modernity through their emphasis on order, planning, and reason to create their own authentic understandings, whether it be in government projects in national parks or local playgrounds, or through nostalgic music, massive expos and fairs, and even in reimagining the hearth and home. Through it all, a new modern way was being promoted, one that promised a better world for all. The 1930s witnessed what Terry Smith has labeled a "domestication of the modern," which was unlike manifestations that occurred before the great crash and after World War II.[6] Within this context, the unique circumstances of modernism/modernity cannot be defined as a single thing but as many things occurring at the same time, which necessitates an understanding of who, where, and how the term was used and understood. *Modernity and the Great Depression* will steer clear of the debates that dominated the interwar period in fields such as literature, poetry, and art, and instead focus on the replication and appropriation of modernism within American society. But we cannot separate the meaning of "modernism" from its usage, and any study of it must be located within a fixed yet circular place, for no meaning can exist outside of its location. Yet that definition must reflect the ideologies that allowed modernist consciousness to flower.

The Great Depression challenged many Americans' understanding of the role of government, economics, the workplace, gender, race, social relations—in fact, nearly every aspect of American society underwent some type of reconsideration. Order, planning, and reason: these were the touchstone ideas that both defined and drove modernity during the Depression era. Given the depth and seriousness of the crisis, people in nearly all facets of life put their faith and hope in this trinity to bring about if not a solution, at least a salve that might point to a better future. The commitment to solving the problems that led to and were part of the Depression focused on taking the best practices of the past and combining them with the new ideas brokered in the midst of the crisis. The modernism present during this time period and the examples given in this volume outline how the ideals of order, planning, and reason became an ontology that aided in the shift of consciousness in American society toward the symbolic and practical advantages of modernity.

One of the primary lenses through which to view this process is the acceptance and appropriation of the tenets of modernist thought, which in most cases involves the role and impact of scientific methodology, reason, and organizational planning on the daily lives of most citizens and how these processes project the future. The modernism/modernity that I examine borrows from a variety of sources but is best drawn from Christina Cogdell's *Eugenic Design*. She places modernity within the Depression era and locates it within the promise of salvation in the future, where "scientists, designers, corporate leaders, politicians and ministers" were joined by the vast majority of the American people to promote, "inspire, define, and create the world of tomorrow."[7] This view encapsulates the most significant aspect of modernism/modernity during the era of the 1930s, namely, to make modernity approachable, easier to accept and understand, and, finally, more relevant to the Common Man's daily life. Americans in the midst of the worst crisis of their era adopted new ways of seeing their world; they trusted and believed that these new means would offer them a solution where others had failed. Scholar Ástráedhur Eysteinsson suggests that the vagueness of the definitional characteristics of modernity/modernism allows for its utility as a lens of analysis for the twentieth century, especially as it signifies a change in consciousness. The debate about its exact definition concerns more its meaning and application, particularly as society becomes more accepting of the benefits and drawbacks of modernization, and becomes in part the definition of modernity. During the Depression era, as art historians Jeffrey L. Meikle, Christopher Wilk, Terry Smith, and others have argued, modernism became normalized to Americans, made up of, as Wilk suggests, a "loose collection of ideas" linking the present to the past and future, locating itself within the broad cosmopolitan space, replicating and, according to Meikle, "incorporating icons of the modern into one's own personal environment."[8] The domestication of modernity cannot be separated from the acceptance and proliferation of the tenets of modernization exemplified by the assembly line and the structural changes—both human and architectural—that came previous to the crash. The 1930s became a time when the meaning of modernity—not in grammatical or definitional terms but in its acceptance, application, and repetition—reached its apogee and served as the foundation for a consciousness shift.[9]

"It is a day of darkness and of light, a day of despair and hope," wrote George Richards in 1934, and "only through judgment can redemption draw nigh, God's order be vindicated, and man's noblest aspirations be attained."[10] Language like this suggested the awareness that a clear break had occurred. Indeed, when accepting the presidential nomination of the Democratic Party in 1932, Franklin Delano Roosevelt invoked this call for renewal: "Out of every crisis, every tribulation, every disaster, mankind rises with some share of greater knowledge, of higher decency, of purer purpose."[11] Earlier crises provided him and many others with extensive evidence that when social, economic, and political events shook the spirit of the country, a religious revival soon followed, or even precipitated the troubling events. When business statistician cum evangelical Roger Babson declared in 1936, after outlining the economic causes of earlier Great Awakenings, that "all signs indicate that America will soon again be swept by a spiritual revival,"[12] he echoed the sentiments of many religious leaders in the country. The collapse created an opportunity, they believed, to return to more traditional values, to distance the country from the humanist and secular ideas that seemingly led to this crisis. Both the first and second Great Awakenings were led by emerging evangelical movements and resulted in their powerful position within American Protestantism and society in general. Also, much akin to the situation of the 1930s, earlier Awakenings were heterogeneous, made up of diverse ideas concerning salvation blended into a paradigm that ensured the primacy of Christianity and encouraged a new way of thinking.[13]

Modernism's epistemology develops out of the transformations of the late nineteenth and early twentieth centuries, including the rise of industrial capitalism; the concepts of social Darwinism, the scientific method, and pragmatism; and the reformist nature of the Progressive Era, all combining to create an atmosphere in which the flowering of liberal humanitarians could blossom. This modernist ideology celebrates and endorses the positive influences of consumerism, industrial production and efficiency, scientific inquiry and application, cosmopolitanism (with a reverence for the past), and tolerance and diversity in social, economic, cultural, and political realms. These attributes define the modernism disseminated in so many varieties during the Depression era, which espoused that human initiative could and must solve the problems and issues created by humans through the application of reason, planning, and effort. Not inherently against organized religion, it advocated for human activism for human concerns and for organized religion for those things spiritual.

Modernity and the Great Depression is a study of being, an ontology, an examination of how the abstract idea of modernism became manifest, replicated, accepted, celebrated, and even worshiped in American society during the Depression era. Its occurrence during this period of economic calamity speaks to the power of its potential—traditional ideals had failed, and new ideas seemed to portend a better and more glorious future. Scholars have argued that during the 1930s, organized religions in the United States underwent a spiritual crisis and even decline. Robert Handy's seminal article from a generation ago, "American Religious Depression," argues that beginning in the 1920s (and carrying through the next fifteen years), religion in the United States suffered a crisis in spirit. For Protestantism, the tenets of modernism were simply too complicated to battle or absorb, and many denominations lost relevance to the scientific, rational, secular humanism of modernity. Even as church membership remained steady or even grew, the role and meaning of religion underwent redefinition. This "observable spiritual lethargy" challenged how Americans viewed their religious beliefs and helped lay the foundation for modernity's acceptance during the period.[14]

"It is clear we are passing through an unparalleled crisis in human history," fundamentalist minister George Richards believed, and the "day of the Lord is at hand."[15] The series of cataclysmic events that shook America to its foundations after 1929 and throughout the Depression era encouraged biblical comparisons. The country had fallen from grace for its sins against nature, it seemed, and was being punished for not following the true path of its covenant. Only through sanctification, or some ritual freeing us from our sins, could we return to the straight and narrow. Many historical accounts of the Great Depression from the crash until the arrival of FDR and the New Deal paint this dire portrait; indeed, the apocalyptical portrayal is one of the long-standing tropes of Depression-era historiography. The decline in industrial output, the collapse of financial institutions, foreclosures, farm failures, suicides, and family breakdowns all suggested that the end time had come. Herbert Hoover's lack of leadership, at least as the people came to perceive him, only reinforced this loss of hope; as Malcolm Cowley suggested, "The secure world of their childhood had fallen apart."[16]

The call for revival in the early years of the Depression era had deep roots that go back at least to the turn of the century as the effects of industrial capitalism, urbanization, immigration, communism, and of course, evolution had a cumulative effect on American society. However, as the Depression deepened, the call for spiritual revival was challenged by secular modernists, who suggested that the path to sanctification came through new ideas made necessary in light of the failure of the old. Central to their argument was the adoption of new symbols and meanings to explain the individual's place within this new world. With much the same enthusiasm afforded to religious conviction, terms such as "belief," "conversion," and "salvation" took on new meanings relating to the here and now, whether in advertising, government policy, or other aspects of the modern world. During the Depression era, it seemed that no matter where one looked, one would see a call for something new, suggesting both a break from the past and a faith in the future.

In many ways, this process held generational appeal, as the parents of what became the Baby Boom came of age and had to make economic, political, social, cultural, ideological, and even religious decisions far different from those of their parents as they faced a rapidly changing world with an increasingly uncertain future. Many Americans recognized the need for an agenda of broad social reform to challenge the status quo, echoing Dewey's sentiments when he wrote that "the only form of enduring social organization that is now possible is one in which the new forces of productivity are cooperatively controlled and used in the interest of effective liberty and the cultural development of the individuals that constitute society."[17]

Modernity and the Great Depression does not suggest that a civil religion replaced traditional faiths.[18] It is clear that during the 1930s the acceptance of those things labeled as modern, under the definitional characteristics described above, reached its apogee. Of course, this process had an antecedent tracing back to the late nineteenth century and was manifest in a variety of ways before the Depression era, but the *break* that was the Great Depression in a way forced or made it imperative that a new way of being, of thinking, of planning for the future be discussed and in many instances implemented for the betterment of all. Modernity, with its emphasis on planning, reason, and scientific methodology, played a central role in this process. In some instances it served many of the same ontological needs for its adherents and even used some of the terms linked with religion, such as faith, salvation, and belief. In other instances modernity functioned in ways that religious organizations had in the past, providing symbolic and real presentations of positive changes that could come about through practical commitment to its ideals. Oftentimes these were made manifest in institutional situations, as in government programs or large-scale celebrations that involved complex planning and encouraged general societal acceptance and approval. And still for others, modernity outlined solutions that pointed to a future that was certain and hopeful.

The role and meaning of modernism during the 1930s is therefore as complex as its multiple definitional characteristics. What this study tries to do is examine how modernism was appropriated and made acceptable during this important epoch and how this process could be linked in a variety of ways to our understanding of American society. How did some Americans come to accept and/or witness modernism as a means of salvation? Was the proliferation of modernist tenets simply a rhetorical device used to signify the changes that were omnipresent in this time of crisis? American society's ability to accept, utilize, and propagate modernism's many attributes (which defines "modernity") encouraged it to link reason and planning with progress and therefore called forth a new way of thinking and seeing the world around it. The link between progress and modernism was inescapable, for as Charles Beard wrote in 1933, they meant "that mankind, by making use of science and invention, can progressively emancipate itself from plagues, famines, and social disasters and subjugate the materials and forces of the earth to the purposes of the good life—here and now."[19] This sentiment was echoed throughout society, and incoming President Roosevelt acknowledged that "this new generation of ours stands ready to help us seek action" in order to remake American society that was languishing in the aftermath of the crash.[20] The decade of the Depression was a clear break, suggesting a new order. As cultural critic Stuart Hall has argued, "What is important are the significant *breaks*—where old lines of thought are disrupted" and new ones are "regrouped around a different set of premises and themes."[21] Unknowingly summarizing this consciousness shift, Kenneth Saunders wrote in the *Saturday Review of Literature* in 1931, "To understand the movements of our time we must have a philosophy which harmonizes the various elements of life. We cannot go anywhere [without] a compass."[22]

On June 28, 1934, FDR addressed the nation in what would become one of the regular features of his administration, the Fireside Chat. Designed as a homespun way to speak directly to the people, the presentation called up the image of a simpler time, when commonsense conversations took place around the family hearth and complex questions were broken down by basic reason and logic. The other side of this bucolic presentation involved the modern means of its dissemination—the radio and its complex interrelationship with electricity, technology, factory management, and coordinated networks. To further muddy the image, FDR delivered the speeches from the less-than-pastoral radio room in the White House (nowhere near a fireplace). Yet to many Americans it was as if the president were right there in their parlor. He used this 1934 speech to defend his administration's early efforts to stem the tide of hopelessness ravaging the American landscape and to suggest that although some critics had attacked his policies as radically different from those used by past administrations, such steps were necessary to build a better tomorrow. In order to better illustrate the situation to his listening audience, Roosevelt related how in the coming summer the White House would undergo renovations to add much-needed space and "modern electric wiring and modern plumbing and modern means of keeping the offices cool . . . [while maintaining] the simplicity and strength of the structure. . . . In the face of every modern test[,] the necessities of modern government business require constant reorganization and rebuilding." Roosevelt concluded by saying that "our new structure is a part of and a fulfillment of the old."[23] In so doing, and perhaps without knowing, the president enunciated the basic tenets to be outlined in this monograph.

Modernity and the Great Depression will explore the ways in which politics, culture, and society witnessed and participated in this transition. What role did language play in the contest for meaning and utility of the terms and ideas of "modernism" and "modernity"? How does the repetition of modernist imagery introduce and reinforce itself and inspire a greater appreciation of modern tenets? What role did specific organizations, institutional structures, and events play in exposing and promoting the social values and progressive impulses of modern society? In what ways were performances (and the many forms of their dissemination) designed to document a shared past and a unified future? These themes weave their way through each of the five chapters, whether discussing the contested definitional terrain of the terms "modernism" and "modernity" among religious and secular leaders, the role and influence of the federal government under the Roosevelt administration in the promotion of modernism through the Civilian Conservation Corps and the National Youth Administration, the six American world's fairs held during the era, or even how the writings and opinions of the nation's leading interior decorators and the advice they gave American women regarding modernity in the home and how vernacular and cultivated music resonated with its generation and harkened back to the past as it presented the salvation of the future. The decades that followed World War II would broaden the appeal of modernity to everyday life, for example, in the laying out and construction of Levittown and its suburban cohort, or the drive to land a man on the moon by the end of the 1960s. However, the convulsions of the Cold War, civil rights, Vietnam, and deindustrialization challenged the core beliefs of modernity and ushered in a new era best exemplified by the election of Ronald Reagan to the presidency in 1980.

In the end, during the Depression and lingering into the postwar era, modernity became one idea that unified the American people with a common belief that the future was theirs, both to define and capture, if only they kept the faith.

THE END OF TIMES

DEFINING MODERNITY IN THE 1930S

I

"The lexicographer of the future will have some difficulty" defining modernism, wrote William Thomas Walsh in *The Catholic World* in 1930.[1] The full effect of the market crash had yet to make itself known to most Americans, and Walsh, like many within the religious community, was more concerned that the current generation's fascination with temporal gratification would lead them from belief and salvation. To him, modernism came from a "half-breed mating of a heresy [liberal Protestantism] and a hypothesis [science]."[2] On the other hand, the liberal Christians whom Walsh and other Christian traditionalists condemned saw in modernism an ethical and responsible belief structure that blended science and the secular world with the ideals of Christianity. There were also skeptics and others who went beyond religion and advocated a secular modernism that emphasized education, reason, and organizational planning as the means to salvation.

"Modernity" comes from the word—and the idea of being—"modern," which is about the present. The past as a collection of events has only one purpose and that is to arrive at this point, whatever the time period. What made the early twentieth century unique in this regard was the proliferation of modernity throughout every aspect of society, from work to home to food to clothing to the way a person thought. To not be modern in any of these ways was to be old-fashioned. While early antimodern critics worried about the loss of individualism and authenticity, it was only later, when some of the negative aspects of being modern—Nazism, war, death, and constant replication—that intellectuals and others looked back and began to redefine modernity, modernism, and modernization. During the 1930s, if the average person on the street were asked to define modernism, they would be hard-pressed to discuss the problems associated with the replication of items or the loss of authenticity. Instead, they would answer "up-to-date," "new," or "current." In the early part of the decade, perhaps some would discuss it in terms related to religion; others, as the decade progressed, would mention the positive attributes of reason, science, and planning. The term held many meanings, but its influence was omnipresent.

The debate concerning the definitions of modern, modernism, or modernity during the Depression era underscores the power and influence of language as signifier. What one labels heretical another sees as liberating. In the years leading into the 1920s, one version of modernism as a term and idea largely existed in the cultural realm outside of the United States. Peter Gay outlines the rise and artistic understanding of modernism as a European movement bereft of definition, except for the "conviction that the untried is markedly superior to the familiar," which encouraged them to be attracted to "heresy" (in their art) and "self-scrutiny." These tenets formed the basis of the modernist movement in high (i.e., cultivated) artistic circles in Europe, especially Paris, from the mid-nineteenth century and into most of the twentieth. However, to the masses this movement seemed exclusive, vague, decadent, and detached from the reality of most people's understanding. And, for the most part, this is what modernists hoped for—a break from the past. These were outsiders, rebels with a cause, self-proclaimed liberators of the mind from the constraints of the past. They saw themselves as missionaries, in a way, of a new way of being.[3]

In the United States, this modernist movement arrived and flowered in the early twentieth century and followed the general tendencies outlined by Gay. Certainly they saw themselves as outsiders, but for reasons different from their European counterparts, primarily in relation to their desire to break from what they saw as the American Puritan tradition. Their work stressed primitivism, expertise, the exotic, and, according to historian Robert Crunden, "instead of a certain and stable universe, they saw an indeterminate and relational one." The American modernists wanted little to do with politics or society in the larger sense. They were, in the final analysis, "socially irresponsible."[4]

This initial modernist bloom ended with the US entrance into World War I in 1917, as many turned their attention to winning the war; however, the sense of artistic detachment continued into the 1920s. "The masses," historian Richard Pells writes, "plainly, were not the modernists' preferred clientele." So although their artistic impact was significant, their presence in the imagination for most Americans was limited.[5] For most citizens in the era leading into the 1930s, modernism came from one of two distinct lines: liberal Protestantism and the Social Gospel movement of the late nineteenth century, or in the modernization movement of the same period identified with Frederick Taylor's factory management techniques (best exemplified and promoted by the Ford automobile company). These two lines rarely intersected in the early part of the twentieth century, even as liberal Christians advocated the "golden rule" in the hope of influencing industrial leaders and uplifting the working class, and as factory designers and company personnel departments worked to improve their employees through tighter controls and simplified work (exemplified in the assembly line).

As the country entered the Depression, the term "modernism" held onto these signifiers, but perhaps because of the failure of industry and its association with the ideals of modernization, the religious aspect of the term dominated the discussion in the early part of the decade. With the crash and the social dislocation that came with it, many religious leaders hoped for a revival similar to those that had allowed for their churches and various denominations' expansion in earlier eras. The time was ripe for a return to God's word to put people onto the proper path. Believers needed to turn away from the world's "over-emphasis on social Christianity," Lutheran minister Frederick Knubel said as he advised his congregation in 1932 to heed "the call for a return to Reformation principles." He pointed out that during tough economic times there was a natural tendency to turn to God; however, the "bigness of material things and the bigness of man continue to control" the people's mindset even in the midst of the economic crisis.[6]

Roger Babson, statistician and former chairman of the Commission on Church Attendance of the Congregational-Christian Denominations, heralded the coming revival. "Much of the 'New Deal' legislation is merely a [cyclical] phase," he believed, designed to satisfy the immediate desires of the population, but that would not solve the problem. Only when people follow the example of Jesus—the "willingness to sacrifice"—will the country begin to prosper and grow again. His book, *A Revival Is Coming*, used statistics to predict a spiritual return to Christ. "America will again be swept by a great spiritual awakening. Nothing can stop it." He compared periods of great economic development and spiritual renewal from the first colonies through the 1920s, suggesting that every period of economic advance came with an increase in religious and spiritual commitment. The Depression era, which he traced back to the early 1920s, came from society's "ease, security, and amusement" guided by selfishness and greed at the expense of the true spiritual qualities of "sacrifice, courage, and faith." His "Prosperity-Decline-Depression-Improvement cycle" proved that "just as certain as day follows night, so religious awakenings follow periods of religious depression. The church is on the eve of its greatest period of prosperity."[7]

Yet there were considerable divisions among the faithful, resulting in extended discussion over the secularization of society and the church's changing role. Some believed modernism separated people from their faith in God and transferred it to man. "The logic of modern thought is the denial of historical Christianity," wrote Methodist minister Edwin Lewis in 1934, and unless some sort of compromise between the two ideas could be found, the schism would continue to widen. Since the latter part of the nineteenth century, this division had grown, evinced by the debate surrounding the meaning of the Social Gospel and evolution, and exacerbated by Pope Pius X's 1907 encyclical condemning modernism for all Catholics. But in America, modernism as a break from the traditions of the past was already a contested issue with a variety of Protestant denominations. This growing schism grew to include discussions concerning women's rights, prohibition, immigration, and civil rights, and it reached its popular zenith in 1925 with the Scopes trial. The stakes were high for all sides, because each believed the soul of the nation—the covenant—was at stake.[8]

"Our problem is to combine intelligence with spiritual insight, reason with piety," wrote University of Chicago theologian Edwin E. Aubrey, before the country recedes "into the barbarism of a popular passion that lacks perspective, because the learned have become the spiritual dilettanti." He echoed many who worried that the modernists, driven by their passion for scientific methodology, ignored religion and its commitment to "God in Christ." Modern science's desire to seek truth without any religious belief attached made their research and commitment to scientific method flawed because it lacked moral grounding. Man's manipulation of nature enhanced the primacy of science and reinforced the humanism of modernism leading to a reliance on man to provide solutions over those proscribed by God.[9]

These traditionalists feared that the increasingly modern society would no longer need God. Presbyterian minister John McComb denounced the followers of modernism as idolaters "worshiping a man-made God, instead of the Almighty God of the Bible." He was concerned that those who approached faith in a rational manner "destroy any system of morality."[10] Believing that all things are relative and truth mutable challenged the basic construct of faith and belief and denied the omnipotence of God, according to Allison Trice and Charles Robertson. Liberal, modern Christians viewed miracles as an "impossible" fabrication designed to convert pagans. Modernist rejections of the Bible as the "inspired word of God" left their followers empty and without a moral center: "Having no hell to fear nor heaven to gain, there is left only the deterrent forces furnished by the laws of the land, and these are so imperfectly administered that the criminal is tempted to take a chance of escaping the penalties of law." This division between God and man's law created lawlessness and a general state of fear, the authors suggested, and was supported by the theories of Freud, who encouraged promiscuity "opposed to chastity and virtue" as outlined by God. The reliance on the flesh weakened the marriage bonds and destroyed the family, ultimately leading to the destruction of society.[11]

Reverend Demetrius Zema of the Department of History at Fordham University gave a series of lectures in the fall of 1933 where he laid bare what he called "The Thoughtlessness of Modern Thought." The media had created a "deluge" of false information over the past generation to the point where it was nearly impossible to discern fact from fallacy. Modernists, religious and otherwise, denied absolute truth and based their ideas on "assumptions [which] require no thought" at all. This was because modernism "shirks definition . . . [and] moves in a twilight of half-intelligence" designed to obscure truth for the purposes of "extinguishing the very lamps which should guide men's feet amid the encircling gloom." The remainder of the lectures, on culture, science, and progress, argued that modernists perpetuated false gods and consciousness and worshiped before a "shrine in the midst of its intellectual wilderness." Their continued reverence to modern ideas during this "thoughtless period" of history would only lead to personal and societal ruin. Only absolute faith in the one true God guaranteed salvation.[12]

That connection to societal and personal decline was central to the argument of many critics who condemned modernism as heresy. William T. Walsh developed a set of modernist commandments that began with "man is an animal" and followed with a list condemning the individualistic nature of society and the prophets of the new order, such as Ibsen, Wells, Tolstoy, O'Neill, Dreiser, Twain, and Haeckel. These ideas and their proponents were responsible for leading "the youth of our day like sheep into doubt and unhappiness." The tract blamed the proliferation of the "perfidious drug" of modernism on liberals who preferred reason, which made them unhappy because there were so many unanswered questions. His advice—"if it hurts so much to think, don't do it."[13]

Zema and Walsh were not alone in their fear concerning the effect of modern ideas on the minds of the young. Many pointed to the media, scientists, and liberal Protestants for the debasement of society connected to modernity. But the center of modernist thought and influence was the nation's colleges and universities, where, according to Baptist minister Cortland Myers, professors planted the seeds of atheism among their students by making fun of the "myths and legends of the Bible." Young people were graduating without a spiritual center and were being taught that man was the center of the universe and not God. "Man has no right," he exclaimed, "to substitute his opinions for this supreme authority." Real Christians must "stand fast" against this intellectual modern onslaught.[14]

Dan Gilbert was exactly the type of young person the traditionalists spoke about. As a young university student, he was taken in by the promises of the modern prophets of progress. He soon realized the fallacies of their beliefs and published a memoir as a cautionary tale for all those tempted by the fruit of secular salvation, titled *Our Retreat from Modernism*. Although initially attracted to modernism, once he realized his mistake, he felt obliged to warn the "vast numbers of lost young people" misled by the "opiates" delivered by teachers, liberals, and Social Gospel–minded ministers at his college. Their teachings, he believed, were designed to bring God "down to earth" and to humanize Jesus as the "first socialist." Gilbert blamed those who advocated that humans were endowed by God to make the world a better place, for this meant that salvation could be man-made as the modernists remade the world in their image, not God's. This revolutionized "every branch of human activity" and worked to transform humanity to fit their modernist agenda. The false faith of reason deflated the power of God and inflated the influence of man. The modernists led their students away from traditional religion and morals and even used the religious language of the past to convert the weak-minded to their ideas.

Gilbert's tale of seduction and deceit, where the aims of the modernists were no less than the "complete negation of all the real fundamentals of life," outlined the schism between the liberal and fundamentalist wings of American Protestantism. His belief that modernists were blinded by materialism and worshiped the truth they created while ignoring the true word of God in the Bible became the dominant narrative of the religious right. By this point they concluded that the ultimate aim of the modernists was to humanize Jesus and transform the Gospels into stories about the possibility of creating a heaven here on earth. Professors promoted a distorted view of American exceptionalism to encourage their students to believe they had the power to transform the world. These young converts were told they were the new Adam, confused into believing that salvation was man-made and defined by social justice. Gilbert's jeremiad ended with a call for the renewal of traditional, fundamental Christian beliefs.[15]

Gilbert, like many others who came to be identified as fundamentalists, believed that the people of the United States had "forgotten God," and the

"The Descent of the Modernists" by E. J. Pace. First appeared in the book Seven Questions in Dispute *by William Jennings Bryan (New York: Fleming H. Revell, 1924).*

collapse of the economy in 1929 was a result of the country's "pleasure-bent and worldly-minded[ness]" for which "modernism has been largely responsible." Many fundamentalists referred to the modernists' rejection of the first and second commandments—to love and worship only the true God—as their most basic sin, for "we who cherish the truth of God's Word will shun modern liberalism."[16] Those who put their faith in man-made truths were deceived by the ideals of Satan, whose ideas encouraged modernism to be accepted by many people under the false pretense of salvation. In the "Lesson for December 4, 1938: The Sin of Lying," the *Negro Star* in Wichita, Kansas, quoted the sermon of L. D. Higley: "The first lie was told to Satan and it brought about the fall of the human race. The last lie by Satan is being told even now in the form of modernism." The lesson advised its readers to "have no part in putting forward this falsehood."[17]

There were other Christians, however, who had come to accept the modern world, advocated for a social gospel, and saw the potential for spiritual renewal in the rise of scientific methodology. They believed that ministers and their churches needed to adapt to their congregations, and to speak to the situations as they presented themselves in the here and now and not ignore the realities of modern society. These religious modernists, in some ways taking their cue from Harry Emerson Fosdick, "insisted that the deep and vital experiences of the Christian soul . . . could be carried over into the new world and understood in the light of the new knowledge." He and others within the liberal Christian wing believed their faith had to adjust to the new social ideas not only to remain relevant to their congregations but also to temper the hubris that accompanied this secular turn. Earlier Christians had weathered greater changes and did so with conviction of faith, without which the scientific modernists lack "the moral grip to lift men above the ordinary levels . . . and give them courage . . . to defy the world." Liberal Christians needed to reinforce their Social Gospel roots and stay true to their creed to recognize and discuss the realities of nationalism, capitalism, and problems of the world around them.[18]

The liberal Christian wing believed that the orthodox reliance on strict biblical interpretation ignored the reality that the faithful had, over the centuries, changed and adapted to human situations. Although they worried about losing their role as moral guides, Christians needed to engage with their world, according to Shailer Mathews, former dean of the University of Chicago School of Divinity and one of the principal organizers of the Northern Baptist Convention. Christianity's connection to "Western civilization [was] organized by the same persons who organized states, waged wars, established industries and commerce and organized scientific investigation."[19] As these people had changed so too had the nature and understanding of faith and its role in society, which made the liberalization of Christian doctrine during the 1930s historically inevitable. Changes that democratized the laity tended to increase the number of faithful and legitimized free will to its believers. The individual held the keys to the kingdom of both heaven and earth, free to choose between sin and salvation through not just sanctification but also social activism and reform. Mathews's assessment was not meant to mimic the Roman Catholic practice of good works but reflected the Christian commitment to prepare for Him the way by improving the world to better reflect the gifts of the creation. "God is to be seen in the creative process in nature and in human history," he wrote, making it possible for Christians to believe in scientific methodology "because we know that those activities we call evolution are in the universe" of God's creation. Modern Christianity reflected the most recent phase in the continued evolution of faith, and those who wished to preserve old and outdated theologies ignored the realities of belief, for it was "easier to promise salvation than to give justice. It is also easier to sway ignorant masses by fear than to direct them by reason."[20]

The core value of modernist liberal Christianity lay in its validation of "free inquiry."[21] Understanding that ignoring the world would result in the falling away of many of their younger members, many ministers worked to build socially relevant churches. They were aware that the zeal of church elders had not been transferred to the youth of the Depression era. "Many fine laymen carry forward their parents' interests," Henry Van Dusen wrote in 1931, but not their steadfast beliefs, and he labeled such people "second-hand Christians." To try to force them to follow the past revivalist "currents [that] have spent their force" was futile.[22] A survey by Professor George Betts of Northwestern University outlined how generational differences divided clergy: active ministers held fast to "ancient tenets," whereas those still in seminary "doubted or rejected" the necessity of the Apostles' Creed, Hell, or church attendance for salvation. It was clear to many that in order to speak to their congregations, ministers needed to make religion part of—not separate from—modern life. Faith had to be honest and meaningful, as well as speak to the needs of its generation, for any revival to occur.[23]

Many ministers and leaders of congregations believed in this coexistence and sought advice from experts to modify their teachings in order to better appeal to the modern world. Canadian religious philosopher

Herbert Leslie Stewart, in his excellent survey of the history and meaning of modernism within the Christian faith, outlined how to unify modernism's ability to use new methods, data, and evidence to understand the word of God. This reification could only result in bringing the faithful "nearer to its Founder's purpose, and more plainly shown to be the highest attainable truth about the meaning of life."[24] George Richards, professor of church history at the Theological Seminary of the Reformed Church in the United States, encouraged ministers to reconcile modern society with the Gospels in order "to live in the power of it in the conditions of a new time." *Beyond Fundamentalism and Modernism* (1934) made clear that Christians must accept modern science because both aspire for a better world. This sense of hope, according to Richards, came at an important juncture, for aside from the economic calamity of the Depression, the encroachment of poverty into the laboring classes invited exploitation and reduction by demagogues to mere "protoplasmic substance," creating a reaction to "stimuli over which he has no control." He worried that unless there was an alliance between science, false prophets in the guise of politicians, military leaders, scientists, or even clergy would drive society away from common fellowship. Clergy had to "put to use all inventions and discoveries as aids for the establishment of a society that will satisfy the whole life." This tolerance of science and its ethos increased the presence of God in the modern world, making His work manifest "through the evolution of the universe [and] in the consciousness of man."[25]

The religious discussion concerning modernity had effects outside the church. For example, President Roosevelt worked to bring clergy into his New Deal network, making speeches before religious bodies and regularly using biblical references. Kenneth Heineman's study of Catholics in 1930s Pittsburgh outlines the tightrope FDR walked in trying not to alienate religious leaders. He points out that the Diocese of Pittsburgh supported many of Roosevelt's programs, particularly the Civilian Conservation Corps and his efforts to legitimize collective bargaining for the betterment of their overwhelmingly working-class congregations, and certainly the Catholic press gave him more positive coverage than secular papers, yet some worried that the state's assumption of social responsibility in the guise of the New Deal made individuals less concerned about their moral responsibility to serve God.[26] FDR found appealing to clergy difficult. For example, when lay commencement speaker John Matthews advised Fordham University's graduating class in 1935 to follow FDR's programs because they matched the social justice ideals of the church, he was followed by the university president, Very Reverend Aloysius Hogan, who warned that "America today has too many modern Pilates in positions of authority and influence . . . [guided by] hidden interests."[27] Matthew Sutton has recently detailed how some within the fundamentalist and evangelical tradition believed that to "support Roosevelt was to support the coming antichrist." They were fearful that FDR's ascension would forever transform the country and its people, believing that the "nation was no longer in the hands of God's chosen people." Their reaction led to increased lobbying and political activism in the later years of the Depression decade that spilled out from the pulpit to the congregation and into the electorate.[28]

Yet, in general, America's religious leaders viewed the New Deal and Roosevelt himself in a positive light. In September 1935, in an effort to both build support for his upcoming reelection and evaluate how religious leaders viewed his efforts thus far, FDR had his staff send a form letter/questionnaire to more than 100,000 ministers, priests, and rabbis, of whom more than 30,000 would reply. The initial evaluation of the first 12,000 responses had 84 percent giving FDR and his programs a favorable review, albeit with some light criticisms. Of the final count, 58 percent gave his programs a favorable vote compared with only 21 percent unfavorable. Certain programs, such as social security, the Tennessee Valley Authority, the National Youth Administration, and the Civilian Conservation Corps, were seen more favorably. FDR closed his letter with a request for their assistance to "solve our many problems," yet many were still concerned that the increased reliance on modernism challenged the place of organized religion and put man ahead of God.[29]

The ongoing debates and divisions surrounding the meaning and import of modernism led some—such as Reinhold Niebuhr—to become skeptical. Niebuhr followed up his *Moral Man in an Immoral Society* (1932), which doubted that any real social change could take place without some element of force, with a question for the nation's religious leaders: Could

Christianity "bridge the collapse of our present civilization?" He spent much of the middle part of the decade ruminating on this idea, most cogently in *Reflections on the End of an Era* (1934), where he balanced his desire for a better world against the realities of totalitarianism. "American capitalism," he wrote, "is like a once robust man who suffers from premature senility but fails to note the critical situation" because he could buy time to obscure "the facts of his present situation." But there were real "limits of our knowledge and power," and unless a solution to the vast social inequalities inherent in the capitalist system could be found, radical alternatives from the right and left would gather force.[30]

Niebuhr's intellectual focus in the middle part of the 1930s expressed his growing skepticism that the divide between the promise of social justice and the realities of capitalism could be breached through either religion or politics. His earlier commitment to socialist Christian pacifism was tempered by his fear that it would not work in the present situation. Seeking to broaden the meaning of modernism vis-à-vis faith, he suggested that unless liberal Christians openly sided with the "victims of racial and social justice," they would lose their legitimacy, because being not quite radical enough to alter the social and economic system and not quite conservative enough to accept the existing social order meant losing any relevance at all. Only when clergy worked to "bring Christian insights to bear upon" the social and economic issues of the day and advocate for real change could a true Christian socialist consciousness emerge. Throughout his writings in the decade before the war, Niebuhr vacillates between optimism and pessimism, or what theologian Robert McAfee Brown labels his "pessimistic optimism." Although he was highly critical of capitalism, which existed "only by attempting to universalize itself but . . . can live healthily only as long as it fails to do so," making its demise "inevitable," he saw little value in those who placed too much emphasis on reason and rational solutions, for they were "unconscious of the fact that they are dreaming of such a moral world in a leisure provided by the privileges" of the very system they sought to modify. These two sides to the same mechanical universe ignored the "irrational egoism in human behavior" and were unwilling to confront the law of grace, which worked with nature and nature's history to outline the paradox of human existence: the perfection of God's love while dwelling in the futility of human imperfection. No human solution to the problem would work, as progress, defined either by the optimistic rationalists or the millennial moralists, ensured the necessary future would unfold. "A social system simply outlives its usefulness," he wrote, "and must therefore give way" to one "better fitted to organize life under new conditions." His fatalistic Marxism suggested that all great epochal change occurs when social, political, military, or economic systems face destruction; then, and only then, do humans seek the repentance that might allow them to work toward a new way of life. Past events, from the Old Testament through the Great Awakenings, proved that only when society and its people fully accepted their sins did change occur. In the era of the Great Depression, these sins were pinned to classic liberal policies rooted in Smithian individualism, which also included in its enlightened circle many of the overly secular ideals of rationalistic modernism.[31]

In 1935 Niebuhr wrote that "capitalism is breaking down in America with no effective radical movement to challenge it or offer an alternative to it." There seemed to be no place to turn; socialism, trade unionism, communism, agrarianism, radicalism—all seemed vacant to him, lost in the rush of "the futilities of Rooseveltian 'liberalism.'" Although he made a serious effort to outline some ideas that might ease the transition and perhaps even prevent the wanton destruction and war that he saw as otherwise inevitable, his skepticism prevented him from believing that Christian idealists could lead the way toward these changes, as they "live under the illusion" that their unselfish belief in justice will automatically be rewarded. They needed instead to become realists, accepting that not everyone is interested in their solutions or ideas. He chastised "eager young radical preachers in American Protestant churches" for trying to modernize their middle-class congregations. "Pure morality divides people," he wrote, making it impossible for Christians at that time to usher in a new era because "modern society is forced by the conditions introduced by the machine to return to the social ideals once held by early society." He advocated a form of "social ownership," where citizens relied on and worked in compatibility with their fellows, but he argued that it could only be accomplished through organized religious, political, and social leadership that challenged the basic assumptions of capitalism. What he called for, in essence, was a change in consciousness.[32]

The shift in understanding concerning the role of the individual within society had accelerated with the rapid advance of industrial and consumer capitalism. As Niebuhr railed against the unwillingness of his generation to accept responsibility for the injustices of capitalism, he ignored the power of secular modernism—first in the factories, then in the homes, and finally in the consciousness—to bring about this reformation. Yet it was all around him. Brinkerhoff Jackson, for example, in discussing the design and building of Rockefeller Center in New York City, pointed to the new way of seeing the world that Niebuhr hoped for. Modernist in its lack of pretension, honest in its design with a practical use of space, its relatively unassuming artifice of reliefs and ornamentation combined with the visual strategy of the uninterrupted vertical lines designed to trace the building's length created an "extraordinarily exhilarating" sense of complete freedom. The building "come[s] to an end without climax," without curves, suggesting that "everywhere a sweet reasonableness and freedom and individualism" resounds.[33]

What those who challenged modernity did not—or could not—see was that the modern world advanced a new way of life. In 1934 the Reverend James Gilkey wrote, "A new liberal religion is emerging in America today," one that would allow all of Western society to progress.[34] It was clear that modernism in the various ways in which ministers defined, attacked, or defended it had arrived. Religion underwent a significant redefinition as a result, one that sociologists label the "secularization thesis." Under this model, introduced by Max Weber and Emile Durkheim, society transferred its reliance on organized religion for things such as rewards and punishment, warfare, work, family relations, poverty, and much more to the larger society represented by government, business, and even individuals. This did not equate to a loss of religiosity, for people retained their traditional beliefs and continued to participate in their denominational services but transferred their faith in the myriad social contracts and relationships that defined their society.[35]

The hermeneutic debate over modernism among religious leaders mirrored secular society's understanding of the various ways modernity was displayed, consumed, and replicated that revealed not only its pervasiveness but also the complicated and heterogeneous nature of modernism's definition. The basic understanding in a way refers back to Peter Gay's work, where breaking with the failed ideas of the past, the need for organized planning on all levels, and an ambivalent appreciation for machine-age technology, both as a symbol of the times and as an example of efficiency and order, came to be accepted. The crises of the era demanded new ideas and actions that better assisted in solving—or at least dealing with—the problems of the Depression era. There was little unity in the religious community's definition of modernism or its affect, and, like other periods of crisis when religious ideas identified and suggested how best to reestablish the US exceptionalist position, the larger promise of modernism, which lay outside traditional religiosity, had been exposed to the people, which helped them recognize they were on the true path to salvation. Robert Handy's seminal article from the 1960s laid bare the depression that plagued organized traditional religions during the Depression era, as they were unable to adequately address the overwhelming problems of economic and social dislocation, compounded by the increased role of the state and the loss of relevance in the face of the scientific rational humanism of modernity. Even as church membership remained steady or grew, the role and place of traditional religion was challenged by an "observable spiritual lethargy," which in its way outlined the supremacy of modernity.[36]

Many people moved outside traditional spiritual solutions and saw in modernism an opportunity to build a more reasonable future. Coming into the 1920s, leaders hailed the machine age as the wave of the future. The organizational and social benefits that came with the application of new ideas and technologies, primarily in consumer goods such as food, automobiles, radio, and household items, was only the beginning of a new world order that was just around the corner. The crash and the uncertainty that followed in the early part of the 1930s challenged this optimism, but believers held fast to the notion that salvation in the here and now would come through the application of rational ideas and solutions. The spread of this new gospel and the conversion of the people necessary to make it a reality mirrored past awakenings, as the modernist evangelical spirit took on many forms and came to encompass a shift in consciousness by the time the United States entered World War II. In fact, the organization and sacrifices necessary to fight and win the war only entrenched the ideals and values of modernism, which remained fixed in the American mindset from that point forward. Of course, aspects of this commitment were present before the Depression era, and traditional religious belief continued to be a critical aspect of the American identity. However, the ideals of modernism, broadly defined, replaced the traditional church in many social, economic, and cultural issues facing the people, allowing the complex and sometimes contradictory message of modernity to become dominant.[37]

It was clear at the time that although still important, the role of the church was losing legitimacy because of the activities of the state. Samuel C. Kincheloe's analysis of religion and the Depression for the Social Science Research Council (1937) reveals that despite repeated attempts, religious enthusiasm for revival simply was not occurring.[38] Religious attendance stagnated and even declined in some denominations. Jewish and Christian leaders tried to inspire renewal in a variety of ways, including the Drive for Religious Recovery in October 1935 and the National Preaching Mission in fall 1936, sponsored by the Federal Council of Churches, but neither of these or other smaller drives seemed to work. Lloyd Cassel Douglas, rector for Saint James United Church in Montreal, recognized the inability of the traditional religions to inspire revival, based primarily on the distance that had grown between the laity and the leadership. "The house of God ought to be open twenty-four hours of the day" with religious volunteers working with whomever came in to help address their needs. The church had to recover its leadership position among the minds of the people, which could only be achieved through "doing rapidly and efficiently a large number of things," and by providing people with something that might make them "forget their workaday cares for a little while."[39] He, like many others, recognized that the people did not view the economic collapse as biblical or the wrath of an angry God, but man-made of greed, avarice, and contempt. Thus, they looked not to church or God for deliverance, but to government and other nonreligious social service agencies for social welfare services. Many hoped for a revival, but when none came the people became, as Kincheloe wrote, more secularized.[40]

The social portrait painted by Robert and Helen Lynd in *Middletown in Transition*, written a decade after their classic sociological study of 1920s America, showed a much-changed community with a "widened [gap] between" strict religious beliefs and "workaday habits." Their survey of Christian churches and their leaders outlined how the initial hope for revival in the wake of the economic collapse failed to materialize, and there was "no marked upsurge" in church attendance. Ministers from higher- and lower-class churches bemoaned the lack of revival spirit and religious belief, and according to one prominent physician, church attendance had become "a kind of automatic" routine. Even more troubling was how few young people found any relevance in the churches. As one young man told the investigators, religion had its place but not "a big place" in his life. One of the principal reasons for this shift, the Lynds pointed out, was that much of what the churches had provided in terms of assistance, housing, and education had become secularized and that church leaders saw themselves only as "spiritual agents" and not the leaders caring for the "needy." The Lundberg study of suburban Westchester County (north of New York City) found similar results. The ministers interviewed pointed out how the people in the community no longer felt that "membership in a church [was] obligatory either to save one's soul or to achieve social status." Church membership increasingly declined because people had too many other options. For those in Middletown, Sundays lost their sanctity to other activities or even work to occupy what had once been reserved for spiritual endeavors. One estimate suggested more than ten thousand residents left town every Sunday for drives in their automobiles.[41]

Several religious leaders recognized their marginalization at the expense of modernity. One minister in Middletown warned that "foolish and unlearned a man may be, ignorant to the wise conclusions of the philosophers" and people will "neglect the spiritual at the peril of their life," whereas another suggested that God meant for "man to change human society." In the end the Lynds found that the "gap between religion's verbalizing and Middletown's life has become so wide that the entire institution of religion has tended to be put on the defensive." And further, that religion had relinquished its authority of "defining of values" to the larger secular world. For those in the Westchester area, Protestant ministers complained that "the wickedness of the city," combined with all of the cultural activities it availed, led many to ignore traditional religion as they believed that they had already "inherited the earth."[42]

By the middle of the decade, many people were introduced to a variety of solutions to the problems of the day under the general moniker of modernity. Whether they first saw modernist ideals and practices in the factory or home, via advertising, or within their community, it challenged their traditional understanding of the role of organized religion, the individual, and the state, suggesting a shift in consciousness. The ideals of rational thought applied methodologically to the situations and problems of the day in order to develop efficient strategies for their solution, and to reevaluate the tenets of the past to develop less emotional responses to human interactions, served as core beliefs of modernity. These general precepts had within them many contours of their specific application, but all those who came to see in them hope for the future were committed to seeing it through. One key proponent was John Dewey. By the time of the Depression, he had fully developed his "intelligent action" thesis in which social and political change in America had to come through a rational, organized, and well-planned approach. Dewey's commitment to understanding cause and effect and dedication to liberal democratic solutions made his version of pragmatism, "experimentalism," more practical, utilitarian, and modern. For Dewey, intelligence was equated to power, and as scientific methodology laid bare the variances within nature, the same reasonable application of ideas, he wrote in 1934, "should be carried into social affairs."[43] Only when intelligence was applied did it become powerful, and society needed to integrate its assumptions into the larger system of wants and needs. Modern intelligence had to address the needs of its society, and in this way, as one biographer has written, Dewey's ideas were "contiguous with religious attitude."[44]

Dewey, already in his seventies in the 1930s, worked to lay out the parameters of his lifelong work (not knowing he would live another twenty years) on experimentalism, which helped identify his understanding of the potential of modernism. In many ways, he viewed modern intellectuals as heirs to religious clergy and the new secular theology, which was rooted in the ideal of problem solving through rational planning and reasonable experimentation. The problems of society were created by its members, not wrought by a superstitious belief in damnation, and therefore should be solved through the application of basic rational principles and ideals. In his 1933 review of *Is There a God?* by Henry N. Wieman, Douglas C. Macintosh, and Max C. Otto, Dewey challenged the authors' vision of God as "one standing in a definitely favorable relation to specifiable interests of mankind" as "totally irrelevant." Those attributes given to God were social definitions of what individuals created in their own world and through their own collective actions to define and refine their world. The expansion of possibilities (or experiences) brought about through the application of scientific methodology and a belief in the social contract formed the outline of the modernist paradigm.[45] He began to more clearly lay out this new consciousness first in *Art and Experience* (1934), where he effectively summarized his experimentalist belief structure and, according to historian Victoria Grieve, bridged the gap "between the metaphysical and social aspects" of his philosophy. Her excellent summary of this seminal work places his attitude about art within the social realm, arguing that for Dewey, the larger purpose of art and those who created it was its social function.[46]

Art and Experience served as the foundation for a more detailed examination of faith and reason. Dewey believed that salvation came from scientific method, planning, and the reasonable application of human resources. And, although he advocated for the social construction of art, in *A Common Faith*, also published in 1934, he argued that people needed to be liberated from the constraints of superstition so fundamental to organized religion. Dewey had turned away from religion in the 1890s but found no fault with those who chose to believe in God, for he understood that religion provided hope to many people. However, the constricting tendencies in religion and its doctrine denied progressive growth. Central to his argument in *A Common Faith* was that the Depression era offered a unique opportunity for "emancipation of the religious quality" that reinforced superstition in place of reason and limited the imagination of its adherents to explore solutions to the modern problems of the day.[47]

Dewey recognized that events resulting from the economic collapse challenged the definition of religion—all of society, in fact—and its meaning to the modern world. "In a distracted age like ours," he wrote, an idea that can "unify interests and energies now dispersed" is "urgently needed."[48] Dewey believed that the advancement of what he called "religious attitude"—the hope that through dedication to a higher principle a better society can be made—over the supernatural concept of religion dominated by pie-in-the-sky salvation was necessary for societal advancement. Dewey saw a clear difference between "religion" ("a special body of beliefs and practices having some kind of institutional organization, loose or tight") and "religiosity" ("attitudes" organized and directed toward a "proposed end or ideal"). In Christianity, the end or ideal relied on "religion" and the faith in things unseen or unproven, which reinforced the belief or ideal. The dependence on things not based on evidence transferred belief from the real to the metaphysical, suggesting that the way things were was beyond human comprehension. When faced with change or a complex problem of humanity, religion turned to the supernatural for explanation and solutions. The idea of "religion" encompassed what Dewey's experimentalist pragmatism argued against, which served as the foundation for modernism as a method of thought and salvation. It granted and relied on free will to address and solve problems using reason and scientific methodology. "There is but one sure road of access to the truth—the road of patient, cooperative inquiry operating by means of observation, experiment, record and controlled reflection."[49]

Dewey advocated a separation from the metaphysical dogma of religion to the methodology of intelligence open to all. This did not deny the mysteries of the universe, for these drove the human imagination toward new discoveries and theories. "The new vision," he wrote, "emerges through seeing . . . old things in new relations serving a new end which the new end aids in creating." Religion, and even the dogmatic atheism, insulated humans from each other as they worked toward some type of personal salvation. For Dewey, this denied the social responsibility of intelligence and limited rather than expanded human capability. A new era had dawned, he believed, one based on the organization of thought and action along social lines and on methodology that opened possibilities rather than a dogma that limited them.[50]

By the beginning of 1935, Dewey believed he had successfully liberated art from mystique and religion from the religious. In *Liberalism and Social*

Action (1935) he cleaved classic liberal economic and political theory from the modern liberal model, which was based on scientific methodology and organization. Dewey concisely outlined the history of liberalism beginning with its earliest application during the age of reason and its interrelationship with laissez-faire economic ideals. Although initially located within the political liberty of the individual to think and act as part of the state, liberalism soon became subordinate to the economic. The edicts of free enterprise released humankind from the constraints of the past and unleashed an era of tremendous change, but with it "an inner split in liberalism" took place. Classic liberals relished the freedom of the new age and sought government action only to protect their liberty and to maintain order.[51] As advocates of individualism—echoed in Herbert Hoover's *American Individualism* (1922)—they held firm to the belief that individual achievement came from an "equality of opportunity" where every person was free to succeed or fail based upon their "intelligence, character, ability, and ambition."[52] By the first part of the twentieth century, classic liberalism failed, Dewey believed, to adjust to the reality of modern society. Liberalism ignored the fact that many people could not progress based on simply their abilities, because they faced restrictions based on race, gender, religion, and class. Dewey chastised their romanticism, for "just at the time when the problem of social organization was most urgent all they could do was assert that intelligence is an individual possession." The modern era called for new patterns of belief, where "organized social planning . . . is now the sole method of social action." The remainder of the book outlined the tactics necessary to bring about this change of consciousness through education, economics, politics, and social relations for the "flowering of human capabilities."[53]

Central to the reformation was education. In a 1936 radio address, Dewey outlined how education could bring about positive social change. He said that his proposals were nothing but a "new version of the very same ideals that inspired the Declaration of Independence" and the foundation of the country. Just as those people constructed a society that fit their needs, "a new version is needed because of the enormous social changes" evident in modern America. Dewey criticized those who hid behind the fallacy of American traditions, which rewarded the few at the expense of the many, pointing out how history was manipulated by the likes of the Liberty League to reinforce classic individualism. Resistance to change would cause "confusion . . . [and] unnecessary human suffering," he warned. How people thought, acted, believed, worked, hoped, and dreamed needed revision, and these "preliminary changes are brought about by education."[54]

Dewey understood perhaps more than others the role and power of education, for by the 1930s he was seen as a pioneer in the field whose expertise had defined a generation of professionals. Yet he was aware that the benefits of education were not evenly distributed among the people, and although his philosophy called for inclusion, more often than not education remained exclusive. This problem could only be dealt with through the effective use of centralized planning, in this case through a federal Department of Education, whereby resources would be equally distributed among all the states and regardless of class and race. Modern society demanded an educated populace where, as he argued some forty years before, education mirrored the society. And, because other areas of society such as banking, government, and even environmental work were now emphasizing rational planning and organization, education should follow suit. Dewey believed that the nation stood at a crossroads. Down one road lay the continued reactionary policies that reinforced the status quo of inequality and division; the other road accepted education's "responsibility to shape the habits of thought and action that in turn shape organized conditions of social action."[55]

Of course, Dewey was not the first to believe—nor was he alone in this belief—that salvation could be achieved in the here and now through planning, organization, and the application of ideas to human problems. Adolph Berle and Gardiner Means argued in *The Modern Corporation and Private Property* (1932) that the form and structure of capitalism had little meaning in the modern economic world and called for more direct central planning to eliminate periods of bust after economic booms in what could be best described as state-run capitalism. Stuart Chase went one step farther in *The New Deal* (1932) by calling for the abandonment of free enterprise and the assignment of economic responsibility to experts in an organized and efficient new society.[56] Charles Beard used many of the ideas that Dewey espoused as part of his modernist discourse on progress. The time was ripe for the "use of science and invention" to "emancipate itself from plagues, famines, and social disasters" for the social good, he wrote. Humankind needed to continue to advance through the application of new ideas and techniques to old problems, move beyond the temporal notion of fatalism and the afterlife, and "develop an orderly economy which will establish security . . . and the widest possible distribution of the benefits flowing from efficient industry."[57] The progress of the machine age, philosopher Ernest Minor Patterson argued, accelerated the pace of change and revealed the incredible power of human thought; however, it also encouraged larger corporations, an unequal distribution of effects, and a higher degree of risk. The fragility of the system necessitated more active and more modern means to achieve and maintain progress, especially through better planning of the economy based on a rational understanding of the cause and effect of industrial and governmental decisions. To delay could bring disaster, for "we have already passed into an era where mere national planning is inadequate" and new methods are necessary; and although "the task is stupendous . . . the alternatives to success are horrible to contemplate."[58]

In order to provide up-to-date information to the nation's young people in high schools and colleges and their teachers, John Greenan worked with publisher McGraw-Hill to summarize for classroom distribution the *Recent Social Trends* study done in Hoover's final year in office. Greenan organized the topics under either "Problems of Our Biological Heritage" or "Problems of Our Social Heritage," each with an introduction outlining the tremendous challenges facing the nation. "Scientific discoveries and inventions," he wrote, "instigate changes, first in the economic organization and social habits which are most closely associated with them" affecting every aspect of life. By learning, studying, and understanding the facts laid out in a reasonable manner, with plenty of charts and statistics as documentation, the nation's young people could become active agents in the quest for a new world. Greenan recognized that the future of the country lay in the hands and minds of these students, for more mature Americans were likely to "cling to ideas, ideals, institutions, blindly perhaps, even when outworn . . . holding to the older and more familiar symbols."

The future belonged to the modernists who believed that through organization, planning, and the rational use of human intellect, new patterns of life and new modes of production would lead to a better world. "In the formation of these new and emergent values, in the construction of new symbols to thrill men's souls, in the contrivance of the new institutions and adaptations useful in the fulfillment of new aspirations," he hoped the information provided in his book would prove "helpful in finding a more intelligent course in the next phase of our progress."[59]

Some of the most vocal and interesting prophets of this new era were called technocrats. Begun in the early part of the century and inspired by the ideas of Thorstein Veblen and others, the technocratic movement and its ideas and influence reached its apogee in the 1930s. By the early part of the Depression era these technocrats believed, as historian William Akin argued, that the "march of science, invention, engineering, and their offspring—the machine and modern technology—possessed the potential for a material utopia." They created the Committee on Technocracy at Columbia University and, led by Walter Rautenstrauch and Howard Scott, advanced the belief that through efficient and organized planning, the issues that caused the economic downturn could be reversed and made to benefit society.[60] Stuart Chase's *Technocracy* (1933) saw it as a "prophecy" that "hinted at a blue print of a possible new society" controlled by technicians made up of engineers and other scientists who would direct and plan the economy to better distribute the innumerable resources that came with modernism. However, the technocrats faced opposition on numerous fronts as they challenged traditional beliefs regarding wealth, energy, and the existing structure of society. Although Chase was not an avid convert, he did hold with many of their proposals.[61]

One of the more interesting advocates of this idea, although he was not a member of the organization, was Lewis Mumford. By the time he published *Technics and Civilization* (1934), he had already garnered a reputation for being an advocate of modernism in its more secular application. With this book, however, he laid out more plainly his understanding of not only the legacy of machines but also their potential to transform and redeem humanity, in much the same way that the technocrats had. The work reads like a sermon for modernity, a homily for the future when "men will be back once more in the Edenlike state . . . [and] the ritual of leisure will replace the ritual of work." This would only come if American society could reorient its consciousness to accept the benefits that the history of technics outline and promise.[62]

Mumford traced the ascendency of modernity to the current generation by dividing its history into three "waves" beginning in the tenth century and continuing into the Depression era. He did not deify the machine or its contributions or imagine its omnipotence, but instead placed the power and meaning of modernity in the hands of humanity. The machine and its attributes of order, efficiency, and reason were value neutral and only operated under the command of humans. The potential of the machine as modernity had yet to peak, necessitating the work to strengthen its "contemporary transvaluation." He began by outlining the basic foundations for the modern transformations, linking developments such as breaking down time into units of measurement abstract of human intent, the rise of capitalism as an unintended spur to the modern transformation, Protestantism's refocus on the here and now, and the changing identity of nature into something that needed "to be explored, to be invaded, to be conquered, and finally, to be understood." Science, of course, played a central role in this process, as it moved from superstitious sorcery to empirical reasoning, liberating humans from the fear of their own choices. People could now adapt and control virtually every situation by applying the basic principles of experimentation, invention, demonstration, and reason. The superstition of the afterlife gave way to the temporal; "mechanics became the new religion, and it gave to the world a new Messiah: the machine."[63]

Mumford labels the three phases of this evolution as the *eotechnic*, *paleotechnic*, and *neotechnic*. In the initial phase, the mastery of wind, water, wood, and glass allowed humanity to welcome "the dawn of modern technics." One of the keys to the success of this age lay in the proliferation of the written word. The book not only standardized aspects of language and communication but also unleashed the redemptive power of discovery and invention to transform the world. The next phase expanded and ultimately exploited these potentials, improving iron and steam power in an era when "the reek of coal was the very incense of the new industrialism."

However, the promise of salvation was usurped by the greed of individual capitalists and, in language and imagery very similar to Pare Lorentz's 1936 Farm Security Administration documentary *The Plow That Broke the Plains*, ushered in an age when "mankind behaved like a drunken heir on a spree." This was an era permeated by fear and war and a search for order. The final stage was still developing. Driven by new sources of power—electricity, oil, and the internal combustion engine—that had radical effects throughout society, the "maggoty corpse" of the earlier period was stymieing the full liberating potential of the new era. All aspects of society were affected by science, not just industry, and "the sense of order became much more pervasive and fundamental." Principles that governed machine inventions were now applied to human problems, and economic planning, urban renewal, and rational solutions to social problems hinted at a promised land. However, "the bankers, the business men, and the politicians" threatened to stall the acceptance of this new way of life in order to protect their position and influence in society.[64]

The second part of *Technics and Civilization*, as Mumford described it twenty-five years later, outlined how these changes were accepted and utilized by society as "a religion, rather than as a means of satisfying human wants."[65] By applying the ideals of uniformity, standardization, and rational planning to all aspects of society, a more equal and balanced society could emerge, and humankind would fully enter the neotechnic age. The machine, or the idea of it, that was so central to modernity could not provide this salvation, for its ambivalence made it neutral. Only with the enlightened application of the modern promise could the full benefit of the new era be felt. The universe was no longer mysterious but knowable through reason: "That a part of the order of the universe was a contribution by man himself, that the limitations imposed upon scientific research by human instruments and interests tend to produce an orderly and mathematically analyzable result, does not lessen the wonder and beauty of the system: it rather gives to the conception of the universe itself some of the character of a work of art." Nature, God, and the universe were constructs of humanity utilized and organized for the betterment of all. The economy of the machine aped the efficiency of the universe as humankind accepted the moral implications of its actions—increased standardization and the elimination of social distinctions. In his final chapter, "Orientation," Mumford challenges his readers to not simply use the language of the machine to exploit and enslave, making the machine the religion, for it was a mere artifact created by humans. It was the acceptance of the *idea* of modernity that promised salvation. The form was less significant than the function, for the assurance of a better world came not from the machine but from humanity itself. The promise of modernity rested within individuals to transform themselves and their world by using reason and logic to better plan, organize, and construct a society where the production of all benefits all.[66]

During the Depression era, the words "modernism" and "modernity" took on many connotations and were discussed by a variety of intellectuals. These contested meanings surrounded the issue of human versus spiritual agency and the division between the solutions posed by traditional religions and scientific methodology. In the early part of the decade, the discussion seemed to carry over from the religious debates of the late nineteenth century within Catholic and Protestant churches over the unity of science with faith. By the middle of the 1930s, the discussion gave way to more secular applications as the divide within Christianity widened. Camps were defined, positions hardened, and any chance of a synod to hammer out a compromise disappeared, to a large degree because of the ascendancy of the secular reformation. For fundamentalists, modernism was a falling away from traditional beliefs of the past that took the people down a road of secular ideology fraught with, at best, temptation or, worse, damnation. To liberal Protestants, modernism meant a commitment to organization, methodology, and reason that would allow for the full flowering of humanity and the eventual elimination—or at least moderation—of social, economic, and political evils. "Man is a part of nature and we must redefine nature in a way that includes man and all his gifts and values," wrote the editors of the *Christian Century*.[67]

Yet their differences also reveal their unity with regard to modernism and its acceptance during the Depression era. Frederic Jameson argues that the tenets and language of theologians writing in the modern era share the same sense of "otherness" with nonreligious moderns: both saw themselves as separate from the past and "somehow distinct from all other human beings who ever lived in the past."[68] That they railed against the tendencies of modern capitalist society and sought to use scripture and a call for more traditional values only reinforced their modernness, for they used the very hermeneutic devices as those they believed were responsible for destroying society. These religious leaders saw their situation as unique, even though in the history of religious thought the onslaught of new ideas has been a constant. And for the moderns, the fodder for their attack of the society was an outgrowth of the machine-age tendencies toward increased organization and efficiency, of which, on the surface, they did not disapprove. But much of their animosity arose from the isolation and alienation that came with modernization and the enjoined secular awakening. New symbols, modern iconographic representations of a more reasonable future, challenged the language and identity of the traditional religions, creating a tension both within their denominations and in the larger society that gave form to the idea of modernism as the agent of a new era of salvation. The normalization of modernism, which at its core is modernity, and all of its multiple replications throughout society, which served both advocates and critics, speaks to its acceptance. Modernism became the new consciousness rooted, not unlike earlier religions, in conflict, division, and debate about its utility for salvation.[69]

Modernism promised a new world, a place created by humans for the benefit of the people. This new belief presented itself in a variety of ways, as the chapters to follow will delineate, as the Depression-era modernism asked people to put their faith in reason, to believe that through free will they could and would build a better place, a more equal place to finally fulfill the covenant of America's destiny.

A NEW MODEL ARMY

THE CIVILIAN CONSERVATION CORPS, THE NATIONAL YOUTH ADMINISTRATION, AND MODERNITY

2

Franklin D. Roosevelt's first inaugural address sounded more like a sermon than a speech. His election came at a time of unimaginable national trauma where every social and economic indicator pointed to a country and its people near the end of their rope. The future seemed perilously on the brink of . . . well, no one knew for certain. FDR pulled no punches in the speech, outlining how events of the past had weakened the country and how the people, the president included, had to adopt new ways of understanding government, banking, business, and even citizenship. Using biblical metaphors such as "we are stricken by no plague of locusts" and "the money changers have fled from their high seats in the temple of our civilization," the newly elected president called on the people to put behind them the evil ways of "a generation of self-seekers" and spread the good news of organization, planning, and regulation so that all may understand that "our true destiny is not to be ministered unto but to minister to ourselves and to our fellow men."[1]

This gospel of modern government, which promised to put people to work, better plan and organize natural resources for the benefit of all, and control the negative effects of security and banking speculation, formed the core of what Roosevelt called his "New Deal." Even the naming of his program suggested a break from the past and echoed the sentiments of modernism. He did not stop with just policies, though; in other speeches, he advocated that people take their cars and travel the country and talk with their fellow citizens so that they might better understand the diversity of America and the need for policies that advocated inclusion and a better social and economic system for future generations. This new American dream would be a covenant between the government of the people, the people themselves, and the prosperity brought about through the cooperation and willingness of business leaders and labor. If everyone pulled together, he intoned again and again in his radio speeches and public appearances, a new day would dawn for the United States.[2]

Central to this new day was getting people to work and by association turning them into emissaries of the New Deal. From the start, FDR's critics argued that the programs were self-serving promotions of his New Deal and the Democratic Party, but they ignored that these programs, both by their actual work and service, and by the sheer numbers of people involved and their activities, pointed to a new order of things and the potential salvation that could come through applying modernist ideals of planning and organization to the structure and meaning of society. Specifically, the new administration knew it had to address the needs of the nation's young people, proving to them that the New Deal and its new, modern approach to work, government, and organization would help usher in a new age of prosperity. Through their activities and the examples they set, the young people in the Civilian Conservation Corps (CCC) and the National Youth Administration (NYA) became symbols of the positive attributes of modernity, what FDR called his "shock troops of the social conscience."[3]

To develop this symbolic new model army, the New Deal needed to attract and retain new members, as well as train them in modernism's key concepts and beliefs. Recruitment and education helped maintain order and stability, and promised that through an acceptance of the basic beliefs, a shared future of hope awaited the nation. Both the CCC and NYA actively recruited marginalized young people not yet cognizant of the advantages of modernism and, through their practical lessons, educational opportunities, and basic hard work, introduced them to its advantages. This conversion experience meant first getting the recruit to commit to the group's belief structure, after which a more practical and focused experience, through work and education, reinforced the basic ideology. Putting the young men into unique situations, some organized, others not, allowed the CCC and the NYA to help young recruits apply what they had learned to their families, friends, local communities, and the greater society. They were encouraged in their training and activities to develop relationships, like brother- or sisterhoods, which would carry them from their indoctrination and remain with them for the rest of their lives.[4] They would use their experiences to inform others of the positive benefits of modernism, whether they came through teaching new skills as part of the NYA, creating natural recreation areas through the CCC, or simply by going back home to their neighborhoods and detailing the positive ideals of modern thought they themselves only recently came to understand. The key to the process lay in their ages.

During the Depression, youth were targeted as at risk from a society that offered little hope. As Percy Hayward, the director of young people's work for the International Council of Religious Education, warned in 1930, because of the precipitous drop in activism between "the mature men and women of the church and that of their own children," young people faced an uncertain future dominated by prolonged unemployment, delinquency, and general antisocial behavior. First Lady Eleanor Roosevelt, whose voice the president listened to very closely, worried that the country was on the verge of "losing this generation" and joined others in calling for the federal government to step in and assist the nation's young people. That the government's desires were linked to modernism comes as little surprise, given that the CCC, NYA, and other New Deal agencies shared modernist tendencies, including common goals and norms (planning), the need for collective identity (reason), and a hierarchical system to which the individual feels an affinity (order). This modernist social phenomenon allowed the recruits to go out into their communities to spread the positive message of modernist thought and practice. The CCC and NYA's message of organization, planning, and hard work pointed to a great and better future and asked its recruits to make individual sacrifices for the betterment of all.[5]

The salvation of the nation's youth became a priority of the New Deal and FDR. Fewer than four weeks after he delivered his first inaugural address, FDR announced his commitment with Executive Order #6101, creating the Civilian Conservation Corps as a vehicle "for the relief of unemployment through the performance of useful public work." A comma in the original text seems to set the CCC apart as the order continues, "for other useful purposes."[6] The central purpose of the CCC was to employ young men in order to provide them life and work skills necessary to contribute to the greater good of their families, communities, and the state. Beyond these economic and practical goals lay the larger task of reclaiming the nation's natural environment, enriching the participants through their involvement in nature, and creating public recreation spaces for future generations. The nation's forests "have been and continue to be a part of the basic pattern woven into our national fabric," FDR wrote in 1937, and the CCC would "rebuild our youth as well as our forest resources," benefiting both the nation's young people and society as a whole.[7]

The CCC was created to provide employment for millions of young men with limited opportunities, and working in natural areas would encourage their understanding of the human connection to nature. Such a policy blended what Roosevelt saw as "the moral and spiritual value of such work" and pointed to his administration's commitment to organization, planning, and other modernist ideas that set the tone for the social and cultural transformation that reached its apex during the Depression era.[8] This also meant seeking the advice and direction of professionals in the field, landscape architects, to help better plan, design, and oversee CCC activities in order to transform "what had been largely a creature of chance into a synthesis of orderly design."[9] The CCC sought to balance the recreational needs of the people with the desire to preserve (or at least maintain) some aspect of wilderness. This directive was applied wherever the CCC operated, in the hope that they could transform underdeveloped or abandoned areas into ones "designed . . . to choreograph visitors' experiences . . . [that encourages] the aesthetic appreciation of landscapes and allows the spiritual communion with nature."[10] Central to this task were young men with little hope who saw in their activities the positive values of planning, organization, and application of reason to the solution of everyday problems.

On March 31, 1933, the president signed the Federal Unemployment Relief Act and created the Emergency Conservation Work agency, more commonly (and, in 1937, officially) known as the Civilian Conservation Corps. The program was renewed in 1935 and 1937, only to be dismantled by congressional action in December 1941, officially ending July 2, 1942. On April 5, 1933, FDR appointed Robert Fechner as the first director, where he remained until his death in 1939. Fechner was saddled with the difficult task of negotiating with CCC advisory boards from the Departments of Labor, Interior, Agriculture, and War, as well as balancing the fears of labor unions and local communities. The initial plan accounted for about 12,000 men, but by July 1933, with more states requesting CCC camps, the number swelled to 300,000 young men, including World War I veterans and local experienced men (LEM). The basic recruit earned $30 a month and sent $25 back to his family. Most were recruited through community welfare rolls or through word of mouth.[11] Carroll Aust remembered that his father told him he had heard something about a program where he could "get some money." As the family was in need—"I had been hungry . . . [and] when you're hungry nothing else matters"—he quickly signed up. For others, a judge made the choice for them. Clinton Dean was "a little unruly" and was encouraged to join the CCC to escape more draconian punishment. Edward Mokan was caught stealing a car and chose the CCC over jail. "That's what they were doing for everybody in" Philadelphia "instead of filling the jails up." Others were like Robert Gonyeau, who joined just "to get the hell away from home" and start a new adventure.[12]

No one was certain the CCC experiment would work given all the turmoil of the era, so Fechner worked to quiet the naysayers by laying a "remarkable" foundation. The first task, after enrolling the young people, was to set them to work laying the necessary infrastructure for the corps to get to their camps. In a very short time they laid more than 25,000 miles of truck trails and strung 15,000 miles of telephone lines. Once these projects were completed, and with the help of the LEMs, the recruits built their work camps in national and state forests and parks. After finishing building their camps, the CCC began a campaign of insect and disease control on more than 3 million acres of land, planted 98 million seedlings, and fought wildfires equaling 678,000 man-days. It was the ability of the nearly 300,000 recruits to overcome their "spiritual and physical depression" that was most significant to Fechner, for in a very short time the

"This boy is happy to be in the CCC." Courtesy of the National Archives and Records Administration, College Park, Maryland.

young men learned the positive virtues of organization, cooperation, hard work, and a "healthful environment."[13]

As important as these social and natural contributions were to the environment and the young men, the impact on local economies was even more staggering. In 1937 alone, more than $90 million went to buying foodstuffs for the camps; another $43 million was spent on clothing and $11 million on medical supplies. Considering that in 1938 the CCC's roughly 273,000 men consumed more than 12 million pounds of bacon, over 62 million pounds of beef, more than 12 million pounds of chicken, nearly 100 million eggs, 62 million pounds of potatoes, 27 million pounds of pork, 31 million pounds of sugar, 74 million pounds of flour, and 12 million pounds of coffee, it's no wonder that recruits like Jack Pollari remembered that he "ate like a rich man. I didn't get that at home. Although I didn't starve at home we never had pork chops and steak and all of that goody stuff." Aside from the ability to provide over 298,935,000 meals for the recruits, the millions of hogs, steers, chickens, and millions of acres for wheat, potatoes, beans, and other commodities at a cost of $159 per man for the year were often locally produced and provided a tremendous boon to an area's economy. Add to this the recruit's wages, which accounted for $123 million mailed home that year alone, and the positive economic benefits of the CCC encouraged local and state representatives to lobby for camps in their communities. The CCC's reach went beyond the transformation of the recruit, as townspeople were quick to recognize the multiple ways in which a CCC camp might help to alleviate unemployment and stimulate local business and industry.[14]

The impact of the CCC was not only felt by the young men they sought to transform into contributing citizens and workers, or the local economies that benefited from the demand for commodities, it also symbolized how a modern vision of nature could benefit the American people. One example of this initiative, which was replicated throughout the lower forty-eight states, took place in an area located between Cleveland and Akron, Ohio—the Virginia Kendall Reserve (VKR).[15] Covering 530 acres once owned by Cleveland coal baron Hayward Kendall, it had been a dairy pasture, and although it was undeveloped, much of the flora and fauna were gone. Kendall willed the land to his wife when he died in 1927; after a few years and some local political jockeying by director-secretary for the Akron Metropolitan Parks Board (AMPB), Harold S. Wagner, and F. A. Sieberling (founder of Goodyear Tire and Rubber), in 1933 the state assembly gave the AMPB authority over Virginia Kendall Park. Shortly thereafter, in early August 1933, Wagner petitioned the CCC for a camp at the VKR to develop, reconstruct, and design the area to fit local usage and, in a larger sense, the image of nature in America. The "main objectives," he wrote, were "in the preservation of the natural features [and] the execution of projects that will serve the greatest number of park patrons and to take them to the places of most interest."[16]

After Wagner graduated from Harvard University's Arnold Arboretum, the most prominent landscape architecture school at the time, he went to work for Warren A. Manning, one-time coworker of Frederick Law and John Charles Olmstead. It was from Manning that Wagner came to see that the use of local flora, especially trees, would heighten the experience of park visitors. As manager of Akron Metropolitan Park (AMP) District he directed the planting of more than 255,000 trees in 1932 alone. Working with the AMP also led to his close counsel with Albert H. Good, one of the leading proponents of "parkitecture," a school of architectural design that advocated for building outdoor facilities in harmony within natural areas. Working together, they utilized an Olmstead brothers' evaluation from 1925 for the AMP and made it fit into their plans to turn the VKR into a recreational destination, a place that would provide the visitor with the best natural experience they could create. With these plans, Wagner requested a CCC work camp be established near the town of Peninsula, Ohio, which took place after approval by the district office. By September recruits were hard at work clearing an area for CCC Company #576.[17]

After two months, the camp was ready. Company #576, made up of eight enrollees from California and two hundred local recruits, arrived on December 11, 1933, initially under the command of navy lieutenant J. R. Tobin. However, delays and discipline issues led to Tobin being reassigned in May and replaced with army captain A. W. Belden. Wagner's initial plans for the area's structures were simplified, as he came to recognize the limited knowledge and work experience of the recruits. Following his training and working with Good, he wanted to use local stone and vegetation to build and cover buildings and to blend the structures as much as possible into the natural environment. Blighted and fallen American chestnut wood provided an excellent resource for the siding and shingles, with locally quarried rock used for the foundations. He made certain that all "the truss timbers . . . and rafters [were] squared, rather than round" to better accommodate the limited skills of the worker.[18]

Company #576's first major task was constructing a two-story structure with one side opening onto a covered picnic area. The building's ground floor would be a large open area for overnight retreats, with restrooms for men and women and a small concessions area. The small second floor would contain living quarters for the caretaker. A trail would be built from this site to an overlook that would provide the visitor with a "180 degree" view of the "tall buildings in Cleveland and Akron." This area—the Ledges—became one of the more popular destinations of the area (although seeing the skyline of either city was not possible), and numerous other trails were laid to reach it from other areas of the VKR. Good's designs for unobtrusive parkitecture restrooms were also located in the Ledges area, making certain that visitors would come to the area and see the large outcropping of rocks, with a view of existing and soon-to-be-planted hardwoods rolling down the valley toward the Cuyahoga River, the town of Peninsula, and points beyond. With nearly two million people living "within an hour's drive of it," Wagner praised the Ledges area as "one of the outstanding operations of its kind in the country."[19]

At the same time these structures were going up and being finalized, Company #576 was hard at work constructing Kendall Lake. The hope was that a small lake would draw people—especially young people—to the area in both the summer and winter. The CCC cleared a thirteen-acre site fed by the Salt Run stream by the summer of 1934 and finished an earthen dam by fall. By the following summer the lake had filled up and became a popular swimming area. After it was completed in 1937, the CCC arranged with the local school boards to bus city children out to the VKR and the lake for their first exposure to the "country parks."[20]

Company #576 and their work at the VKR was, like so many other CCC projects, astounding to not only the experts who planned the natural transformation but also the young men who accomplished the task. By the time the camp closed in the fall of 1938, the company had built two shelters, eight latrines, a dam, a bath house, seventeen footbridges, a 40,000-gallon well, a 600-foot toboggan slide, and 208 tables and benches; graded and developed five acres of campground; moved more than 15,000 plants and trees for "effect"; and planted 122 acres of trees to create a natural space dedicated to the visitors' enjoyment. The transformation of the area, which only a decade before had been denatured, symbolized the modernist ideal of transforming undeveloped nature into a useful park. The VKR, like many other CCC projects across the country, began with experts logically laying out a plan, applying parkitecture theory to the design, and then applying these concepts to the construction using the organizational structures of the CCC. The result preserved the beauty of nature while providing pleasure to the people who visited. Although there were camping areas and dormitories, these were for young people bused in from nearby cities for a taste of nature. Most visitors came to the VKR by automobile for the day and saw in nature an organized, consumable product, like a zoo or a circus. Professionals maintained the area. The trails, vistas, shelters, and lake were created to enhance the visitor's understanding of nature. What had been undeveloped land had been transformed. Nature, left to its own design, needed the young men of the CCC to make it modern.[21]

The CCC in the VKR, as well as throughout the country, sought to direct and redirect the viewer, to determine how the visitor saw nature. By the end of 1936, the CCC boys at VKR had laid out nearly five and a half miles of trails throughout the reserve, planted or moved more than 57,600 trees and shrubs, and cleared debris and dead growth from forty-five acres. Most of the dead trees they cleared were American chestnut that was recycled for the construction of the shelters. Kendall Lake required 6,000 cubic yards of earth to be moved—mostly by individual wheelbarrows—for the earthen dam, along with enough sand for a 1,000-square-foot beach. Visitors who came to the VKR did so believing they were experiencing a natural, real, or authentic place. Yet it was a modernist creation, designed to fit the CCC's directive to make nature accessible to and usable by the general public. The success of this mandate, combined with the speed at which it all operated, was not lost on the young men who did the labor. They were witnesses to the great things that could happen through planning, organization, cooperation, and hard work. They too had been transformed and through their work became part of FDR's new model army.[22]

The activities at the VKR fit into the larger goals of the CCC perfectly. Given Wagner's influence, it had strong local ties, and it was clear that people from the nearby towns and cities would benefit from the park. People visiting the VKR, as well as the fact that many of the young men who were part of Company #576 came from surrounding communities, ensured that it would serve as a testimonial to the power of experts, organization, and planning, key components to modernism. The CCC transformed land into a beautifully designed natural experience. What took place at the VKR was replicated throughout the country: by 1938, in 4,500 CCC camps, 2.3 million young men planted more than 1.5 billion seedlings on 1.5 million acres of land. The immediacy of these numbers were overshadowed in Fechner's mind, for he believed the larger contribution would come in the future, where the people and government would support a policy ensuring proper planning to lead to a "goal of a balanced natural resource budget."[23]

FDR recognized the social value of the CCC. He cited the agency's ability to rehabilitate the nation's young men, linking their activities "in our forests, parks, and fields" as a benefit for all citizens. FDR had long believed in the positive attributes of nature, identifying it as central to the American character. He worked, both as steward of the family home in Hyde Park and as governor of New York, to make sure that this resource was preserved and utilized in a reasonable manner. FDR created the CCC with the express purpose of serving the "American people" by ensuring that future generations would enjoy and benefit from the civilizing tendencies of nature. In a 1936 NBC radio address, he praised the CCC and its young men for their "promptness" to seize "the opportunity to engage in honest work," to perform their duties in a "fine spirit" that won "the respect of the communities in which your camps have been located" and "merits the admiration of the entire country."[24]

But nature is not orderly, it is wild and unyielding. Before people could enjoy its benefits, an infrastructure of roads, trails, latrines, and even creeks had to be arranged in an organized manner while at the same time maintaining their natural state. The CCC, with input from the experts in the Department of Forestry, understood that "nature does not always work for the betterment of a forest," and that competition among trees, brush, and weeds did not allow for the best or most beneficial flora to emerge. The task of the CCC was to "produce better forest products in less time" than natural selection might allow. This is where the CCC relied heavily on the expertise of landscape architects. The field of landscape architecture developed in the mid-nineteenth century and flourished in the United States under the leadership of Frederick Law Olmstead. Like other professions, it formed an accreditation and oversight organization, the American Society of Landscape Architects, in 1899. This new profession blended the mathematics of engineering and drafting with the aesthetic of the gardener, architect, and naturalist. As a technical profession, its practitioners applied scientific principles to the design and arrangement of natural spaces, resulting in environments that were "useful, safe and enjoyable."[25]

In general, the CCC followed their advice and applied it to projects. In order to better ensure that CCC projects throughout the country were applying these same principles, Wagner's partner Albert Good was asked to compile an edition of best parkitecture practices and designs. *Park Structures and Facilities* was published in 1935 (and revised and republished in 1938 as *Park and Recreation Structures*) and distributed to CCC units throughout the country. It provided a compilation of structures designed in harmony with the natural surroundings, blending in with local flora, and utilizing as much local product in construction as possible. "Through the use of native materials in proper scale, and through the avoidance of rigid, straight lines and over-sophistication," Good advised, the structure should "give the feeling of having been executed by pioneer craftsmen with limited hand tools . . . [to achieve] sympathy with natural surroundings, and with the past."[26]

The designers of CCC projects understood that their task was to employ reason, logic, and an understanding of basic natural laws to transform natural areas into places responsive to the needs of people. The design and layout of CCC projects such as the VKR ensured that visitors would find the park useful, beautiful, and natural to the point where it was almost impossible to differentiate between what the CCC created and what existed beforehand. By utilizing the American style of landscape architecture, which sought to "harmonize with the natural setting" and create usable natural areas, the CCC planted native shrubs, used native rock quarried from local areas, and blended facilities into the landscape so that it seemed as though it has always been there.[27]

At the same time that the CCC was using the ideas of landscape architecture to transform nature to fit their designs, leaders at the local, state, and national levels also understood the limitations of their labor force and thus sought to transform these young men as well. Most recruits to the CCC were unskilled and undereducated. In 1937–1938, for example, the national percentage of those enrolled in the corps who had completed at least eighth grade was about 25 percent, but only 9 percent graduated high school. They were also young, with most recruits falling between seventeen and nineteen years of age with little or no occupational experience. Elden Sessions's study of six hundred Ohio CCC members in 1936–1937 revealed that most came from families "unsuccessful in their struggle for independence and security." Nearly one-third came from traditional working-class backgrounds and another one-third from families who could not list an occupation, were on relief, or were working on the WPA. Seventy-two percent came from urban areas with limited schooling. He cited an earlier Pressey Senior Classification Test (a mental alertness test used by educators at that time) of 786 Ohio corpsmen where the median score was 33, translating into an intelligence level akin to a thirteen-and-a-half-year-old in the eighth grade. Of these, more than 25 percent scored in the twelve-year-old and sixth-grade category, and only a handful came close to their chronological age. Although Sessions labeled a few with a "high degree of mental ability," most left high school before they turned sixteen, and only a handful stayed long enough to graduate. Furthermore, only 28 percent held jobs before they joined the CCC.[28]

Another study, done by Helen Walker, an associate professor of family case work at Western Reserve University, in 1938, provides an interesting portrait of Cleveland CCC recruits. She and her students found that 60 percent of the white enrollees came from families whose head of the household was foreign born, and of the sixty black enrollees studied, only one came from a family born in Ohio. Nearly all came from what Walker's team labeled "lower economic ranges" and from neighborhoods described as "run-down," "congested," and "very close to the factories." African American dwellings were described as "crowded, unattractive. Poorly kept, and sparsely . . . . furnished." Many of the young men ran with "gangs of boys and young men" and frequented pool halls, theaters, and bars, and hung out in city parks. In general, they joined the CCC between the ages of seventeen and twenty with a median age of 18. They fared better educationally than those at the state level in Sessions's study, as 72 percent went beyond ninth grade and 15 percent graduated high school. Some left school because they didn't like going or disliked a particular teacher or class, but others left because of economic pressure at home. They had to work. Yet only 38 percent held full-time jobs upon entrance to the CCC, with another 11 percent employed part-time.[29]

The generational characteristics described in the Sessions and Walker studies fit the national pattern for CCC enrollees. Paul Grooms recalled how he had "dropped out midway in the seventh grade, and then in the CCC when I went to Pennsylvania, I completed the elementary school. I completed the eighth grade. I got a certificate from the Somerset County Public Instruction, public school services." His was not an unusual story, for as Charles Lord told his interviewer, "[a] lot of the boys never had any work experience at all" and had to be trained specifically for each job they did once they were in the CCC. Their lack of work experience was compounded by the reality that they had to adjust to the difficult circumstances of working outdoors, far from home, and under tight, almost military, control. And they had to deal with the issue of cooperation. "I learned to get along with people from all walks of life," CCC recruit John Kochan recalled, "because in the camps that I was in, there were Jewish people there, Irish, Italian, German . . . all nationalities." Being together, far from home built a sense of camaraderie that bound the recruits together. Although there were the occasional fights and disagreements, for most recruits the experience taught them "how to get along with other people."[30]

Roosevelt wanted the Corps to be "a builder of the kind of men this Nation needs," with "good moral character, hard work . . . physical hardihood, active citizenship, and love of country." They were to be models of the new American. The nearly three million who enrolled in the CCC were called his tree army, and through their efforts the positive force of planned nature was open to all. Furthermore, they found the corps changed them as well. Historian Neil Maher argues that recruits came into the CCC, learned about conservation, and took what they learned back to their communities, primarily the idea that "landscape" meant the alteration of nature by humans. Their experience taught about the power of man to make nature more useful and efficient and gave witness to their conversion to modernity. They saw and were involved in transforming nature, both externally and within themselves as the CCC made them stronger, more conscious of their ability and power, more convinced that any problem could be surmounted.[31]

It was clear to all concerned that those who enrolled in the CCC needed training, education, and discipline. The CCC would provide employment, money, and potential job skills, but the larger purpose was to take the recruits and mold, shape, and transform them into "ideal American citizens."[32] This meant teaching them how to work and get along with a variety of ethnic groups to build a sense of inclusion and solidarity. The similarities of their backgrounds helped bond them as a cohort and encouraged a shared identity. The CCC leaders were hopeful that the individual recruits would recognize that their shared economic, social, and emotional values would encourage them to work together, and after seeing the success of their hard work, they would accrue a self-respect that they could project onto their peers, families, friends, and those in their communities. The projects with which they were involved demanded they work together as a group to achieve a common goal, and central to this solidarity was a commitment to the discipline and order of the CCC. The young men recruited into the CCC were part of what the president's wife had called the lost generation, and combatting their generational hopelessness was not lost to them. The pride they experienced while working as a group, completing projects that would benefit large segments of the population, provided them a glimpse into a tangible future. A 1941 FSA/CCC publication, *The CCC at Work*, reminded its readers that to "work and play successfully with other boys their own age is an important part of CCC training," which built the character necessary to be "proud of yourself—and your country."[33]

Central to their rebuilding process was recognizing the positive virtues of discipline and order. Given their backgrounds, they had to be taught how to not only follow orders but also understand how following those orders made them better men. They had to want to change. "It taught me, and I know it, discipline. You learned how to take orders, and you didn't go in there and do it the way you wanted. You done it the way they said to, you know what I mean," recalled Lurtie McDonald of his CCC days.[34] The recruits were often reminded, as VKR's Captain A. W. Belden wrote in 1935 in the camp newspaper, *The Kendallite:*

> Discipline and respect for authority will be impressed upon you. It will not be sufficient to do what you are told—you must do it in the way specified. Follow all orders of those placed in a position to give them.
>
> Remember that you are important, individually, only to the extent that your efforts improve the company as a whole. You can become a very important cog in a well-oiled machine.[35]

The reality of fifty to a hundred young men living together in barracks created some issues, such as discipline and basic hygiene. Some recruits at the VKR got into trouble because they were "running up and down the streets and dark alleys at all hours."[36] Many who came to the CCC were not well versed in personal hygiene and were shown how to take care of their bodies in this way. Regular showers, shaving, and washing and wearing clean clothes were central to the daily routine of the recruit. They were also young, growing strong and healthy, and had pocket money for perhaps the first time in their lives, so the CCC had to play a role in dating and sexual relationships as well. Many had few experiences with courtship or the aftereffects of sexual liaisons. For example, in a letter to the advice editor of *The Kendallite*, one young man asked about his inability to hold onto a girl after the first date because of his apparent shyness. The young woman he was interested in rebuked him because he "can't make love to them the right way." Whether he meant intercourse or convincing a girl of his ardor, his letter revealed the confusion that beset many of the young enrollees. The response from the newspaper's "Voice of Experience" advised him to turn the lights low and, for more specific advice about what to do next, talk to "Pete, [as] he makes all 16 year old girls heart skip a beat."[37]

The adverse effects of sexual relationships were a concern for the CCC leadership across the country. Officers instructed the recruits of the "gravity of venereal disease" on their mental and physical health as well as the negative toll it took on the camp itself. The chaplain chided the young men for their desire to engage in sexual activities, reminding them of "the moral aspects of the circumstances leading to infection." CCC leadership advised abstinence but understood the reality, and many camps did as the

VKR did by scattering "prophylactic stations" in the camps. "All men who have had illicit sexual intercourse" were to report to a station for "such cleansing and prophylaxis as may be prescribed." The issue was a serious one, for aside from common respiratory issues (colds) and flu, venereal disease was the most reported illness in the forty-one Ohio camps during 1936, with 120 cases reported. This meant 18 percent of men in the CCC in Ohio in 1936 were diagnosed with a sexually transmitted disease, a slight decrease from the year before. The problem was exacerbated by the fact that several of the surrounding towns still condoned houses of prostitution, which "did a good business on liberty nights."[38]

The CCC leadership also hoped to transform the lives of youth through education, either via on-the-job training or specific vocational after-work courses. The *Manual for Instructors in the Civilian Conservation Corps Camps* detailed the low educational level of most recruits and advised instructors to adjust their basic teaching methodology toward practice and repetition until it became a "habit," for the mind was like a "switchboard" that needed training and reinforcement. The teacher's role involved the "processes of controlling, directing, or managing [their] thinking." Given the CCC recruit's background, they had "developed bad habits" and needed instruction on making better choices, which in turn would lead them to become better men. They needed to learn how to accept authority and with it the advice of those in positions to give orders—experts. The recruits needed to have faith in those who were trying to make them better, to save them from their own actions and substitute their poor judgment for the authority of expertise. Charles Lord recalled that the "majority of the boys wanted to learn something and prove" they were worthy. Many others were "educated to the job," he said, sometimes taking "special classes in plumbing, carpentry, electricity, [or] blacksmithing" so that when they got out of the corps, they would have better job opportunities. This ethos fit one of the key education program aims, which was to develop an "understanding of the prevailing social and economic conditions to the end that each man will cooperate intelligently in improving these conditions." And what better way to improve their society than improving their skills.[39]

Through a variety of activities, from the hard work in the field to classroom work and recreation, they were taught that they were in control of their own destiny. They were taught practical vocational skills such as auto mechanics, typing, forestry, and diesel engineering. CCC member Gilbert Sanders recalled that he and the other recruits "learned a lot . . . other than actually how to work. They, most of them knew how to work, but they didn't know how to get out and try to find work." The CCC training gave them "confidence" to go out and make it in the workforce. Carroll Aust agreed, telling his interviewer that "it seemed like when they did get discharged and go home they were more confident, I think. They figured if they could handle [the CCC] then they could handle anything." One former recruit called it his "Civilian Conservation College," for "that's where I learned all my, uh, good things, that put me on through life." They were witness to not only how they could manipulate nature to their own ends but also how they held this same power over their future. It was this sense of confidence that was reflected back to their families and communities as examples of the positive attributes of modernity. VKR camp commander Belden captured the attitude in 1935 when he wrote: "For the future we have the bright outlook of continuing this spirit to the end that the company and this project may maintain their rightful place on top . . . so that the final result may be an everlasting monument to all of us."[40]

The building of confidence in the CCC boys was important as it was connected to a larger fear that because of the economic crisis, American masculinity was at risk. The CCC promoted itself as the builder of modern men and was dedicated to saving the nation's manhood. This meant strengthening the recruit's bodies through plentiful and healthy meals and plenty of hard work. Most of the recruits were underweight and unhealthy. Three-quarters of the recruits would not pass the basic army weight requirement, and according to historian Neil Maher, "many young men felt both emasculated and infantilized before joining the CCC."[41] Through hard work and the education and training programs, the corps transformed the frail, skinny, and weak young boys into strong, tanned, muscular, and healthy American men. The strenuous outdoor labor combined with the bountiful food available at mealtime made them modern workers and citizens ready to operate the machinery of the factory or the farm. As Jeffery Suzik argues, the "boys were definitely not being encouraged to 'make' technology themselves. . . . Technology was definitely 'making' them."[42]

The young boys enrolled in the CCC were transformed and convinced that through planning, hard work, and a healthy scientific diet, anyone could be made into a better, stronger, healthier man. This new man became a model citizen, projecting the positive attributes of modernity by making nature better through simple tasks, done with expert guidance, and organized for the betterment of all. The modernist ideology they absorbed and witnessed applied both to the forests in which they toiled and the transformation of their own bodies and minds. The average corpsman in Ohio gained almost sixteen pounds and developed a tanned and muscular body, as did recruits from all over the country. That the CCC built men, in the most masculine of terms, was something that administrators, including the president, pointed to as one of the CCC's greatest successes. In a story all too familiar, recruit Albert Petoski quit school after the ninth grade, fell in with a bad crowd, and ran afoul of the law. He joined the CCC to escape this life and stayed in for two years, leaving with specific skills he could apply in the private sector. When interviewed after his discharge, he said the corps built his "self-respect," gave him a sense of "pride in accomplishment," and "improved his health." He emerged from the CCC a new, better man, one ready to tackle the hard problems in life and willing to sacrifice for the betterment of society. Petoski, like the nearly three million other CCC recruits, became part of the new model army of American citizens dedicated to making nature over in a more useful and efficient manner and, in the process, transforming themselves.[43]

"As muscles hardened," the president told the American people in his radio address honoring the third anniversary of the CCC, the recruits became "accustomed to outdoor work [and] grasped the opportunity to learn by practical training on the job." Thus as they were transformed, they also transformed nature for the betterment of the American people. "We built a lot of men," CCC veteran Leonard Tulloch told his interviewer. "They came in here skinny, scrawny, underfed" and within a few months were transformed into men who more resembled "weight-lifters." The physical transformation was matched by a change in the way the boys saw each other and the work they were doing. They took great pride in what they were part of and saw in their labors a benefit to not only their generation but also the future. Because many of the young men came from troubled backgrounds and lacked positive reinforcement, they looked on their accomplishments as proof that through hard work, sacrifice, and planning, anything or anyone could be saved. "I am confident," wrote Robert Fechner in 1938, "that this program has been of great social significance" to the recruits as it built their self-respect and dignity and brought pride to their families and communities.[44]

The situation was more complex for African American enrollees. Walker's interviews with some of Ohio's black enrollees reveal that many came away from the project with the same sense of pride and accomplishment as their white cohort. One recruit, Paul Smith, said he "came away proud to have learned something constructive," which aided him in getting employment after his discharge. However, of the fifty-nine African Americans interviewed, nearly all complained of racism within the officer ranks and discrimination from fellow white recruits. That the CCC officers came from the regular military, with a few from southern states, meant that some had a hard time leading black recruits. One particular officer, who was later removed due to complaints filed with the state office, called them "insulting and derogatory names" and treated them very poorly.[45]

This was not unusual, as the CCC's record regarding black enrollees was spotted with inconsistencies and downright intransigence. The original act contained language that specifically said no American should be discriminated against because of color, race, or creed, yet Fechner let it be known that blacks would constitute no more than 10 percent of total CCC enrollment to correspond with their place within the American population. This quota system was not implemented for any other ethnicity, and because blacks faced higher unemployment and poverty rates, their percentage of the total CCC should have been higher. The corps was not unique in this, as most New Deal programs had racial quotas to limit the number of African Americans on government programs, except relief. Often, black recruits were sent to segregated camps and to distant national park camps. One such camp was in Libby, Montana, where twenty-five young African American men from New York and New Jersey were sent in 1933 and 1934 to dig firebreaks, plant trees, and build trails—all the things other CCC camps did. Yet they were viewed as "hoodlums" and had frequent run-ins with local law enforcement officials, and almost half were sent home or given dishonorable discharges for refusing to obey orders or work. Perhaps because of situations like this, in late 1934 Fechner issued an order that required all black units to be employed in their home states—again, a policy not implemented for white enrollees.[46]

The continued segregation, and the fact that by 1935 only 6 percent of the enrollees were African American, forced Roosevelt to issue a new order requiring that African Americans be given positions of leadership and that target quotas be met. By the end of 1936, more than 145,000 African American young men had served in the CCC, sending $28 million back home to their families. Also by 1937, the 31,000 African American young men listed on the CCC rolls filled the 10 percent quota for the first time. The central office also made an attempt to place more African Americans in leadership positions, although these were as education advisors in all-black camps. Fechner did little to redress the rampant segregation and left the day-to-day operations to local officers and advisors. Not until 1940 were black officers put into leadership positions, and then only for all-black units. In total, more than 300,000 African Americans served in the CCC by 1940, yet few served alongside whites, and the black workers often faced resentment from local communities. Recruit George Childress remembered that there was an all-black camp close to his CCC camp near Mammoth Cave in Kentucky, but he acknowledged that "we didn't mix. . . . [We] didn't work together. They worked by themselves and we worked with ourselves." Even in the face of this overt exclusion and separation, most of those Ohio recruits interviewed by Walker spoke enthusiastically about their CCC experience, echoing white enrollees' comments that the experience taught them how to work, transformed them into better individuals, and taught them the values of sacrifice, planning, and organization.[47]

It seems that regardless of race, class, or region, the CCC had a transformative effect on the nature the boys worked in, the communities they came from and interacted with, and their own identities. Their consciousness shifted from knowing little or nothing about the conservation of natural resources to being advocates for the planned and organized use of nature. They became converts to conservationism and witnessed the positive value of planning, efficiency, hard work, and sacrifice as they made nature better and more useful; at the same time, they were transformed physically and given the power over their own bodies, minds, and spirits. They experienced a new way of being and, in a larger sense, became living examples of the effectiveness of modernity. "When you return to your homes," a company commander remarked at one of his camp's monthly citizenship ceremonies, "interest yourselves actively, as citizens and taxpayers, in your communities affairs, its institutions, its public schools and . . . inspire the youth of your community to play the game of life honestly and uprightly." He continued to extoll the virtues of "justice, health, democracy, and loyalty" and asked if they were ready to accept the responsibility to spread the good news "in the service of conservation of human lives." They were more than ready.[48]

This transformation was not accidental but the result of the training and reward system designed by CCC administrators. Abundant food, a safe place to stay, and money both for the family and for themselves helped create a sense of security that most had lacked before and gave them faith in the system. Combined with the daily physical labor and the education program, the CCC transformed men Fechner and others considered "raw material." The systematic education of these young people, who James McEntee, Fechner's successor, labeled "conservation evangelists," allowed them to take their new bodies, identities, and attitudes into the larger world as representatives of the future. The CCC had successfully taken those who had fallen out of place in society, saved them, and then sent them into their communities as examples of the positive impact of modern thought and action.[49]

The larger lesson, of course, was that nature could be made better not just through landscape architecture but by recognizing that nature begins with man. Through planning, reason, and cooperation, any problem could be solved and every person saved if only they had faith. Many CCC veterans concluded that they benefited from the "intangible and broad" values concerning personal transformation that came through their time in the corps. Doing work that would outlast them and had value for society motivated them to give witness to the positive virtues of the corps. "To me," said one enrollee, "the Civilian Conservation Corps is the beginning of a new era in America."[50]

This new model army connected their work in nature with the personal pride it instilled in them as individuals and as a country as a whole. Enrollee Tulloch pointed with pride to all the trees in and around the VKR and told his interviewer that the CCC had "planted all the trees you see there . . . hundreds of thousands of trees." Corpsmen expressed gratification mixed with humility when discussing their efforts, confident they had worked to construct a version of nature that best utilized the visitor's time and was useful, efficient, spacious, and controlled—all things modern. They saw their work as "speedier and more efficient [than] Mother Nature," while at the same time awed by their own physical and intellectual transformation. The CCC encouraged most of the three million men who served to recognize the importance of conserving natural resources and the power of planning, organization, hard work, and the development of an ethic that valued cooperative work. In his final report in January 1944 to Interior Secretary Harold Ickes, Director Conrad Wirth connected the transformative nature of the CCC to the larger society: "It brought to the minds of the people of this country the need and value of a sound, active conservation program. . . . The nation cannot afford to have its resources neglected or wasted. . . . This can be done only by careful planning and hard work." The CCC succeeded in not only constructing nature but also sending out into society examples of the positive attributes of their organization and planning.[51]

The success of the CCC and the good news of federal organization and planning encouraged FDR and his advisors, principally Harry Hopkins, to consider expanding the idea of work relief to other programs. The continued problem of unemployment and the sluggish economy certainly played a part, but Hopkins had come to the conclusion that an outright dole, like that paid through the Federal Emergency Relief Administration (FERA), encouraged apathy and suggested a failure on the part of government to find a reasonable solution to the economic crisis. If the new era promised better planning and organization, and if the New Deal hoped to bring this reformation to its full bloom, then FDR had to turn loose the power of the federal government to get people back to work in a way that not only provided them succor but also reaffirmed that salvation came through modern solutions to age-old problems. The New Deal promised planned, organized, and modern solutions, and the outline of the new system—the welfare state—took shape.

Hopkins tested this new vision during the winter of 1933–1934 under the auspices of the Civil Works Administration (CWA). Designed to assist the massive numbers of unemployed through that year's harsh winter, the CWA provided work for those on relief in occupations related to those they held in the private sector. This allowed them to maintain their skills, feel like productive members of society, and earn money for their families. In its five months of operation, the CWA employed more than 4.25 million people and pumped, through wages paid to them, $860 million into local and state economies. Hopkins authorized all sorts of projects to alleviate the problem of the nearly 11 million people still out of work and provided the president a clear blueprint for a much larger and comprehensive work-relief project. When the Democrats swept the congressional elections in 1934, creating a supermajority in both chambers, and given the lack of success of FERA and the National Industrial Recovery Act (NIRA), the administration asked for new legislation in early 1935 that made federal work relief a reality. On April 8, 1935, the president signed into law the Emergency Relief Appropriation Act, which provided $4.8 billion in funding, and, through Executive Order #7034, he created the Works Progress Administration (WPA) on May 6, under the direction of Hopkins, to spend it. He had little difficulty finding adequate projects to spend this largesse, working day and night to get as many people onto the WPA rolls as possible—from more than 1 million persons in 1935 to a high of 3.3 million in 1938. By 1943, 8.5 million Americans had been employed by the WPA.[52]

The WPA created public projects to provide immediate benefits and pay future dividends. These workers were also part of the new model army, spreading the good news of government organization, planning, and a new way of being by telling their friends and family about their contributions to their "community that no depression can take away." They built icons to modernity, whether it be the 650,000 miles of roads resurfaced or created, the nearly 100,000 streetlights they installed, the 95,000 community public buildings—at least three for every county in the country—or the 1.2 billion hot lunches they served to schoolchildren.

Their work served as living examples of the positive attributes of the New Deal, not as a political agenda, but as a new way of being that was saving America. In New York City alone, for example, the WPA helped refurbish or build eleven swimming pool complexes by September 1936. These modern structures included three in-ground pools built to, according to historian Marta Gutman, "up-to-date technical standards." More than 1.79 million people enjoyed them that summer, with those under age fourteen (some 600,000) entering free of charge. The ability to build this many complexes, some with entire recreation centers and many in low-income or at-risk neighborhoods, reaffirmed the WPA's commitment to represent the "New Deal vision of modern childhood," which "embraced a central insight of modernism" through planning, organization, standardization, and high quality regardless of the neighborhood or the skills of the workers. Three-quarters of all WPA projects involved these types of community building activities and favored un- or semiskilled workers making an average of $82 a month. Ordinary people creating spaces for ordinary people certainly did suggest a new order, a clear break with the past. Without programs like the WPA, as Tom Skelton of rural Georgia later recalled, "we would have fought among ourselves" rather than work together.[53]

There were literally thousands of examples like this in nearly every community in the United States. The WPA contained multiple kinds of projects, from sewing to art. One area of special concern, and this policy reverberated through all WPA projects, was the plight of young people. Although the CCC employed desperate young men to reclaim the environment, one WPA project sought to give all the nation's youth "their chance" to stave off despair and hopelessness. FDR issued Executive Order #7086 on June 26, 1935, creating the National Youth Administration (NYA). Certain it would yield positive benefits to young people and the country, the president—advised by his wife, Hopkins, and Hopkins's appointee to lead the NYA, Aubrey Williams—outlined four basic goals: (1) help high school, college, and graduate students stay in school by providing funds to create part-time jobs; (2) provide work relief and job training to school-age young people not enrolled in college and over the age of 18; (3) lobby educators to modify their curriculum to better prepare the nation's young people for the real world through job-specific training; and (4) encourage positive citizenship and leisure-time activities.[54]

The problem of youth unemployment, which in 1933 necessitated the creation of the CCC, grew worse by 1935, demanding even more dedicated intervention. One estimate had more than three million young people between the ages of 16 and 25 on relief rolls and eligible for NYA funds, and a great many of them lacked the basic educational background to successfully operate in the country's workforce. The private sector simply could not absorb the nearly 1.7 million new workers entering the workforce each year. In 1930 unemployed youth accounted for 27.5 percent of the total unemployed; by 1937 this had grown to 35.9 percent, where it hovered until 1942. Mrs. Roosevelt's fears of a generation lost to hopelessness and despair seemed certain unless positive steps were taken to educate, train, and teach these young people how to be contributing members of their society. In essence, they needed to be converted to the American way of life.[55]

Charles Taussig, chairman of the Advisory Committee for the NYA, believed America's youth would be lost because they were born into an "abnormal world" and "know only chaos." He chastised the traditional policies and ideas that brought the country and world to the Depression crisis point and feared that it offered young people "no opportunity to live" or "the integrity, spirituality, and reasonable moral code" to help resolve the problems. He had faith, however, that within this darkness a light of "social consciousness that did not exist in previous generations" had begun to shine and that young people would become modern "explorers in a world [in] which even their elders fail to recognize familiar landmarks." This meant training the youth to lead the country by empowering the NYA to help fill the employment and training gap between high school or college graduation and employment. Young people were the vanguard for the modern society, and new teaching and educational techniques would enrich them with positive life skills to the benefit of all.[56]

The NYA leadership understood that until the Depression era, the affairs of the nation's youth, other than the CCC, were generally ignored. In the past, when land was readily available, opportunity awaited those young people willing to chance a new life farther west. With that opportunity gone, and with one-sixth of the population between the ages of 16 and 24, and with more than 37 percent of them unemployed as of July 1936, a plan was needed to address this "lost generation." This became the NYA. The initial impetus came from FERA activity begun in 1934 when monies were first allocated to students at the University of Minnesota and then extended throughout the country. In the late spring of 1934, resident camps and schools for unemployed youth were established. These ended with the establishment of the WPA in May 1935 and were resurrected in June with the creation of the NYA. The number of young people who enrolled quickly ballooned, increasing from the initial 34,924 in September 1935 to a high of 628,713 in April 1937, before settling at 405,671 in November of that year.[57]

Central to the NYA was the student aid program. Begun under FERA, it helped young people stay enrolled in high school, college, or graduate school by providing paid positions averaging $20 per month for undergraduates and $40 per month to graduate students for up to thirty hours of work. High school students earned between $6 and $15 per month depending on their activity. In its eight years of existence (1935–1943), 2,134,000 young people benefited from this program, costing $166,838,741. During its peak year of 1937, more than 24,000 educational institutions participated. High school students received the majority of NYA aid, with graduate students in the minority. One report indicated that those receiving college aid were "at least equal if not indeed superior to other students in scholastic achievement," a tendency replicated at the high school and graduate levels. The NYA achieved some gender balance, especially in high schools, where females outnumbered males (52 to 47 percent), but fell behind in the collegiate ranks by nearly 20 percent (59.9 to 40.1 percent). In keeping with many of the WPA-based programs, African Americans made up 11 percent of enrollees in high school but only 5.7 percent in college. African American students numbered under 140,000 over the eight-year span of the agency, but for most, without the NYA, their ability to remain in school—high school or college—was problematic. More than 90 percent of all participants came from relief rolls, with 70 percent of these from homes that earned less than $900 a year. They did clerical, research, survey, or community service work, while others worked with the ground and building maintenance crews or in a variety of staff positions through their schools. Community service NYA youth helped with theater programs, playgrounds, tutoring, social service agencies, nursery schools, museums, and health facilities. They became positive examples of the potential of youth to those in their communities and, within larger governmental circles, how organized relief could help create a more modern America.[58]

The other side of the NYA involved the work projects program, which assisted young people over 18 (initially 16, but changed in 1936) who were not going to college or trade school but needed assistance to acquire the job experience necessary to gain private employment. Like its parent organization, the WPA, this wing of the NYA built and repaired roads, trails, and streets; constructed or repaired public buildings and recreational centers; did conservation work; worked in nursery schools; served school lunches; and performed a myriad of other services. This part of the NYA served fewer youth, peaking in 1937 with 184,727 young people; paid less (an average of $15 per month); and was skewed significantly toward males (69 percent to 31 percent) but retained the WPA-mandated 11 percent of African Americans, even as their unemployment numbers, regardless of age category, were nearly double that of the national rate. The impact of these projects, where many of those enrolled also took advantage of educational opportunities to achieve literacy, could be seen in the communities they served. "The program has contributed to the improvement of local communities," an NYA report concluded, which demonstrated "the constructive ways of engaging out-of-school unemployed youth and improving their morale." The NYA also challenged traditional educational policy, which did little to prepare the nation's young people for employment in the private sector. The NYA felt that their work programs, where young people "are maintained in residence at institutions and undergo a course of training related to their employment" to both their own and their community's benefit, pointed to the future of American education and outlined the possibilities for a more rational, organized, and well-planned curriculum. Recognizing that the youth constituted a "lost generation," the NYA believed its program "contributed significantly toward the solution" and salvation of the nation's young people.[59]

There was pressure to grow this program, which led in 1938 to the NYA's creating work-training facilities as resident projects. Here young people, much like in the CCC, lived in dormitories that they built and maintained for six to eight months while receiving instruction and training for jobs in the private sector. They were paid $30 a month, less $20 for room and board. These facilities produced clothing, toys, and other items to be distributed to needy families, and youths worked in parks, playgrounds, and community centers where they took on leadership roles in athletic activities for children, worked in neighborhood centers and libraries, built and maintained school bus shelters, provided research for civic government, and did whatever they could to prove their worth, dedication, and belief in America. One of the requirements for acceptance into these NYA facilities included the "oath of allegiance" and a strong statement against any "organization" that advocated the overthrow of the US government.[60]

These were the programs, but the success of the NYA could only be determined, according to Director Williams, based on the willingness of the young people to accept what was being offered to them. In his *Final Report* (1943), Williams wrote proudly that the NYA's success rested with the "hopes, ambitions, strengths, and weaknesses" of the youth who not only accepted the responsibility for their jobs, training, and education but went far beyond the pale by serving as examples of the positive benefits of the NYA.[61] They served as representatives of a modern government unwilling to allow a generation of young people to fall through the cracks of a failed economy or a broken educational system. "Under Government auspices," he wrote, the "NYA succeeded in developing arrangements by which young people could learn the essentials" to be employed in America. Previous eras had left American youth "stranded in a world where rugged individualism" . . . closed "the door of opportunity" on them. Past ideas pitted each citizen against each other and hampered the entrance of young people into the American system, which needed to give way to "collective forces" designed to use "cooperative social action" to guarantee equal opportunity.[62] According to historian Richard Reiman, the primary goals of the NYA included encouraging the nation's educational leaders to modify their curriculum to be more open to modern society and its needs, and more importantly, to "superintend and guide the mindset of young people." The NYA both transformed the institutions that educated and trained the nation's youth and instructed them on "the practices, responsibilities, and rewards of citizenship." As stewards of modern society they represented the ideals of the government's modern prescription for the ills of the economy. As the chairman of the National Advisory Committee, Charles Taussig, wrote in 1933, the relief policy for youth needed to prepare them for the "new and revolutionary economic and social concepts"[63] or face a return to failed classical liberal economic theory.

In order to determine its effectiveness, and staying true to its connection to modernity, the NYA conducted many in-house and external studies. Helen Harris, director of the NYA for New York City, conducted a study in 1936 to detail the significance and meaning of the NYA to the city and its youth. She and her team interviewed and surveyed 6,500 NYA enrollees involved in various projects, from the YMCA to parks and recreation, and concluded that the NYA had a positive effect on how the young people viewed their government and society, adding that the young people believed they were "needed and wanted [to] make their contribution to the community." Nearly 90 percent of the participants reported that their time on the NYA increased their self-confidence and saw it as a "great advantage to the younger generation." They also said that the NYA kept them off the streets and helped build positive character that would benefit the future of the country. Although Harris's study was primarily quantitative, her team also collected comments, and although there were some complaints about low wages and lack of hours, the vast majority of the comments echo a young woman from the Staten Island project who said the NYA helped prove that she "had the capability of holding" a job. Most commented about their increased self-respect, responsibility, and citizenship as positive benefits of their participation in the NYA. But one young man put it other terms: "It took my mind off why it was we live in a system where privilege counts more than ability—freedom of opportunity is just a phrase—and why the government only goes far enough to give only temporary help—rather than reform our social institutions so that capitalism can be allowed to work for everyone and not for a chosen few." Although his comment was not the norm, it indicated an awareness of the larger issues of the NYA and other government projects.[64]

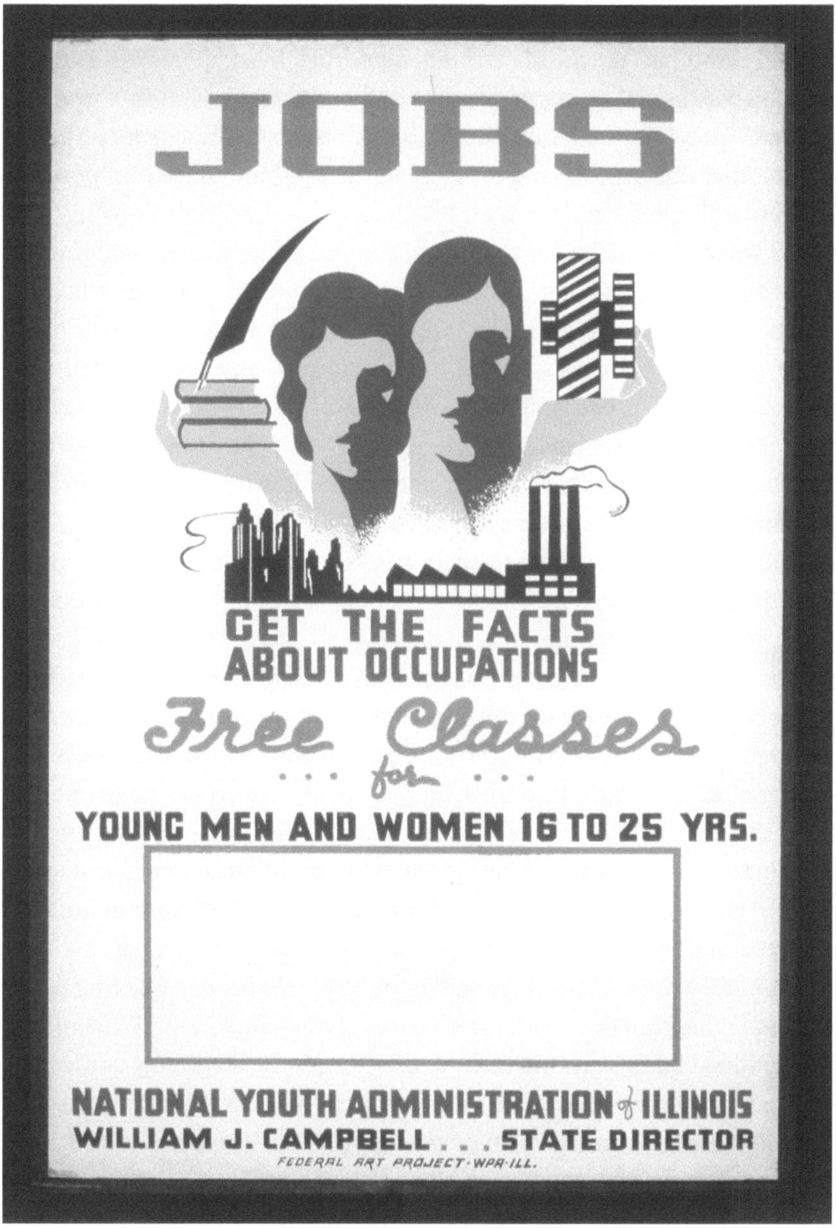

"A Poster for the NYA of Illinois." WPA poster by Joseph Dusek, Illinois Federal Art Project, WPA, 1941. Library of Congress Prints and Photographs Division, WPA Poster Collection, courtesy of the Library of Congress, Washington, DC.

Another study came from the private sector. In 1938 Betty and Ernest Lindley, who had previously written supportive biographies of FDR, undertook the task of trying to describe and evaluate the NYA in *A New Deal for Youth*. They admitted the difficulty of the task in the first chapter, pointing out that the largesse and diversity of the program made it impossible to draw a single portrait. After a brief photo essay section showing NYA youth working in fields, at recreation centers, schools, harbors, forests, classrooms, hospitals, agricultural centers, libraries, retirement homes, vocational centers, college labs, factories, mills, workshops, and many other places, the analysis turned to how these young men and women, black and white, urban and rural, were learning skills that contributed to the betterment of society. These were clearly not the "sentient, restless, and explosive" youth that Taussig feared would be lost, but engaged and involved members of the citizenry.[65]

The Lindleys spent most of their analysis comparing the goals of the NYA to its achievements. The first goal—to provide hope and opportunity to desperate young people—was met with great success. They reported that 95 percent of the young people on the NYA came from relief homes where the youth had little hope for the future. "I had to quit school when I was in the eighth grade" to help out the family, an eighteen-year-old NYA member reported, but without proper training he drifted from one to another meaningless and low-paying job. This young man's story was not unique, the Lindleys argued (most likely for an adult middle-class audience uninformed about the plight of youth), for more than half of those in the NYA dropped out before high school. The salvation of earning a paycheck for meaningful work was plain, as one young man related that "the first time I walked in the front door with my paycheck, I was somebody." What makes the Lindleys' book most interesting, however, is the testimony of the NYA youth. They tell how they valued the paycheck—the first for many—as well as their pride, commitment, and dedication to the ideals of the NYA and, by extension, the country. In a section titled "These Are Their Stories," the authors present thirty-four pages of young people testifying to the positive benefits of the NYA.[66]

These stories confirmed that many of the nation's youth saw a new modern order to their world and wanted to tell others about it—by their

"Young Black NYA Workers." Courtesy of FDR Library, Hyde Park, New York.

actions and images. One young Italian girl from a family of fifteen came to the NYA unable to read, write, or tell time, but with training she learned the basics of these skills as well as sewing to support herself. Another young man lived in a canvas tent with his family and subsisted on a diet of walnuts. With NYA training "he proved to be very capable at almost any job" and secured private employment as a carpenter's helper making $110 per month. Mary Lou and Emma were the eldest of eighteen fatherless children who lived in a four-room cabin with no furniture and survived on a diet of locusts and hickory nuts. They never attended school. But these young African American women were "eager to learn and improve themselves," which resulted in their moving the entire family to a better locale nearer to a "white community" where both of the girls found domestic employment. Arnold, a young man initially seen as a "hopeless, ignorant, Southern farmhand" who finished fifth grade when he was eighteen years old, was transformed with NYA vocational assistance into a respectable young farmer interested in modern farming and animal husbandry techniques. He became an "independent farmer." A letter from a young African American woman in Florida described how before the NYA she was "almost blind in one eye," but with seamstress training and the pay from the agency, she regained her sight with glasses and got her first job.[67]

The stories of NYA-inspired salvation document young people's understanding that the future was theirs and that the ties to the past had to be loosened and a new path traced. These modern pioneers, or as Taussig labeled them, "explorers," were both dissatisfied with the world as it existed and open to the potential that new ideas offered. They were introduced to many of these new ideas through nonmandatory yet highly attended evening or weekend classes designed not to be "anything that smacks of the old-fashioned schoolroom where a superior teacher ruled over inferior children." The NYA understood the "inequality of educational opportunity" in both theory and practicality. The percentage of youth who participated in these extra training sessions ran from 70 to 100 percent.[68]

In 1945 William Levy, a former NYA supervisor of research and program evaluation and work-education director, submitted a dissertation to Ohio State University evaluating the role and effect of the agency in Ohio between 1938 and 1943. He used letters and interviews to allow enrollees to outline the NYA scripture: (1) "respect for individuals as human beings"; (2) cooperation between the individual and the group; and (3) "faith and confidence in the ability of the people" to make a better society. Through enriched work experiences and directed activity, which reflected a new educational directive designed to bring a "new attitude toward forgotten youth," Levy argued that the NYA brought about significant changes in the way the young people viewed themselves and their world. This modern outlook taught the nation's youth that salvation lay not just with the individual; there is also an "obligation toward others . . . regardless of their different social and economic backgrounds." One student wrote that the training he and others received would be beneficial "the rest of their life"; another congratulated the NYA for its willingness to accept the responsibility for those who "might have been lost." All of their testimonials reflected their commitment to have, as one young woman said, a "chance . . . to make good at it."[69]

Levy's understanding of the tenets of the NYA and his findings—that those on the project came away convinced that they had been saved by this modern governmental agency—were not unique. In 1937 the NYA worked with Ohio State University's Gerson Chertoff to study whether the agency was having any effect on the young enrollees' understanding of social problems and their role in helping solve them. Employing scientific methodological terms, the investigators laid out their desire to get "reliable data" to determine the way in which the ideals of the NYA had become incorporated into the consciousness of their young recruits. Chertoff's team studied five Cleveland-area NYA projects to assess if "their attitude towards certain social problems [have] been liberalized." Through interviews and looking at NYA records, the team determined that the 120 young men and women studied did change their minds about the meaning and importance of social problems. Upon entrance, most had only a "vague and general" idea about social problems, which the investigators linked to the fact that most had, at best, a tenth-grade education and came from "families of low educational standing." However, after only a few short weeks the "workers tended to develop a more specialized interest in and understanding of the social problems" of the day. Further, they determined that their exposure to the positive influences of the NYA meant that their "interest in these problems will be deep set and lasting."[70]

These studies documented how the NYA was making young people more aware of the social problems of the day and, more important, how they could help solve them. As Ralph Tyler, director of the Progressive Education Association, wrote, the studies "demonstrate one means for developing in youth intelligent interests in social problems" and provided "evidence" that through proper "planning and supervision," young people could be made active agents in their world. The final section of Chertoff's report included NYA youth responses to specific interviewer questions. These read like recitation lessons. When asked, "What do you think of work relief as a form of assistance to unemployed people?" their responses could have come straight out of Williams's or Hopkins's mouths: "Work relief is better because people have more self-respect," said one; another said it was "good because people could hold their pride and feel more independent." When asked if they saw the need for relief, most agreed it was necessary "until everyone has a job." And finally, as the NYA projects stressed work in recreational facilities, they were asked what recreation meant, and the responses seemed almost rehearsed: "Organized recreation makes people useful, helpful, able-bodied citizens, and helps them get the best out of the environment they are in"; or, "The purpose of recreation is to divert attention toward relaxation and using leisure time profitably."[71]

These reports, primarily from Ohio, represented a snapshot of how many youth viewed the NYA across the country. The state ranked fourth in total expenditures at more than $8 million by the end of 1938 and regularly provided about twenty thousand young people with either student aid or employment on work projects ranging from working in the maintenance department in Springfield's city garage to being play leaders in the Montgomery County Children's Home. Also, working through Ohio State University, the state's coordinators spent considerable time documenting and studying the workings and effects of the agency. The state NYA director, S. Burns Weston, wanted to make certain that as many young people as possible were aided by the NYA and that as many communities as possible witnessed its benefits. To this end, he strongly encouraged NYA off-campus projects for those students receiving aid and boasted that more than "twelve per cent of the total number of students in participating institutions are employed in off-campus projects."[72]

The Ohio NYA was unique among states as it worked with various graduate programs at Ohio State University, where many students also received benefits, to investigate the effectiveness of the agency and help write evaluation reports. One master's thesis in public administration examined the effectiveness of a service rating system to better see in "black and white the qualities which the management wants" NYA recruits to possess. By accumulating this listing, the recruit had a better chance to "measure up to a supervisor's standards" and get the job. This ranking system helped build self-confidence and improved morale, and its advocates concluded that in order for a rational and meaningful service rating system to work, NYA supervisors and private employers needed to determine the basic positive qualities an employee must possess, which could then be shared with the NYA recruit to better guarantee they understood what was expected, how to accomplish their goals, and how to focus on being a great employee. Another master's degree study, this time in social administration, surveyed the economic background of the young people on the NYA to evaluate the ratio of relief to nonrelief workers. Recognizing, as others had, that traditional policies had failed to "offer hope to the great mass of youth," the thesis outlined how previously unambitious youth who "hardly allowed themselves" the privilege of pursuing career goals began to view their future with more optimism and saw in the relief effort the willingness of the country to integrate them into society. The study analyzed those in the Ohio NYA who came from relief families and were employed on work projects—more than 90 percent—and concluded that the dominant society had failed these "custodians of the future," and that an "organized society" must accept the responsibility to provide jobs, security, and hope.[73]

The educational tie-ins with Ohio State University validated and scientifically proved that the NYA was working. The NYA believed that the nation's educational system needed significant reform, and these studies outlined specifically how the agency was helping the nation's young people address the failures of traditional schooling. The fear of losing this generation was turned on its ear as the NYA used empirical evidence to show that providing basic work skills and functional educational courses brought a shift in consciousness among the youth. In 1938 the Ohio NYA, again working with Ohio State University, submitted a brief but detailed report on the effect of the NYA on the morale of its workers. The team interviewed and surveyed both supervisors and youth to get an understanding of whether the ideals of the agency had a positive or negative effect. It would be hard to imagine how the NYA could reduce morale, so the study was directed in a fixed positive direction. However, there was the chance that the research might show that the NYA had no effect on morale, which in effect would prove a negative. There was a lot riding on the report. State director Burton set the tone by reminding the reader that "perhaps the most fundamental" objective of the NYA was building self-confidence and that this report would "eliminate guesswork in determining whether the NYA" was building more confident and optimistic citizens. It is fortunate that the study showed a direct correlation between the NYA and improved health, economic status, personal appearance, self-esteem, self-respect, attitude toward work, cooperative social behavior, and social value. "This means," the evaluators concluded, "that most youth workers have improved their individual development of self-confidence and morale." Using the most recent social scientific methodology, reports such as these documented how the NYA was not simply providing economic relief but rebuilding the nation's youth and sending them out into the larger world as examples of what could be done through reason, planning, and effective social legislation. Those who served in the NYA, like those who came out of the CCC camps, became examples of the power of modern ideas and policies and served in their families, neighborhoods, and larger communities as members of the new model army marching to the new order.[74]

The Depression left the nation's youth behind and weakened their ability to work or contribute to society in a positive manner. Many in the CCC and NYA were literally the dregs of society: illiterate, undereducated, and from questionable home life and neighborhood backgrounds. Their future, even in the best of times, was pocked with doubt, but in the 1930s there seemed little hope for them. There were some within and outside of government who understood the value of these young minds and bodies and believed they could be reformed to meet the needs of the modern society. The young, they understood, served as the foundation for the new order, or as FDR called them in 1938, the "shock troops." Some European countries used their young people as the foundation for their dictatorships, and although there was some fear that FDR was using his policies in a similar manner, the experiences of the CCC and NYA revealed that the real goal of the administration's focus on youth was to transform and modernize their way of thinking. The CCC and NYA served as models of modernity's potential and made plain the true path of democracy and citizenship. As FDR said in a 1936 radio address, we have "dreams and visions about a greater and finer America that is to be . . . blessed beyond anything we know, with these spiritual things—material and spiritual—that make man's life abundant." They were the new model army of modernity.[75]

The seriousness of the youth situation during the Depression era signaled a concern for what many felt was a falling away from core ideals and values that defined democracy and the United States. These "ethical priorities," as Paul Weaver wrote in 1944, provided meaning for life and helped define the "nature of the universe."[76] The CCC and NYA, as well as other agencies created by the government in response to the economic crisis of the 1930s, guided the nation's youth to identify and internalize the modern core values and ideals of social commitment and service. With proper planning and rational human implementation, the young people were shown how modern ideas (modernity) worked to save not just them but also, through their labors, their families, communities, and nation. Those enrolled in the CCC and NYA came away from their experiences transformed both physically and intellectually. They were excited by what they had experienced and what they now felt life held in store for them. They incorporated the values impressed upon them and projected these onto their family, friends, and coworkers, making them in many ways the new model army of modernity.

SALVATION AWAITS

EXPOSITIONS, WORLD'S FAIRS, AND MODERNITY

3

"Between 1933 and 1940," writes historian Robert W. Rydell, "an upthrust of modernist world's fairs broke through the crust of Depression-Era America and transformed [the cities where they took place] into blazing beacons of light and hope." He goes on to point out that these fairs and expositions drew more than a hundred million visitors and that their mix of nostalgia and utopianism were projected onto an American population hoping that a new era was imminent. Hundreds of millions more shared these visions through movie newsreels, newspaper and magazine stories, radio broadcasts, and, of course, old-fashioned word of mouth. In light of the devastation and the pallor of death that hung over world societies in the aftermath of World War I, many countries turned to expositions, Rydell suggests, buttressing "their own authority." Fairs in Paris, Barcelona, Seville, Antwerp, Stockholm, Liege, and various cities in the United States featured their contributions to world society, often using their imperialist gaze as a lens for introspection, and more often than not backed with state funding, documenting the progress of civilization.[1]

In the United States, the trope of empire was trumped by the ideas and philosophies of modernism, especially as they related to the positive attributes of science and technology. Faith in reason promised a future that would once again make the United States "the city upon the hill" for the whole world to view. "American modernism," Rydell argued, "was not just about style or a way of living; it was not just about surfaces. It was about the substance and meaning of modern life itself."[2]

Rydell's focus on the fairs' triumvirate of business, government, and the modernist designer's attempt to revive the American economy and point the way to a more stable and modern future is not incorrect. Yet the fairs in the six US cities—Chicago (1933–1934), San Diego (1935–1936), Dallas (1936), Cleveland (1936–1937), San Francisco (1939–1940), and New York (1939–1940)—resembled a variety of celebrations, from religious tent revivals or camp meetings to carnivals of consumption and even amusement parks as much as they played on the serious nature of their initial ideas.[3]

World's fairs as events had always detailed the promises of the future in the present. But they had lost much of their luster during the 1920s, and to risk capital resources and investments during a time of economic and social crisis in the 1930s was quite a leap, encouraging organizers to draw on the traditional message of unity and salvation. The fairs presented during the Depression era were designed to introduce new ways of seeing, of experiencing the world around them, asking people in their visual presentation and arrangement to put their faith in the ideals of scientific methodology, reason, and planning.

The call to organize these expos and fairs came from a partnership of political and business leaders who felt that social and economic circumstances in their regions necessitated an event to remind people of their collective past and outline the possibilities of the future. The speakers, location, landscape design, and social function of the events were planned and organized to make the experience a transformative one. The attendees would leave refreshed and ready to spread what they had experienced with those who were unable to attend. In this way, they became emissaries of the salvation of modernity. But the fairs also held symbolic importance. Organizers put great thought into the setup of the camps, making certain that the layout allowed the speakers and pavilions to project their message to the people, many of whom had little hope for tomorrow, given the drudgery of the reality of the economic situation. The organizers knew that in order to be successful, they had to keep the layout and the message basic and easy to digest. The structure of the meetings sought to connect to other aspects of American culture. This resulted in expos and fairs that were part carnival, tent show, circus, vaudeville, and even Hollywood and radio. As historian Christina Cogdell has written, beginning with the Century of Progress (COP) in Chicago and carrying through all the expos and fairs in the 1930s, the overriding ideal presented reassured the "American public that they were under enlightened leadership . . . whose plans to control the future were backed by the authority of scientific knowledge." The future would be better because of their faith in science and the ideals of modernity.[4]

When the largest and best known of the six fairs of the Depression era was being planned in 1937, Grover Whalen, president of the New York City Fair Corporation, told anyone who would listen that the keystone for success lay in the simplicity of the message. Salvation would come through "a perfectly ordered mechanical civilization."[5] Certainly his comments, like many that he made publicizing the 1939 event, were more hyperbole than real; yet they underscore the message presented by the fairs held during the Depression era. In the midst of the worst social and economic crisis in the nation's history, hope was in short supply. President Roosevelt and his advisors knew full well that only part of the problem lay in providing sustenance to the dispossessed; the larger issue dealt with providing hope for the future. This ideological desire lay at the foundation of many of the more successful New Deal programs, such as the Civilian Conservation Corps, the Works Progress Administration, or even Social Security, because they all provided hope along with security. The world's fairs and expositions of the 1930s served this purpose as well, giving people a glimpse into a future that awaited those who believed in the power of progress tied to modernity.

The 1930s saw more world's fairs and expositions than any other time period before or after, as a reaction to social and economic circumstances. The economic collapse and the subsequent social crisis called for a new way of understanding the past and how the present situation offered hope for the future. While religious leaders believed this might come through some revival-like atmosphere, no such revival took place. Even though there were religious camp meetings throughout the country, these failed to excite the masses as they had in the past. Into this breach came the six American expos and fairs that linked the struggles and successes of the past to the hope and security of the future through organization, planning, and reason. These were modernist spectacles, testaments to what could and would be done to alleviate the suffering, uncertainty, and crises of faith that in many ways were the Great Depression.

The fairs and expositions of the 1930s offered salvation in exchange for belief and even faith in reason exemplified through science. Starting with the COP in 1933 and finishing with the New York World's Fair (NYWF) in 1939, Americans were called forth to witness the salvation available through the methodology and reasoning of science, making the dreams of tomorrow real for the here and now. The process of sanctification began by recognizing how science had positively transformed human existence, followed by a vision of what the future might hold if only the people applied these same scientific principles to other areas of their life. As Gerald Wendt, director of the NYWF Department of Science, wrote in 1939, "Even present-day science can be intelligently used to enrich the content of life, that the methods of science are applicable to larger human problems, and that the attitude of science expresses the highest reaches of the human spirit," which testified to the overall theme of the decade's celebrations. No less than a shift in consciousness was necessary, as too often people accepted the products of science, which greatly improved their way of life, but held firm to the superstitions and unreasonable ideas that dominated human understanding. The fairs offered them a glimpse of what the future might look like.[6]

The six fairs and expos of the era brought the supremacy of science and reason to more than a hundred million people. The national events, such as the COP or the NYWF, displayed the wonders of science and technology to millions, while the regional fairs reached millions more who were unable to get to the host cities. The first of these spectacles took place in Chicago with the COP in 1933, at a time when science and scientists needed to redeem themselves in the public eye, as the economic crash and subsequent hardship of depression were partially laid at their feet. They had been the early prophets of mass production through the application of scientific methodology and technology; these same ideas contributed, according to many ordinary citizens, to the problems plaguing the nation and the world. In the first decades of the century, science's aspirational visions suggested the power to understand and manipulate nature, whether it be in the formulation of social policy based on its discoveries, like understanding bacteria's role in disease, or the potential for long-term transformation through the application of genetic theories most commonly associated with eugenics. Science touched every aspect of American society, and the number of scientists and the funding they received grew exponentially. Although World War I tempered some enthusiasm, the abundance of the 1920s, brought about by the application of scientific methodologies to technical and commercial problems, saw science once again in the limelight. New theories, like that of relativity or quantum mechanics, led some within the scientific community to question their certainty and encouraged most to continue with the faith that their theories and methods would aid in the betterment of society and its people. The crash and the social frustration of the early Depression era forced many within the scientific community to redouble their efforts to project the advancement of society through science.[7]

Historian Glen Scott Allen suggests that the American public's perception of science and scientists, as represented in popular culture, is divided between the "heroic figure" who used his (the genre has rarely portrayed women as scientists) genius for the good of all humankind, or the "villain" who sought only power and control over others. During the Depression era, the image of science and its scientists underwent a redefinition in the public mind from "independent Master Mechanic" to a servant of society, as pulp magazines such as *Amazing Stories* and *Wonder Stories* joined the ranks of the more respectable *Popular Science*, *Popular Mechanics*, and others to present the future through applied science. The American public had little understanding or use for the theoretical sciences, preferring the more practical, engineering-based sciences often manifested in consumer goods. The people consumed and enjoyed these, Allen argues, without understanding "why we actually needed [them]" or their larger transformative power. People put their faith in science without a rational justification, needing only representations to mark their acceptance.[8]

For the fairs and expos of the 1930s, science needed to detail how the more theoretical sciences such as physics, chemistry, or even biology provided tangible benefits to humanity. Perhaps this helps explain why, as the decade wore on, they relied more on corporate sponsorship to detail the specific benefits of science. Explaining how the development of electricity, whether from hydroelectric dams or atomic energy, provided for a better future through new consumer items outlined how science was linked to their consumer liberation. David Nye, a historian of technology, writes that the NYWF, and, by association, earlier Depression-era fairs, provided "complete environments . . . where human needs would be met by electric machinery."[9]

This desire to bring the people back into the fold of modernist scientific hope lay at the foundation of the world's fairs and regional expositions that dot the 1930s. They displayed the advantages of science and its modern methods for those whose faith had been challenged by the crisis. For the many people who had lost hope, the fairs and expositions reminded them of modernism's promise. The twenty-five-cent COP *Official Book of the Fair* explained that progress through science and reason were chosen as the event's theme to outline the "transformations in mind" that occurred over the previous century and to "pay homage to these higher things of the spirit."[10]

At the center of the COP was the largest structure at the exposition, the Hall of Science. Initially called the Temple of Science, it resembled a place of worship and represented "the spirit of scientific achievement." The modern design of the structure formed a U, welcoming visitors to its center. The center stage of this three-acre site exemplified the "order and massiveness" of modernity and made it difficult for the visitor not to feel awed by the salvation promised through science. It even had a carillon bell tower, with chimes to announce special events and call guests to the center. On opening day in 1933, as visitors perused the official guidebook with the epigraph informing them that "Science Finds—Industry Applies—Man Conforms," the Hall of Science welcomed the masses to its center with tones emanating from the carillon tower. A choir sang "The Prayer for America" after the pealing of the bells, and to make certain that the connection between religion and science was not lost, the diocese's auxiliary bishop delivered an opening invocation.[11]

Outside the building, a large statue of a robot with its hands on the backs of a man and woman helping them move forward welcomed the visitors. The message was clear—modernism in the form of science and its methodology would move those who believed into a glorious future. And to better convince those of wavering faith of the majesty of science and modernism, the organizers decided to open the COP with, as Charles D. Stewart wrote in the *Atlantic Monthly*, power "extracted from a star beam . . . [whose] magic touch will now be accomplished by means of a hookup with a star. Instead of earthly force, there will be heavenly light" from Arcturus, one of the brightest stars in the night sky and the same star cited in Job 9:9. Drawing its light onto a forty-inch lens and then refracted into a sixty-three-foot tube and photoelectric cell, the current obeyed "man's behest at every crook and turn" and traveled the eighty miles from the observatory to the COP where its power opened "wide the gates, . . . start[ed] up the machinery, and [said] most effectively, *Here we are!*"[12]

The science exhibits in Chicago were designed to show how science, through the application of reason, had transformed human life and promised an even better future. The exhibits were consciously designed to outline how science made the world a better place over the past hundred years as well as give the meaning and importance of the scientific method to each of the basic sciences so that the "visitor may acquire a permanent interest in the link connecting science with progress." For example, the chemistry exhibit explained how the use of reason allowed scientists to transform matter and come to understand the fundamentals of life. The central mural in the Great Hall featured the Tree of Knowledge with the names of various applied sciences as the fruit to be picked and used by the people. But, as Robert Rydell writes, instead of being "expelled from paradise . . . [they were] invited into a scientific Eden."[13]

The exhibits in the Hall of Science were divided into seven sections—chemistry, biology, mathematics, astronomy, physics, geology, and medicine—with the hope of drawing both lay and experienced persons into the exhibits to demystify nature and to project optimism that through reason and applied science, solutions to all problems only awaited human action. J. Franklin Bell, chief of the applied science and industry division for the exposition, wrote in the March 1933 issue of *Scientific Monthly* that the National Research Council appointed a science advisory committee—a sort of synod of science—to not only outline what areas should be displayed

"Man at the Center of the Future." Photograph identification number COP 17 0023 00000 025, Century of Progress World's Fair, 1933–1934. Special Collections and University Archives, University of Illinois at Chicago Library. Used with permission.

but also specify what they should detail about the significance and meaning of science to human development. Within this council all aspects of science, applied and theoretical, had equal voice, so the exhibits were to feature not only what has come as a result of science but also what might yet come through the application of modern methods.[14]

The COP advisory team asked each science section leader to publicize their exhibits in leading popular science magazines. Reviewing the creation and reception of the earth sciences exhibit at the COP, University of Chicago geologist and exhibit curator Carey Croneis noted the transformative nature of geologic advances over the past century and the social ramifications for human society. He reported that the earth sciences section was filled with "dynamic individual exhibits calculated to tell completely the complicated story of the origin and growth of our planet." He had no doubt that the "man in the street" would come away understanding how the earth evolved and how science tapped into these earthly resources to make life better now and even better in the future. Professor Arthur B. Lamb of Harvard University, president of the American Chemical Society and curator for the chemistry display, crowed that "never has such a galaxy of scientific exhibits been gathered before," and that during the previous hundred years, unshackled from the constraints of religion, the number of organic substances grew from virtually zero to more than three hundred thousand. These discoveries altered the physical world around humanity, he wrote, leading to medical and social advances unknown to earlier generations. The key to these advancements lay in science's ability to understand "the structure of matter" and the development of mathematical formulas necessary to group and alter molecular structures. Lamb summarized the science exhibits as they related (and all things did) to chemistry, reaffirming the role it plays as creator, in many instances, of life.[15]

In the foreword to the COP *Medical Science Exhibits* book (1936), William Allen Pusey, the chair of the medical advisory committee and past president of the American Medical Association, outlined how the exhibits provided a foundation for understanding the scientific and rational need for medicine in modern life. They also detailed the technology necessary for this progress and ensured that their exhibit gave no quarter to "charlatanism." Pusey and his team of medical and scientific "experts" created displays that drew 80 percent of the visitors who came to the fair, or roughly 15 million persons. The exhibits were, he wrote, "the most successful undertaking of this sort to enlighten the public in the art and science of medicine."[16]

For each science exhibit, the focus was how to translate complex scientific information into a format that ordinary people could understand, apply, and take back with them to their families, homes, and communities. In order to meet this goal, the COP exhibits were arranged and organized along strict guidelines. First, the exhibit had to create a "dignified" atmosphere guaranteeing no doubt as to its intention. The facts and images were to be arranged, in step two, so that the "appropriate response" would come almost universally from all viewers. This involved making sure the exhibit conformed to the most modern ideas regarding color, form, and structure. The third step reduced boredom or fatigue by eliminating waste spaces where the route might deviate. Steps four and five made certain the exhibits caught and maintained the focus through "vividness of presentation" and a reduction of complex ideas and theories into their most common understandings. Finally, each exhibit needed to maintain a connection to the whole, so that the "repetition" encouraged an enlightened viewer. The COP wanted to make the exhibits complex enough to impress but understandable for an average "twelve year old child."[17]

The exhibits proved successful to both practitioners and laypeople alike. *Hygenia*, a widely distributed journal for those in the medical fields, praised the COP medical exhibits and reminded its readers that "without the contributions of public health and medicine," none of the advances celebrated in Chicago could have reached fruition. The Transparent Man, one of the more popular exhibits, lifted the veil of mystery from the body and detailed humanity's knowledge of its inner workings. Each of his organs lit up as a voiced-over narration explained its significance to the overall health and maintenance of the body. The point of the exhibit was not to get the viewer to learn or even know about anatomy but to reveal how science understood the form and relationships among the organs and tissues within the human body. Other exhibits alongside the Transparent Man allowed the visitor to manipulate joints and see how muscles worked. The medical exhibit showed, *Hygenia* suggested, how the work of modern science had freed humankind "from the fear of pain, disease, and death." The tenets of salvation were tangible for any "human being fortunate enough to" experience the COP.[18]

Working with these guidelines and with the help of professional advisors made up of architects, designers, and marketers, each exhibitor set up their display with clarity and easy access. To fix the viewer's gaze they prohibited empty spaces, competing lighting, or carnivalesque hawkers inviting visitors to their stalls. This format made certain that the greatest number of people could pass through exhibits unfettered yet informed. The exhibit "A Million Years Ago," which told the story of human evolution, guided the viewers through the entire story with the use of a circular "revolving sidewalk" that guaranteed the "continuous movement of people through the building." When Lincoln Kirstein reviewed the COP before its second season in 1934, he pointed out the "staging, as spectacle, as a show of power in the conscious control of an industrial dynasty" of the Ford display. Although not the pure sciences, exhibits by Ford, General Motors (GM), and Chrysler stressed the science of their automobiles, not only in the design of the car but in its construction and operation as well. The use of fused glass, chromium-plated parts, and many technical aspects of the engine and drive train, made with precision instruments and the most advanced products available, impressed the visitors, as did their view of the workers who appeared clean, organized, and as "innocent of personality as of dirt," yet with "smoothly run, and youthfully imaginative efficiency."[19]

Perhaps the larger point of the COP, and adopted by all the expos and fairs that followed, was best outlined by historian Charles Beard in 1933. Beard made it clear in his introduction to *The Century of Progress*, published by the Committee on Publication, the positive role science and scientific methodology played in America's progress and the salvation of a modern future. Beard linked the COP with the uniquely American notion of Jonathan Winthrop's "city on the hill," but Beard's modern sermon extolled the virtues of modern science and its reliance on reason to "emancipate" believers from the trials and tribulations of past societies built on superstition and to create "the good life—here and now."[20] Beard convincingly argued for a commitment to the faith in reason as manifest through science. He understood that many people blamed science for what they saw as technological unemployment, but to him and many others, this blame was misplaced. Science lay at the foundation of the salvation from the many problems plaguing the nation. Progress "is founded on the belief" that human civilization can and must continually improve to create not some "remote heaven" but a society dedicated to eradicating the "calamities" of the present society. Beard traced those ideas that shackled people to the past to primarily European or Asian sources, arguing that their fatalists' shrug of shoulders and belief that nothing could be done to alleviate the problems confronting modern society forced people to toil under the yoke of false promises, all with the hope of rewards in the afterlife.

Linking the new modernism to American exceptionalism, Beard posited that as America matured and became a world power during the first part of the twentieth century, its historical development presaged its adoption of modernism as salvation. America's democratic development since the Revolution pointed to its uniqueness and served as the foundation for the new faith, a rational new way of being, whether that be political, economic, or technological. Beard was clear: the future belongs to this country whose people are "incessantly engaged in subduing nature and in seeking to develop an ordered economy which will establish security . . . with the widest possible distribution of the benefits flowing from efficient industry."[21]

With so many people moving through the COP, a variety of what Assistant Director of Operation and Maintenance Clarence W. Farrier called "gadgets" was necessary. These were the shelters and decorations that guided the people through the exhibits. The trees that lined the Electrical Group exhibits were artificial and 100 feet tall. The "Clock of Ages" told the story of evolution through forty-two color pictures displayed on its face. Visitors watched the 10-million-year evolution of the earth and human beings that was paired with a 240-foot-tall thermometer, both depicting how science both explained and illuminated human existence.[22]

When the *Christian Century* visited the COP, they admired the hope that the exhibits presented, calling them "a mirror of modern life" and "the epitome of our culture." Although their review denied the promise of an earthly "Paradise," they did recognize within the COP's secular attributes the "practical" modernist ideals that appealed to the visitors. They noted that the exhibits were presented in a way that required little contemplation—one had only to "passively expose yourself to" the secular reality being presented. The editors were cognizant that times had changed and the religiosity of the past had given way to a new temporal sense of salvation based on the COP's "vast exhibition of machinery." They wondered, however, if people could be "rescued from the welter" of their own technology, science, and modern ideas. Were these the vestiges of salvation to replace the older and more traditional symbols? Their final analysis was mixed but hopeful that the COP symbolized the dawning of "an era in which the spirit shall come into its own" like never before.[23]

The initial success of the COP pointed to a second year of operation and also encouraged officials in Cleveland, San Diego, and Dallas to consider fairs of their own. In his final report, Charles G. Dawes pointed out that "no fair, ever held in the United States, attracted more visitors" than the COP in 1933, with 22.5 million paid entrants. When free admissions and employees were added, the total came to nearly 28 million, with another 21 million in 1934. This number made other fair organizers push even harder for their shows to get off the ground, for if they could draw even half of the 49 million who went to Chicago, their regional fairs would be successful. The millions who came to Chicago also pumped more than $100 million into the economy, resulting in the employment, albeit temporary, of more than a hundred thousand workers with an estimated weekly payroll gain of $2 million. The COP's success suggested not the past but a future where the problems of the day would and could be solved using modern faith and beliefs. The World of Tomorrow, the slogan of the New York fair held at the end of the decade, although not yet official, was already born in the minds of many. The COP served as the inspiration and foundation for other cities to hold expositions of their own, and even New York City's Grover Whalen sought the advice of Second City planners as his committee began outlining plans for their end-of-the-decade fair.[24]

Several local leaders in San Diego saw in the success of the COP hope for their own plans to hold an exposition in 1935 using many of the exhibits exported directly from Chicago. San Diego had hosted the Panama-California Exposition in 1915, and the organizers hoped to replicate that fair's success but with an up-to-date, modern theme. However, their desire to hold a fair was met with some skepticism and concern, especially given the depressed economy and a city government hampered by accusations of graft and corruption. When Frank Drugan, a friend of FDR and a newspaper writer, secured commitments (with the help of his friend Cyrus McCormick, Jr.) to move several of the COP exhibitions lock, stock, and barrel to San Diego, interest among those in the business community congealed to form a committee to plan the California Pacific International Exposition (CPIE) for 1935. Three shifts of construction workers repaired and built up the Balboa Park exposition area to resemble, according to the *Official Guide*, "the most modern architecture, blended, harmonized and suited to the Southwest."[25]

The CPIE opened at the end of May 1935 and remained true to the COP's theme of the positive transformative effects of modern science on society. CPIE reminded the faithful and sought to convert those with little faith in the promise of modernity with "palaces" dedicated to better housing, education, science, transportation, and Pacific relations. When visitors entered the Palace of Science, a steel giant named Alpha who talked, sat, stood, and blinked his eyes greeted them. The 2,000-pound chrome-plated giant hinted at what might be the future.[26]

President Roosevelt officially opened the CPIE in modernist fashion via the telephone. Unable to make the trip in person, he reminded the people that it was "dedicated to future generations." The Depression had brought serious challenges and questioned the very nature of our society, he intoned, but events like the CPIE were a testament to the faith the people had in solving their problems through reason, planning, and the power of modernity. "A new public conscience is demanding" that the ways of the past be replaced by new practices and ideas, the president said, and the people were "becoming increasingly conscious of their obligations to the citizens of tomorrow." Sacrifice was necessary for salvation. When he and Eleanor finally visited in October, near the end of the CPIE's first season, he spoke highly of the benefits of science and technology to the nearly sixty thousand people in the San Diego stadium. They were examples, he said, of "what the nation can achieve on a broad scale" if they put their faith and trust in those things that humans could control. Modernity, although not a term specifically used by the president, served as the foundation for his speech, given that it focused on reason, planning, organization, and scientific methods as the means to future salvation. More than 4.7 million people visited the CPIE in its first year. It opened for a second year with a scaled-down agenda and more varied theme, attracting another two million visitors.[27]

The regional success of the CPIE encouraged other regions to move forward with their own plans for an expo. The organizers of the Texas Centennial (TC) used the centennial of the Texas Republic as their theme. They began planning in 1923 for a celebration in 1936, but with the onset of the Depression, the reality of funding and drawing visitors worried the organizers. With the success of Chicago and events building in San Diego, however, the organizers were encouraged, and in late 1934 the Centennial

Commission chose Dallas over Houston and San Antonio to host the event. Over the next ten months they embarked on an extensive building project with Donald Nelson, who had worked as chief designer on four exhibits at the COP. He later related that what took Chicago four years to complete, his team in Texas accomplished in ten months.[28]

The TC, like San Diego, tapped some key individuals from the COP, most notably Nelson as chief designer. Nelson was hired by chief architect George Dahl, who had studied the COP before offering him the position. Nelson quickly hired Major Lennox Lohr, former manager of COP, and Louis Skidmore, who had served as chief of design there, to join him in Dallas. The final Chicago connection came with the hiring of lighting design coordinator C. M. Cutler, whose opening night light display stunned the Texas crowds. When Fort Worth announced that its rival Frontier Exposition would run concurrent with the official Centennial, those planners also looked to Chicago for guidance in the form of Sally Rand and her sensational fan dance. Such a hit in Chicago proved a major draw for the rival Frontier celebration. They also hired Billy Rose to organize the amusement area, who coined the phrase "For education go to Dallas, for entertainment, come to Fort Worth."[29]

Texas wanted visitors to come away from the Centennial convinced that a better future would arrive because of modern science and technology. The Department of Labor used a "mechanical man" to address the question of technological unemployment, telling visitors to the exhibit that the scientific application of reason through machines created more jobs and inexpensive commodities, and that modernism was "making life easier and better for men." When President Roosevelt came to the Centennial on June 12, 1936, he spoke at length of the value of science and technology working together for the good of all people. He delivered a sermonlike speech to more than a hundred thousand people who crowded into the TC that day, extolling the Centennial as evidence of the "return of confidence" and the desire of the American people to see "things first hand." His speech invoked the idea, as had others he delivered previously, of chasing the moneylenders from the temple, only this time it was to ensure the salvation of democracy operating under the aegis of reason. The "prophets of evil" were those business and industrial leaders who continued to operate under the flawed belief that humans were incapable of reasonably constructing a stable and efficient society. They sought to divide the people against one another, preventing the full flowering of American society. The unity displayed by the TC as well as other fairs, FDR pointed out, revealed how the country was breaking down these barriers and restoring "democracy in opportunity."[30]

The TC exposition was the first to inch away from the pure modernist appeal of the COP and suggest, through its close work with corporate sponsors, a more applied version of modern salvation. Although science and technology were great things in their own right, their application to the daily problems detailed the faith organizers had in the future. There were more than 130 exhibits and concession buildings in Dallas organized under industrial banners such as "Electricity," "Communication," "Transportation," and "Housing and Building Materials." As historian Kenneth Ragsdale points out, the 6.3 million visitors to the Centennial in 1936 "discovered on every hand that a better and more rewarding lifestyle awaited somewhere beyond the Depression-wracked era in which they were living." All they had to do was open their eyes and minds and witness how their salvation came through modernism. Under Dahl and Nelson's leadership, the overall design was ultramodern, promoting new technologies such as air-conditioning and television. The publicity department actively recruited people to come to the fair to be educated, sending out more than 8.75 million flyers encouraging visitors to witness a better tomorrow in Dallas. They also published the biweekly newsletter begun in 1934 called the *Texas Centennial News* and encouraged each of the 254 Texas counties to develop their own versions of the celebration. In September 1936 Governor James Allred declared a two-day school holiday so that the state's schoolchildren could make a pilgrimage to the site. The state superintendent estimated 275,000 children made the trip (although a lower estimate places the number closer to 117,000). In addition, more than 45,000 people a month came from outside of Texas to visit the Centennial.[31]

In June 1937 the Centennial opened under a new title, the Greater Texas and Pan American Exposition. Like the other fairs, it hoped to match the success of the first year, albeit in a less grandiose manner. The theme was a little different and the focus on modernity and science less prevalent, but it did draw several million more people to the exhibits that remained and served as a testament to the new era.[32]

The Cleveland exposition, like the regional ones in Texas and San Diego, was small in comparison to the COP and NYWF. And although it focused on regional industry and its peoples, the Great Lakes Exposition (GLE) used its facilities and space to reinforce the idea that modernity, in this case primarily scientific industrial development, laid the cornerstone for the future. Begun like the others to stimulate business and industry, and tied to the centennial of the city's incorporation, leading businessmen such as Dudley Blossom understood the advantages the COP brought to Chicago and wanted the same type of positive infusion for Cleveland. Construction began in the late winter of 1936, and after only a few short months, the GLE opened on June 27. Over the next several months nearly four million would visit—almost seven million over a two-year span—pumping more than $60 million into the local economy during its run.[33]

The GLE hoped to use the enthusiasm of the closing of the Republican Party's presidential convention held earlier in June as the springboard for its opening. Designed as a "cross between," according to the *New York Times*, "an exhibit and a frolic," the focus was on how science related to the iron and steel industry so important to the region. And, like the TC, the focus in Cleveland was on applied science. This move away from the purity of scientific presentation at the COP toward a more applied and commercial vein signaled a schism of sorts that had begun to develop in the dissemination and appropriation of modernity. No longer was science promoted for its own sake, but much like many other manifestations of modernity during the era, there had to be a social commitment. As President Roosevelt said when he visited GLE on August 14, 1936, "These expositions further strengthen that purpose of national understanding and national solidarity" regarding the problems facing society and the solutions, technological as well as human, that were available.[34]

Entering the Romance of Iron and Steel exhibit, for example, visitors passed through the evolutionary stages of human control of metallurgy, beginning with a primitive furnace and carrying through to the modern open-hearth Bessemer furnace. There was no mistaking the power of

"Great Lakes Exposition." Cleveland Press Collection, Michael Schwartz Library, Cleveland State University. Used with permission.

making the product, but without modern science and reason, the advances would have never been possible. When Secretary of Commerce Daniel Roper spoke at the opening of the GLE, he reminded the audience that "what you think and do here affects the rest of the nation," and the success of the GLE reflected the general atmosphere of change sweeping the country. He outlined how cooperation, fair play, and justice were displayed at the fair and told the people to keep their minds open to the possibilities of change and "social justice."[35]

The GLE featured a variety of exhibits that outlined the applied use of modern science. As Blossom wrote in the 1936 *Guidebook*, the point of the exposition was to both document the progress of the Great Lakes region over the last hundred years and "indicate the paths of progress for the future." The design was modern to show the visitors that by using reason and scientific methodology, towns and cities could "fulfill perfectly the purpose for which they were built." The central stage was ringed with seven majestic pylons within the Sherwin-Williams pavilion. Other attractions lay within view just beyond this grand entranceway. The GLE design followed the pattern begun in Chicago and mimicked by each of the other fairs, all of which took their cue from the large entrances used at camp meetings, carnivals, and even modernist movie palaces.[36]

Two key areas at GLE focused the visitor's gaze on the future and the benefits of modernity. The Hall of Progress featured a variety of displays outlining the myriad ways in which modern devices increased "convenience, utility, safety, and economy" in people's homes. Using electricity as the focus, the exhibit detailed through lighting and appliances how modern "science and invention [brought about] higher living standards" for all people. A huge "television theater" impressed visitors with advances in modern communication and entertainment, where they watched themselves and other fair goers on a large television screen. The Iron and Steel hall guided the visitor through the progress of science via a walking tour of the entire steel-making process, from mine to blast furnace. Sponsored by the nation's steel companies, the murals and overall design left no room for interpretation other than that modern science and metallurgy were responsible for the improved way of life for most people in the Great Lakes region, if not the entire country. Other modernist features included a hidden light projector on the top of the Marine Theater that produced an Aurora Borealis–like light show onto the night sky and the design structure of the Hall of Transportation.[37]

One of the principal attractions for GLE came directly from the COP, reflecting the unity of ideas that underscored the success of the expos. Once established with the COP, the theme of the 1930s fairs focused on progress derived not from the idea of manifest destiny or any connection to the supernatural but to the ability of humans to solve natural problems using reason and scientific methodology. Modernity, even when not spoken about directly, was the god worshiped. One of the many fairs' and expos' featured events that reinforced this idea without really mentioning it was Edward Hungerford's history of transportation in America.

Hungerford's affinity for the history of transportation reflected his own belief that progress was linked to technological and scientific advancements. The story of transportation, in his view, was the "the story of American ingenuity, faith, vision and courage in conquering the problem" of moving people and goods from one place to another. Nearly two million people viewed the more than 1,100 presentations of his pageant,

The Wings of a Century, at the COP, which was based on a limited version he presented in 1927 for the centennial of the B&O Railroad. Hungerford's show was a hit and next went to Rochester for its 1934 centennial as *The Pathways of Progress*. The next stop was GLE, where Hungerford brought the same general manager, stage directors, and stage designer he had used in Chicago and Rochester to put on the *Parade of Years*. The story and visuals were hardly changed from the COP show, with authentic wagons, coaches, trains, planes, and automobiles to document the ingenuity and progress of humanity through invention born of necessity. The highlight was the sheer volume and size of the artifacts, especially the trains, as well as the spirited music provided by famed African American composer Dr. Nathanial Dett.[38]

Many other features from the COP were reproduced at GLE and the other fairs. For example, they all erected model homes with modern devices and building materials, tracks for automobiles to "prove" their mettle, exhibits for horticulture, electricity, and communications, and, of course, the amusement zone. The similarity of the Depression-era fairs and expos was not accidental, for the organizers were all in communication with each other. They all wanted to draw big crowds, stimulate commerce, and promote the future. For example, when the buses for the NYWF made their way to the city from the factory in Lansing, Michigan, in January 1939, fair president Grover Whalen asked Cleveland's mayor, Harold Burton, whom he had contacted earlier about helping promote the NYWF, if he would "inspect the caravan" when it came through the city. The buses proved a good publicity moment when the mayor inspected them. In March, Burton spoke at the Waldorf Astoria in New York City and outlined why he and the people of Cleveland were going to support the upcoming NYWF. "The future of democracy depends on the success of the American people as a whole in understanding the facts and needs of the future," he told those in attendance, linking this vision to technology whose influence was "infinitely multiplied." Burton also secured from Whalen a commitment to have July 22, 1939, be declared Cleveland Day at the NYWF.[39]

There were other connections between the fairs. Because of the central role New York played in the development of the Great Lakes, primarily through the Erie Canal, GLE had an office in New York City to sign up corporate sponsorship and promote tourism to the exposition. Whalen and the NYWF board sounded out the ideas of the GLE organizers for their own event, then in the planning stages. Also, the man responsible for the general construction for the GLE, Albert N. Gonsior, had been chief of construction for the COP. A NYWF group led by General Manager E. Earle Andrews, including city officials and engineers, visited the GLE in August 1936 to examine the facilities and general layout before heading down to Texas to review the expositions in Dallas and Fort Worth. By the time of the NYWF, the method and layout of the fair had been based on the best practices of early fairs. In this way, the NYWF served as the final event of the decade-long celebration of modernity.[40]

But 1939 brought forth two fairs, one on each coast, each presenting their own vision of modernity's promise for a better tomorrow. The San Francisco Golden Gate International Exposition (GGIE) began like the other expos as city organizers sought a way to bring people to the Bay Area and stimulate the economy. After outlining the basic idea and focus for the fair, they began the more difficult task of creating a four-hundred-acre island in the middle of the Bay. This meant dredging millions of cubic yards of silt, dumping nearly 300,000 tons of boulders, and adding millions of yards of sand and topsoil, all before the planting of thousands of trees and shrubs and the general transformation of the whole island. The theme for the GGIE was man remaking nature to fit his desire. The architects and architecture of the buildings projected an ideal of what California would look like in the future, blending Pacific Rim themes with modernist sentiment. One of the more spectacular examples of this mixture was Ralph Stackpole's massive sculpture at the entrance to the Court of the Pacific. Historian Kevin Starr writes that "Pacifica loomed overhead like an Art Deco Buddhist-Cubist mother goddess, her hands positioned in prayer . . . [behind which were] seventeen groups of steel panels [ten stories high] which were electrically rotated in such a manner as to create an eerily beautiful wind-sound meant to suggest the prayer of the universe for peace."[41]

Richard Reinhardt recalled how when he was a boy "they built an island in the center of San Francisco Bay that was a capsule of my dreams . . . [and was] an earthly paradise" called Treasure Island. In the early

"Pacifica welcomes visitors to Golden Gate International Exposition." San Francisco History Center, San Francisco Public Library. Used with permission.

1930s several business and government leaders lobbied for an exposition in Northern California much like the one held in 1915 to stimulate business and employment and to show the area's resolve to make it through the hard times. Although there was support for the Depression-era event, lack of financing prevented the project from moving forward until 1935 with the creation of the WPA. City leaders appealed to Harry Hopkins to get the WPA to help create the island in the Bay; he approved the project with a nearly $4 million allotment. The final cost would be much higher and made up with private investment, but with federal support, the island, which sat in the midst of two other testaments to man's ability to reason and control nature—the Bay and Golden Gate Bridges (completed in 1936 and 1937, respectively)—began to develop. As the island took shape, a causeway was built to connect the off-ramp of the Bay Bridge on Yerba Buena Island to the exposition site, making the connection between all the man-made structures complete.[42]

Opening day promised a better future and used technological mastery as a means to start the festivities. At exactly noon in Bombay, India (10:30 p.m. Pacific time), the sun struck a photo-reactive cell, which sent a radio signal to the island, switching on the lights of the exposition. The bells pealed triumphantly from the Tower of the Sun, which rose 392 feet in the air and, like a church bell tower, served as the central focal point for the grid that made up the GGIE. The carillon included a six-ton Bourdon Bell along with forty-three other bells ranging in size from 13 to more than 5,000 pounds. A keyboard at the base that played a variety of simple melodies controlled these bells, beckoning visitors to the GGIE. The next day, May 30, 1939, Undersecretary of State William Phillips gave the opening speech, reminding the audience that the GGIE represented "the goal [toward] which the peoples of the earth" were working, namely, the elimination of the drudgery of labor through the application of science and technology. The problems of the world, which often led to war (and here he referenced the already growing fear in the West), were caused by the inequities created when modern ideas were shunned in favor of superstition and nationalism. He appealed to visitors to take the message of good news presented at the GGIE back to their neighborhoods and hometowns, promising them that "Your State Department" would carry forth the ideals presented at the Expo to "bring a more abundant life to the American people" and understanding throughout the world.[43]

The WPA's Federal Writers' Project helped promote the GGIE by compiling a listing of events and daily activities for tourists coming for the fair. The comprehensive list, published a full year before the GGIE opened and available throughout the West Coast and the nation, outlined the extent of support from local groups and organizations in the region. It also documented the desire of the GGIE's organizers to get as many different people to buy into the expo as they could in the hope that their message of salvation would reach the largest number of people.[44]

The GGIE held to the design formula established at Chicago and utilized by the other fairs. The fundamental modernist ideology that through science, technology, and the power of humans to control, manipulate, and understand nature, the world was made better remained the central theme. The basic layout for the Depression-era fairs had been formalized by 1939. The entranceway opened to a series of arteries directing the visitor through exhibits sponsored by corporations that outlined the benefits of modern society, rational thinking, and logical organization. The organizers were proud of the layout and design, for once inside the "gridiron," as the chair of the board of architects for the GGIE Arthur Brown described the layout, specific "magnets" drew the visitors' attention and moved them efficiently toward informational exhibits. Nothing was left to chance, as the gate the visitor entered determined their route. This guaranteed they saw all that the GGIE had to offer and came away convinced of a better tomorrow. The plan, Brown maintained, was based on the COP and laid out by the organizers in early 1935, well before final plans had even been accepted. For youngsters Patricia F. Carpenter and Paul Totah, GGIE was a "city of hope" where the future promised that "technology would make life easier" and "that something good lay in store for us" based on what the GGIE displayed.[45]

Treasure Island itself was the first and most obvious example of the testament to modernity, but visitors were also impressed by the exhibit halls, their lighting, or, off in the distance, the great Bay bridges themselves. "As the visitor approaches the Exposition by automobile and rounds the last curve of the causeway leading down to the gates, the architectural ensemble reveals . . . its monumental scale," wrote art critic and historian Eugen Neuhaus in 1939 about the GGIE. He waxed enthusiastically about what he saw and the symbolism he felt the event captured, comparing his feeling of the sublime when he visited Venice and the Church of San Giorgio Maggiore. He related how the exposition was more than the sum total of all of its parts and felt the GGIE had the power to liberate "the spirit" of the visitors to help them "forget the routine of ordinary life in an environment that transports them to enchanted isles, distant arcadias, or synthetic utopias." His book, *The Art of Treasure Island*, presented a glowing description of the art, architecture, horticulture, and lighting, even the entertainment zone called Gayway. Because the GGIE emphasized the Pacific Rim, there was an eclectic mix of styles, yet they were unified in their "honest presentation of a scientific-mechanistic civilization—of its speed, efficiency, economy, hygienic requirements, and others of its typical qualities." Neuhaus believed the GGIE had the ability to transform those who attended if they were willing to open themselves to the wonderful art and celebratory feel of Treasure Island.[46]

The GGIE featured, like the NYWF and the COP, a Temple of Religion and a Tower of Peace. "It is inconceivable," said California attorney general Ulysses S. Webb, "that man shall create an island in the middle of the Bay and find no place thereon for God." An ecumenical coalition, led by Rabbi Rudolph Coffee and six Christian clergymen, formed a committee to make sure that the GGIE had a Temple of Religion and promised that it would make plain the link between democracy and religion. These leaders recognized the modernist ideals that were being promoted at the expo and wanted in on the fair. Aurelia Henry Reinhardt, president of Mills College and an advocate for the exhibit, wrote that "if modern ingenuity should create an eighth wonder of the world, what sort of unique rejoicing might acclaim its completion and herald it as man's most godlike achievement?" She knew that the visitors who came to the GGIE would be amazed and awed by the man-made island and all that it had to offer. "This is a new world and we must celebrate these marvels in a new way" by blending traditional worship with "the march of modern science." A Temple of Religion was necessary as a reminder that humility is the foundation of faith and belief in the one true God.[47]

In the entertainment areas, both Billy Rose and Sally Rand showcased their talents, maintaining the connection to earlier celebrations. Although their shows were not in and of themselves connected to the modernist ethos promoted at the Depression-era expos, their inclusion connects to the formula of drawing people to the fair who might normally not attend, and then using their curiosity to introduce new ideas to them. Fair organizers from Chicago to San Francisco held close to this tactic, using the entertainment zones as a means to drive greater traffic to their modernist fairs.

The GGIE failed to draw the millions hoped for and lost money, as did the other fairs. It reopened in 1940 for another run, also like the other expos, but the theme of a better tomorrow was sacrificed to the desire to try to make back some of the initial investment money. Treasure Island became "Pleasure Island," and the focus turned from information to amusement. However, the focus on profits of the fairs obscures their significance. When the GGIE shut down in November 1939, Tom Moriarity reminded his readers in *California, Magazine of the Pacific* that the success of the expo should not be judged by the amount of money it lost but by how many "of the ten and a half million in attendance who left the island with the conviction that the visit had not been one of mental and spirit-lifting gain." That people's consciousness was raised by what they saw at the GGIE was the same conclusion given the other fairs in the era, for they all lost money, yet they all promoted a positive view of the future tied to the ideals of modernity. In this way, they were a great success because visitors came from many of the surrounding states and took back with them the good news of what they had witnessed. None of the fairs in the era did as well as their promoters hoped. But a focus on the number of people who came through the gate or on receipts fails to take into account their transformative effect. First and foremost, they brought people together and offered them a glimpse of hope in an era when many felt despair. They promised a better tomorrow and perhaps left most people feeling better about the future, even as the world was tilting toward war. These fairs promised salvation and they delivered.[48]

When NYWF planners discussed their vision, they too hoped to preach the good news of modernism. They were going to use their fair to promote the role science played in the everyday lives of American citizens by featuring the consumer advantages brought via pure science. Their commitment to portraying technology and science as the salvation for the present and future was even more obvious than the COP's, even as it held to the same general script of the 1933 event. Whereas the light from the star Arcturus opened the COP, Einstein threw the switch that turned on the lights at the NYWF. The Science and Education Hall in New York celebrated the value of reason and rational methodology, made plain through a series of transparent and colorful illustrations within the rotunda that, much like stained glass in churches and cathedrals, inspired awe by those who viewed them for their beauty and promotion of truth.[49]

The difference between the 1933 event and the capstone 1939 fair concerned the changes in how the salvation of modernity would become manifest. Chicago preached the good news of the pure sciences and celebrated science for science's sake that would benefit all of society, whereas the NYWF had a greater focus on the applied nature of modernist salvation through consumer applications. The New York exhibits, unlike those at the COP, came under more direct control of corporations rather than scientists, widening a schism within the academy and some of the various denominational divisions among the modernists. Some thought the focus on pure science, outside of commercialism, needed to remain in order to promote the best part of the democratic experience. Rational thinking, the reasonable application of ideas, and problem solving came through hands-on experiments, these advocates argued, and pointed the way toward the salvation of all society. Modernity was universal and open to everyone as a belief, and its practices should be learned and applied throughout the country through education, which would then create a more rational and organized society. Those on the other side saw the potential of science to develop, manufacture, and sell goods that would provide immediate salvation. Science and its methodology pointed the way toward a future where the application of its basic principles could alleviate and even eliminate many of the problems plaguing human society. The two sides—one that believed that through the daily practice of modernity salvation awaited all of society; the other, that salvation could be had through the application of modern ideas to consumer goods—battled for legitimacy and space at the NYWF. The side advocating immediate salvation, perhaps driven by both economic and foreign policy considerations present in the latter part of the Depression era, ultimately won.[50]

The comparison between the COP and the NYWF can be read as a battle within the idea of modernity. The division between "fundamentalists" (who wanted science to be presented and promoted as pure) and "applied science believers" (who wanted science to be shown as something magical and consumable) outlines the arc of modernist thought in the Depression era from a pure and open focus on science at the COP to a more stylized and commercial science by 1939. This trajectory was aided by the several regional expositions that were held between Chicago and New York, spreading the good news into the hinterland (not to mention the expanded role of advertising and radio) so that by 1939 people had come to recognize the advantages that modernity as a pure science and methodology would bring to their lives, and they wanted specific representations of its power added to their daily experiences. The applied focus of the NYWF reinforced their faith in the power of modernism. Both wings promised salvation through modernity, but they differed on whether this conversion should be individual, through experiments and pure study, or collective through corporate/consumer applications.

Pure reason versus emotion defined this schism. At the Chicago exposition in 1933, science hoped to salvage its image and build support for the future; by 1939 the NYWF used radio, newsreels, films, celebrities, business connections, government support, financial investments, outreach to schools and colleges, and a national publicity drive to make it the capstone of the decade. Although socially conscious–minded scientists lost out in their quest to make the NYWF about their belief that reason and modernity could be a part of everyone's daily life through education and would bring about intellectual equality, the fair's promotion of modernity as a consumable belief open to all citizens reinforced their faith that modernity could and would provide salvation to those who believed—in this case, through their active participation in the commercial economy. George McAneny, chairman of the board of directors for the fair, envisioned the NYWF as serving as a conduit of information to reaffirm the organizer's belief that a better world could be created utilizing materials of the day. The world of tomorrow was not a pipe dream but a plan that could be realized if "the average person . . . [who] is frequently uninformed, and uneducated to the potentialities that surround him" could be made to see, and therefore convert him from "confusion" to "order."[51]

Science was the foundation of all the fairs and expos of the Depression era as it served to celebrate the advances brought about by human reasoning, scientific methodology, order, and efficiency—all attributes connected to modernity. The creators and directors of the exhibits made clear their purpose was to show that commitment to the modernist, rational, and scientific thought process brought about positive human transformation. Perhaps because the NYWF was the capstone of the modernist expos, or because of the primacy of New York City in the American mind, or even understanding that as this final fair was being celebrated the reality of war was threatening the optimism that permeated the ideals of modernism, the NYWF was, as Grover Whalen wrote in 1939, organized to give a "bird's-eye view of the evolution of human activities" and to encourage the visitor to "look forward" to a better tomorrow. Design historian Terry Smith has written about the work of the men who designed the buildings that gave the fair its iconic modernist look, suggesting that their creations underscored the larger theme of promoting a "City of Plenty . . . just around the corner." The whole plan, Smith argues, hinged on the "ideology, practice, and the developed imagery of industrial design which here drew together all the elements of the US modernity into a striking, generalized, and ambiguous visualization" of the World of Tomorrow.[52]

The NYWF planning committee did everything in their power to project this transformative ideal. Like the other expos and fairs, this one began with the basic transformation of "useless" nature into a useful, modern site for the event. For the NYWF, this meant transforming more than 1,200 acres of marshland being used as a dump for refuse and ash into a model for the future. The landscape architects and engineers brought in thousands of tons of fill dirt, dug out two lakes, and created the foundation for not just the fair but also a park that would be used by local citizenry afterward. Now safe and secure, what had once been waste was transformed through reason, planning, and man's ability to manipulate nature. Like the other fairs, the NYWF began with the basic ideal of modernity—man's ability to control nature—so that everything that followed and was built on this foundation (literally and figuratively) reinforced this belief.[53]

Next came the exhibits themselves. In his 1939 book, *Science for the World of Tomorrow*, NYWF director of science Gerald Wendt laid out in ten chapters the fundamental ideals, actions, applications, contributions, and larger meaning of science on display at the NYWF. He acknowledged that the people needed conversion, for even as they adopted and adapted to the by-products of science, they still held onto beliefs that came from the "authority of a great name or of an ancient book." Although the masses of people continued to look at life and the social and political problems around them "with the eyes of yesterday," the tools for radical transformation were all around them. They just needed to see, to witness, how all the things that they accepted as normal came as a result of science, from steel, glass, vitamins, and the advances in communication and transportation to virtually all aspects of life, were not limited to commodities but part of a spiritual transformation. "Science and clear thinking have," he argued, "laid the basis for wisdom that has enabled" humanity to confront and overcome its "natural ignorance and stupidity." Science, and its modernist lessons, did not convert through force, hostility, or nationalism, he wrote, but through inherent "creativity" that was tolerant, truthful, and open to all people.[54]

Eight of Wendt's ten chapters presented a concise overview of the process and application of specific scientific-based technologies that he believed were connected to the "continuance of [human] evolution." What is fascinating about these chapters is the detail he provided regarding the manufacture of items such as glass or steel. He utilized this tactic because he wanted readers to comprehend the basic scientific principles behind the commonplace items they used daily in their lives. In this way he straddled the denominational debate between purity and applied salvation, but he believed it necessary to facilitate the break from the past. "The most striking characteristic of America today is the contrast between our eagerness to accept the new and the fashionable in things that can be bought for money and the antiquity of the political and social ideas under which we stagger." Wendt echoed the sentiments of the scientists who helped create exhibits in Chicago, San Diego, Cleveland, Dallas, and San Francisco when he reasoned that humanity had "been impressed with the impossibility of achieving a beautiful and purposeful life on this earth and have fixed their attention upon a life to come." With modernity through science came salvation, and in this way the fairs and expos that spanned the 1930s called forth the weak in faith to come and experience the salvation that awaited in the here and now.[55]

Perhaps no exhibit at the NYWF exemplified the power of modernity more so than those at the Medicine and Public Health pavilion. The basic ideas behind the exhibits were taken from those on display in the latter part of the 1920s at the Dresden Museum of Public Hygiene. The NYWF organizers, influenced by the American Public Health Association, the New York Academy of Medicine, and others, and underwritten by large insurance companies and the Carnegie and Rockefeller Foundations, wanted the displays to "effectively disseminate to the public" the role of science in the medical field that benefited the human race. The committee created the exhibits to eliminate the superstition regarding public health and suggested that any illness or problem associated with the medical field was understandable, manageable, and solvable through the application of "intelligent coordinated effort."[56]

The creators of these exhibits recognized that if left to the scientists, much of what the visitors would see regarding health and medicine would be nearly incomprehensible. The NYWF was designed as "Everyman's Fair" with movement through the seven zones—Amusement; Communications and Business Systems; Community Interest; Food; Government; Production and Distribution; and Transportation—based on the ideals of efficiency of space, logical presentation of ideals, and enjoyable and understandable exhibits. The Medicine and Public Health exhibit contained the Hall of Man and the Hall of Medical Science, both of which battled against ignorance and superstition to enlighten the "ordinary layman." The creators and designers employed a variety of tactics to get their modernist message across, blending the expertise of science with showmanship. For example, upon entrance to the Hall of Man, described by the editors of the official book of the exhibit, *Man and His Health*, as "cathedral-like," out of the darkness a twenty-two-foot human body with a pulsating red heart was "rising above a great panorama of sky, clouds, mountains and water." This ascension highlighted the apotheosis of man and the conquest of nature that was at the center of all the expos and fairs of the Depression era. Here was man—and, in this case, gendered as male—above all things, controlling the destiny of not only himself but of all dominion. This "Wonder of Nature" was boundless, conquering all aspects of the natural world. There was nothing that humans could not or would not accomplish using science and its methodology.[57]

The Transparent Man, a life-size plastic figure with internal organs that lit up inside a full skeleton, was another tactic used to awe the spectator. Historian Christina Cogdell has argued that it represented, coupled with the variety of other sculptures created during the 1930s, an example of a more pure Nordic body type. At the COP's Hall of Man, millions viewed Malvina Hoffman's sculptural display of eighty men, each representing a different racial type. Although these figures were also males, during the 1930s the advertising industry did develop and promote an ideal female

"Sketch of Exhibit on Man," rising above the crowd. New York World's Fair 1939–1940 Records. Manuscripts and Archives Division, New York Public Library, Astor, Lenox, and Linden Foundations.

type. There was even a Transparent Woman on display at the Buffalo Museum of Science. All of these body types were connected, according to Cogdell, to the widely held belief that through scientific genetic engineering, a more perfect human—better than the one created by God—could be created. The Transparent Man, which she describes as the "Christ-like male of the Nordic type," served to remind the millions of visitors to the Hall of Man that science was at the forefront of improving humanity for the future.[58]

The final tactic seems almost carnivalesque. Sponsored by the drug manufacturer Bayer and located in the Hall of Medical Science, the superstition exhibit challenged most of the popular folk beliefs of the "layman" by moving them through the "Maze of Superstition." The entranceway held a large rotating metal sculpture of a shaman outfitted with all the talismans associated with this ancient and soon-to-be-discredited practice. As the visitor walked through the maze, they confronted folk remedies, old wives' tales, and other superstition-based cures for illnesses and ailments. Each section poked fun at what, in light of the rest of the exhibits surrounding this one, seemed ridiculous. After walking through "the wishbone gate from the Maze of Superstition [the visitor] enter[ed] the Hall of Medical Science—the Hall of Truth." The maze challenged the people's reliance on superstitions because they were not rooted in science or reason and fed on people's ignorance. Entering into the Hall of Medical Science was designed to convince visitors that real truth lay in man's ability to control and use nature to solve the problems that in the past were addressed through prayer or were manipulated by charlatans, witch doctors, and traveling medicine men. The future meant "leaving the bewildering maze of Superstition behind" to accept the belief that disease "can be controlled by science."[59]

Everything at the NYWF promoted modernity, starting from the largest reclamation project ever, to the engineering and design feats that outlined the power of reason, logic, and the human mind. The official program promised people "a new layout for a richer life, predicting and even indicating the shape of things to come." The program indicated the location for all the exhibits and connected them with the fair's theme: the world of tomorrow. The Trylon became a "symbol of the Fair's lofty purpose," serving much the same purpose that a church steeple serves for churches, the domed roof for synagogues, or the minaret for mosques. In fact, looking through the program, the visitor could not help but notice the many steeples and minarets that pierced the NYWF's sky, whether it be the stainless steel worker atop the fifteen-story-high tower fronting the Soviet building, the Star Pylon made of varnished wood and rising 130 feet into the sky, or even the twin 160-foot-tall pylons that flanked the entrance to the Court of Communications. Even the Electrical Products Building had a 100-foot ultramarine-colored pylon. All of these and many others made it seem as though the visitor were walking through a main street dotted with denominational buildings, all promising salvation through different practices. Artist Gordon Gilkey described the two moving platforms leading to the Perisphere and evoked the religious symbolism present during the fair's operation. "Above are the heavens," he wrote, "while below is Democracity—the city of tomorrow, constructed from the materials and with the tools of today." It is interesting that the one place where there was no tower was the Temple of Religion, which also held no formal religious ceremonies and more resembled a Greek temple or art museum.[60]

The 1930s-era expos and fairs were truly an expression of the times that clearly arose in response to a need for hope. Just as the New York and San Francisco world's fairs were set to open, the New York and Buffalo Museums of Science created a survey to determine the ability of the NYWF exhibits to convey their intent. They were certain that what was displayed at the World of Tomorrow would set the tone for future exhibitions, and their detailed survey would prove invaluable to designers as well as business people. They also evaluated the 136 exhibits with on-sight qualitative reviews. Their findings reinforced the success of the modernist ideal of all the fairs and expos held during the 1930s, of which the NYWF was the culmination. The exhibits, influenced and sampled from COP, CPIE, GLE, and TC, inspired more than 80 percent of people "to look further into the subject," whereas they "mystified" another 19 percent. The exhibits were able to accurately transmit the positive role science, technology, and modern thought had on society's progress, and further, continued faith in these three elements ensured a better tomorrow. They found that the appeal of the exhibits came from their ability to show in detail how individuals benefit on a daily basis from technology or science. Unlike the COP, which focused almost exclusively on the purity of the science behind the technology, by 1939 the conversation changed to focus to the tangible rewards of modernity.[61]

The investigators estimated that each visitor spent about seventeen minutes at each exhibit, meaning that the exhibitor had to focus its message to introduce, discuss, and outline an idea documenting its role, meaning, and application to modern society. To ensure this, designers used modern techniques in lighting, color, and overall design. Lighting played a central role: 79 percent of the exhibits used it to augment the information they wanted to get across. Given that 77 percent of the exhibits were educational in design, with 30 percent introducing entirely new ideas to the visitor, it was imperative that the exhibit be exciting, eye-catching, and easy to follow. "An exhibition is a short cut to knowledge," the reviewers argued, with "the exhibitor com[ing] to the fair to inform and persuade." The designer had to take into account the viewer, the time they might spend with the exhibit, and whether they would be able to understand what was being represented. In general, the designers were successful, because the reviewers found that more than 50 percent of visitors were "stimulated" to know more about what they saw, and the exhibits piqued their "interest beyond the exhibition."[62]

The latter half of the book contains drawings of how specific exhibits worked through the manipulation of light, space, and time to captivate and convert the viewer. The GM exhibit, for example, detailed a "three-dimensional dream of a future America" brought about through science, technology, and organizational planning. The reviewers outlined step by step how the Futurama exhibit manipulated space and time through lighting and perspective to awe the viewers into believing that the future they were seeing was somehow tangible and achievable through committed belief. Through its exhibit, GM brought its audiences to heightened states of expectation and "climaxes," leading visitors "from the familiar to the unknown, [giving] them a homespun idea of research, and illustrat[ing] the marvelous in terms of the commonplace and vice versa." The Borden milk exhibit wanted its viewers to come away convinced that their milk was "pure and wholesome . . . [through] cleanliness, modern scientific method and rigid control." The Ford exhibit featured a large mechanical mural detailing how scientists had "utilized the laws of physical science in harnessing the forces of nature." In the Communications and Business Systems section of the NYWF, the Drug Store exhibit provided the history of drugs and cures and, using a giant medicine cabinet, reinforced the idea that pharmaceuticals were the first line of "defense against infection or disease."[63]

Many exhibits used new lighting technologies to mystify and amaze the visitor. Using grouped slide projectors from behind, for example, they were able to illuminate and outline organs within the human body in a transparent woman while a sound recording provided detailed explanations as to what was being shown. In another exhibit, a crystal ball, seemingly detached from the Life Expectancy Quiz Table, lit up to reveal the answer, leaving the visitor in amazement as to how it worked. By manipulating light, space, and materials the exhibitors at the fairs made science consumable and interesting, and as their surveys attested, most visitors came away impressed, inspired, and encouraged by what they saw. The future was right before their eyes, and, it seemed, they believed.[64]

Like the other fairs and expos, the NYWF did not record a profit and reopened the following year focused less on the future (after all, war had broken out all over the world) and more on the past. This switch was not unusual, for modernism relied on this ambivalence or nostalgia. The past was necessary in order to understand the present and project the future, and a usable past was essential to maintaining the conformity of belief in modernity. That the capstone fair of the era chose to focus on a nostalgic view of the past rather than the heaven of the future was the perfect conclusion for the Depression era. New sacrifices were going to be demanded as the country moved toward war, and reminders of a unified past with hope for a better future seemed fitting. Faith came with responsibility; the 1940 fair, which promoted itself as almost a national county fair, outlined the struggles and successes of past Americans in order to prepare the contemporary fairgoers for what lay ahead. The future was still all around the NYWF in 1940, but now it was mixed with a clearer connection to the past and the foundational beliefs that made the country unique and great.[65]

The promise of modernity displayed at these expos and fairs held tremendous influence over the millions who passed through their gates, as well as the millions of others who heard about what others had seen, watched newsreels describing the wonders just around the corner, and read newspapers, books, and magazine articles that promised salvation on display at these events. This should not imply that they came away believing everything they saw would come true. But it does suggest that they witnessed the wonders of science and modernity and that what they saw encouraged them to recognize that the future had come to the present. Cogdell concludes her study of 1930s eugenics and design by suggesting that the idea of the future permeated American society and culture because of the difficult situations that the generation's people, government, and society experienced. They wanted a better tomorrow and understood that it could only come through faith and commitment to organization, planning, and the methodology and application of science. The people took their cue from their leaders. "Scientists, designers, corporate leaders, politicians, and ministers were the ones most vociferously promoting a better future," Cogdell writes, "in part because they possessed the vision, power and means to inspire, define, and create the world of tomorrow."[66]

The world's fairs and expositions that marked the American landscape during this tumultuous era put the ideals of modernism on display. Each fair was built on the apotheosis of science begun at Chicago and modified to meet their specific purposes. There was no conspiracy of modernity by the organizers to make each of these meetings areas of conversion, for each had its own rationale for its creation and promotion. Regardless of their desires to revive business, make money, put people to work, or even create a generation of passive consumers, these ambitions paled in comparison to the ideas and images of modernist salvation surrounding and inundating the visitor. The fairs did not make money, they did not transform local economies, nor they did turn Americans into consuming robots. But they did restore the people's faith that had been shaken by the realities of their generation—with even greater changes looming in the near future. These fairs and expos were universal in their promotion of modernism, reminding people who had lost faith what commitment to reason, order, and scientific methodology had brought to their experiences, and sending them home with not only iconic trinkets reminding them of the modernist wonders they witnessed (the Perisphere and Trylon symbols appeared on more than forty thousand different types of souvenirs) but also a renewed faith that a better day awaited.

A WOMAN'S PLACE/A FAMILY'S HEARTH

INTERIOR DECORATORS AND MODERNITY

4

Men such as Raymond Loewy, Norman Bel Geddes, Henry Dreyfuss, Donald Deskey, Gilbert Rohde, and others dominated much of the American design world during the first half of the twentieth century. These experts "fathered," according to a 1937 article by Maurine Shaw in *Better Homes and Gardens*, the modern designs for factories, machines, and consumer packaging, as well as staples for the American home such as beds and other furniture, refrigerators, stoves, lamps, and ashtrays. Predominantly male designers transformed everything that went into the American home, creating examples of modern efficiency, reason, and order. Their designs used distinct sharp lines and combined machine symmetry with the efficiency of nature to transform the home into a modern, comfortable, and affordable abode for all citizens. Much of what they designed was mass produced to allow the greatest distribution to the greatest number, and, given the economic context in which they were most active, the 1930s represents the peak of their influence as interior designers of the American home.[1]

Although men designed, the decoration of the home was the purview of the women. Responsible for making it a warm, cozy, and efficient hearth for her husband, family, and guests, the woman of the house chose which pieces of furniture to buy, decided where they were placed, picked what colors for the curtains, and made the bedroom both fashionable and relaxing.[2] Elizabeth Burris-Meyer, one of many women interior decorators during the Depression era who published comprehensive volumes to better "acquaint the consumer with the basic facts" of home decorating, advocated moving away from the more ornate interior decorations of the past for modern designs. Women, she believed, had to adopt a "new state of mind" by appropriating modernity into their homes.[3]

The responsibility for informing America's women about modernist designs fell to the many women decorators who advised their primarily female readers on ways to blend modern designs into their homes. In dozens of books written by leading interior decorators, in more than a thousand articles in the country's leading women's magazines such as *Good Housekeeping*, *Ladies' Home Journal*, and *Better Homes and Gardens*, and in countless local and syndicated newspaper decorating columns, American women were reminded that their gender-defined world—the home—was undergoing a major "Transformation in the Modern Manner," as *Ladies' Home Journal* announced in 1936, or as interior decorating maven Dorothy Draper wrote in 1939, "The Drab Age is over." The time had come for women to break from the limitations of the past to create, experiment, and develop new looks and convert their homes to fit the modern times.[4]

Women had long been responsible for making the home warm, cozy, and the hearth for their husbands, families, and guests. The establishment of a separate domestic sphere for women meant they were responsible for creating a shelter for their husbands and children away from the amoral nature of the dog-eat-dog world of the emerging capitalist society. Much like Pierre Bourdieu's concept of *habitus*, many women internalized their role as the pious and submissive preserver of family values and saw their homes as sanctuaries. Although men lived an outer life outside the home, women dominated the inner life of the home, including the cooking, cleaning, child-rearing, shopping, decorating, and everything else that went into making the home a sacred space. This control over the definition of the home space opened opportunities for some women, such as those who organized and made powerful the Women's Christian Temperance Union in 1874, which would have two million members by the end of the century, or those who through active participation in their churches carved out a feminine space for American women. These efforts, combined with the rise and proliferation of department stores, mass-circulation magazines, and advertising suggested that women's mastery of the home was central to the fulfillment of their destiny and calling.[5]

As their place in this sphere solidified in the latter part of the nineteenth century, American women turned to decorating professionals for advice regarding their home interiors. The plethora of available styles and designs for home furnishings encouraged the rise of the decorator as expert, helping women navigate the myriad of advertised goods to select those that would make for a comfortable and modern home for their families. These manuals empowered women's role in decorating the home through the appropriated language introduced by experts documenting the positive social and familial attributes of their home decor. In this way, home-decorating books provided practical advice on making the "place into a home," while also fanning the flames of consumption.[6]

The major decorating texts written by women leading up to the Depression era, beginning with Edith Wharton and Ogden Codman's *The Decoration of Houses* (1897) and Elsie de Wolfe's *The House in Good Taste* (1913), spoke of women decorators as amateurs but emphasized their power in defining the family living space. The home defined a woman's roles as wife and mother but also signified her authority, for it was her responsibility, as architectural historian Adrian Forty argues, "to care for her house as she cares for her body." With this in mind, the division between maternal instinct and expert decorator took on larger issues of agency and identity within the home. Women in the early twentieth century were supposed to have some training in making their homes warm and welcoming for their families, early decorating advocate Candace Wheeler argued in 1895, but this should only occur through the advice of professional decorators, who also needed to be women.[7]

To help educate women to meet this challenge, in the late nineteenth century more colleges, universities, and high schools created specific departments and courses focused on the science of homemaking. Industrial urbanization challenged women to acquire and apply up-to-date information concerning advances to make their homes comfortable and modern. Women's traditional methods of cooking, sewing, cleaning, and caring for children were being transformed by modern technology and science, making it essential for women to learn new terms and techniques. In previous eras, home instruction came largely from informal relationships among women rooted in religion under the more general cult of domesticity. This direction was given authoritative voice, at least in term of decorating, by Catherine Beecher, whose books, *A Treatise on Domestic Economy* (1841) and *The American Woman's Home* (1869), effectively made the home the place of salvation for the family.[8]

It is interesting that many of those teaching household sciences at universities and high schools came from same-sex relationships. Megan Elias's study of the domestic partnership of home economics pioneers Flora Rose and Martha Van Rensselar argues that although they taught how to "provide ideal homes" for their husbands, the fact that so many came from same-sex female relationships suggests a more ambitious desire to manage the house and home as a means to advance society. The women who created and ran home economics departments were activists who saw themselves as scientists committed to improving the workplace where most women toiled without recognition. As perhaps the only women tenured at universities at the time, which as institutions were dedicated to pure research, they were on the cutting edge of the modernist revolution, advancing the application and understanding of new industrial commodities in the home while empowering women to use critical thinking and problem-solving skills in their daily routines. Women were taught they were in charge of the household, and through their covert activism, they transformed the masculine living space of the home to meet their own feminine identity.[9]

Coinciding with the addition of the new home economics curricula, more women looked for decorating guidance from experts trained at the nation's colleges and universities. These decorating experts were usually women who taught other women how to apply the new advances to make their work at home easier, more efficient, and better for the entire family. By the 1920s, as the number of interior decorators had increased dramatically, they were seen as essential guides in the arrangement of the home's interior. They generally advised their clients to adopt more classical styles such as the resurgent colonial or the traditional dark, carved furniture indicative of the Spanish or Italian tradition. But the crash and its aftereffects altered many decorators' vision of the home, causing them to adopt a more open mind on modernist designs, largely due to mass production, which translated into lower purchasing costs.[10]

American women were initially introduced to modernist design innovations during the 1920s in several ways. The most vivid representation came in the introduction of art deco and moderne styles displayed at the 1925 Paris Exposition Internationale des Arts Decoratifs et Industriels Modernes and exported soon afterward. These modernist styles blended ancient patterns of sunbursts, lightning bolts, and other geometric designs with those inspired by the machine age with its distinct lines and angles. Moderne design styles utilized metals, glass, mirrors, chrome, exotic woods, and other materials to signify a break from the ornate decorating tradition of the past. Department stores adopted this avant-garde look to draw women customers into their stores. The vibrant colors mixed with chrome and mirrors were invitations into the world of consumption, and these palaces of feminine consumerism introduced many women to the emerging modern design. The department store had become a loci of feminine power as nearly 80 percent of its clientele were women, and this new space became an arena for the promotion and propagation of the new ideal for women, which was tied to modernity. American female consumers' initial reaction was a mixture of fear and excitement. Some worried that what they deemed a radical European import might erode traditional American standards and that women in particular should have no part in this absurd movement. Many decorators saw the designs as cold, plain, or out of touch with the desires of most American home decor consumers. This *style moderne* "design was the product of a nursery," wrote *Arts and Decoration*, reflecting back a decade later in 1934, and was indicative of a "perennial schoolboy." There were others, though, who saw in the designs liberation from the stuffiness and overexaggerated tones of Victorianism. This decorating difference echoed the larger feminine generational division that emerged at this time, where some women wanted fresh ideas that looked to the future while others wanted to retain the ways of the past.[11]

The crash encouraged many American designers to revisit some of these styles and recast them as modern by softening the lines, toning down the flashy and expensive materials, and generally warming the furniture and fixtures to better fit the American woman's concept of home. Women's magazines played a central role in this process. Monika Obniski has argued that the adoption of modernism by mass-circulation women's magazines began to build in the early part of the Depression era, as the more experimental designs of the 1920s were tempered for the new generation. The magazines' initial lukewarm adoption of modernist designs early in the 1930s gave way to greater acceptance as the decade wore on, endorsing the modernist connection to more traditional interiors. But by the middle of the 1930s, magazines such as *Ladies' Home Journal*, *Good Housekeeping*, *American Home*, *Vogue*, *Harper's Bazaar*, and others disseminated modern styles, oftentimes in advertisements, and advocated for the new age. Whether through cosmetics, jewelry, or other fashion-related items, magazines and catalogues served as the central medium by which the modern ideas reached the female consumer. It was from these magazines, as well as the likes of *Better Homes and Gardens* and *Woman's Home Companion*, that the women from the business and middle classes of Middletown garnered their information about what was new for their homes and learned about new items for consumption. The stories and advertisements in these magazines appealed to a broad group, suggesting that the ideas and images were egalitarian, as though the salvation of modernism was available to all classes. Interior decorating played the primary role in the magazine's definition and usage of modernity, as it "marketed *merchandise for the home*," design expert Lucy Fisher suggests, "whose decoration was considered within the purview of women." Corresponding with the general Depression-era impetus to stimulate consumption, designers needed to make modern merchandise more palatable and more affordable, or, as design historian Kristina Wilson has written, create a "modernity of the pop-culture world, not that of the removed modern artist."[12]

Women, it was argued, controlled the plurality of the household income and were responsible for the majority of consumption. The National Recovery Administration estimated that they accounted for nearly 85 percent of what was consumed at retail outlets. They were also often viewed as supple in their willingness to accept what advertisers presented. Women decorators used their power as experts in home economics to educate their readers in the best colors, materials, and items for their homes. The principles of modernism—using reason and organization to create efficiency and a better product—that had been applied to the factory were being applied to the home, and women used the advice provided in these magazines and books to help them become informed and cautious consumers. And because the recovery hinged on increasing consumption (with women in the forefront), it was essential that they rely on experts, or through the advice of experts become educated themselves, in order to determine the right choices—economically, for their families, and for themselves. Modern furniture fell right into this model, because it was designed to be mass produced using affordable materials and, given its decorating pliability, available and applicable to virtually every home.[13]

One component of this recasting and branding of modernism concerned the overwhelming number of male interior designers. They encouraged, argues Wilson, the "public to interpret modernism as a symbol of an optimistic future." They were part of the modernist triumvirate of "scientists, engineers, [and] architects" helping women "create new forms" and patterns for living, wrote the editors of *Good Housekeeping* in 1937. Their job was to develop new fixtures for the modern home utilizing contemporary materials developed from modern techniques that emphasized efficiency, reason, and simplicity. Some American home designers experimented with the new designs originating in France and Germany that stressed the efficacy of natural materials combined with the clean, simple, and utilitarian order of machines. These items were often handcrafted, because the rise of the designer was in many ways connected to the arts and crafts movement that began a generation earlier, and they were often created and sold as pieces of art out of the reach of most consumers. The Depression forced designers to redirect their focus for both practical and ideological reasons. On the side of practicality, they recognized that in order to make a living they had to, as industrial designer Arthur J. Pulos said, "get with it" and stop being so "self-indulgent." Theirs was not a solitary profession, for designers, like so many other artists, craftsmen, and professionals, came to believe that their creations must serve a social purpose and that those who created and designed needed to coax harmony out of the tension of Depression-era American society.

Which style shall I choose?

"With so many choices, women decorators felt responsible to provide advice." From Florence B. Terhune, Decorating for You *(New York: M. Barrows, 1944), frontispiece.*

The artist as isolated individual creating art without reflection onto society had little value, so designers became creators of affordable consumer goods. In this way, they played a foundational role in the acceptance of modernity.[14]

Designers began to see themselves as being on the front line of a social and cultural transformation. They were in the vanguard, as Paul T. Frankl wrote in 1928, of bringing the "modern spirit" to the home, which he labeled the "man's castle."[15] Russel Wright, one of the leading designers at the time, believed that home furnishing design was not about selling furniture but a "social force straining for better home environment and happier people."[16] This new focus, which Kristina Wilson aptly labels "livable modernism," combined a belief that a "simplified aesthetic could facilitate an enlightened lifestyle" with a recognition that the new designs could also provide "physical and psychological comfort" for the people. Modern designs lacked ornamentation and built a sense of harmony between the design and the function of the piece, a recognition that the machine could serve as both producer and symbol of the new design, and that efficient, functional, and reasonable home furnishings were the goal of the design process. Designers believed, as did Gilbert Rohde, who designed for Herman Miller and Heywood-Wakefield, that their home designs brought harmony to the home:

> [Modern design] is a design solution to living, a solution that is absolutely necessary it you are going to live gracefully, comfortably, and naturally in the world at the time at which you happen to be born into it. Thus if our homes are planned for modern comfort by means of modern materials, it is possible to achieve a new kind of beauty—not the pictorial beauty of the past, but the honest practical beauty of the present, which is the only true refuge in these harsh and strident times.[17]

Their focus on practicality, simplicity, and utility of design were modernist exemplar. The designers also understood that the items had to be priced low for the average housewife to consider using them in her home. However, many of the modernist interior designs at first blush appeared cold and so different from the furniture, colors, appliances, and coverings that women had grown up with and felt comfortable replicating in their own homes. Women decorators were part of this process, because their advice and direction encouraging their primarily women readers to be open to these new modern decorating concepts were essential to stimulating the economy, providing more employment to a myriad of workers, and making their homes the bastion of modernity. By the end of the Depression decade, designer Gilbert Seldes could announce with some authority that over the last ten years "nearly every common object" in the home has changed "for the better."[18]

So "what does the professional designer suggest" to make a woman's home "more practical and enjoyable?" asked decorator Shirley Ware rhetorically in a 1940 issue of *Independent Woman.* Aside from the practicality, efficiency, and functional use of space, modern decorating using these designs created a "home that is attractive enough to be inviting, colorful enough to be interesting, [and] quiet enough that it is not distracting." Women decorators accepted the responsibility of disseminating and domesticating the modern designs for American homemakers, who sometimes felt conflicted about modernism's use of sharp lines, bold colors, and its break from traditional designs. Women professional decorators had to convince their readers that it was the female homemakers' job to incorporate and make normal the modern interior designs in their homes.[19]

Women interior decorators recognized their influence, and, knowing that women would turn to them for advice, they sought to legitimize both their profession and the significance of the home. The sphere of the home had been ingrained as feminine with the traits of nurturing, reproduction, and the cult of domesticity, but with the expansion of capitalism, urbanism, education, and consumerism, what had once been a quasi-private sphere, even as they considered representation to others as important, was transformed, as historian Cheryl Robinson points out, "to the profit sector in the person of the female interior decorator."[20] Men were responsible for the "ingenious use of architectural principles," wrote *Home and Garden* writer Martha Delano in 1934, whereas women applied the "ornament."[21]

By the early 1930s the decorating profession was divided along three lines: those with academic training, those with practical training, and those with no training at all. Some women in the first two categories wanted to legitimize their contributions by advocating for increased professional standards through quasi-licensing organizations such as the American Institute of Interior Decorators. Nancy Vincent McClelland, a pioneer in this development, believed it essential that decorators create specific licensing requirements in order for the profession to achieve professional equality with architects or designers. In her book *An Outline of Careers for Women* (1929), McClelland suggested that decorators' commitment to extensive training would increase the public's acceptance of decorators as professionals and posited that decorating experts be accredited and approved by a governing body such as the American Institute of Interior Decorators (AID), which she helped found in 1931 (its name was shortened in 1936 to the American Institute of Decorators). If the interior decorator were a licensed professional, those taking the advice of the home decorator could be assured that they were getting it from someone "qualified to plan, design, and execute structural interiors and their furnishings, and to supervise the various arts and crafts essential to their completion." McClelland believed that by being recognized as professionals, interior decorators would garner the same respect and deference given to those in male-dominated fields such as architecture and industrial/interior design. The educational home economics movement begun in the latter part of the nineteenth century aided in this process, as it created a number of trained professional women ready to lead their cohort into the future.[22]

However, many others became decorators through their social connections, inherent eye for style, or a need to appropriate their space. Dorothy Draper is an excellent example of the first two tendencies. Born into wealth, she stumbled into decorating after repeatedly moving her family and decorating each of their new homes during the 1920s. Her friends, also from her class, were witness to her skill at decorating her many homes, leading to requests for her to "decorate other people's homes and buildings." Through her social connections she acquired several key decorating contracts in New York City, which she parlayed into a business, a syndicated newspaper advice column, and status as celebrity that lasted until her death in the 1960s. Other lesser-known decorators followed this path, where the beauty of their own home decorating combined with familial connections, wealth, or social status led to professional employment and the creation of their own decorating businesses.[23]

Most women lacked formal training or social connections but wanted to decorate their own homes. Professional decorators understood this and worked to inform the novice of not only the basic principles of modern design but also the tradition behind the newer styles. "Taking advantage of the new movement, they have tried to cover up their lack of culture and taste by attempting to be different. . . . One must know the rules before one can break them," said British interior decorator Derek Patmore in 1934. They needed guidance and information in order to properly utilize the "modern style that really is the mirror of the age in which we live," he added.[24] This was part of the impetus for the licensed expert decorators to write instruction books to explain basic design principles. These books challenged women to abandon the traditional notion that decorating was the result of their intuition and instead promoted the use of science, reason, and organization to make their homes more beautiful. Alice and Bettina Jackson, for example, updated their 1928 book, *The Study of Interior Decoration*, in 1934 to outline how the more experimental moderne designs of the 1920s had been adapted and made practical in the Depression era. The Jacksons reminded their readers that interior decorating was the "result of careful and systematic planning." Women needed to recast their image of an old-fashioned woman decorator with the modern image of a professional woman who applied her intellect and reason to the practice of interior decorating.[25]

In their penultimate chapter, the Jacksons discuss modern decorating by pointing out that modernism developed out of the desire of many people to break free of the past and create designs that would "be in harmony with the greatly changed political, economic, and social conditions of life." In order to distance themselves from the power of tradition, some early designs and uses of color or furniture were startling, abstract, and not very practical, as exemplified by the designs displayed at the 1925 Paris exhibition. The Jacksons used terms such as "daring," "blatant," and "vulgar" to describe some of these creations, but they quickly reminded the reader that these were the "initial force necessary to start the new movement on its way." By the time of their revised edition, these abstract and outlandish decorations had been toned down and made modern and acceptable to the decorator's palette. Now their descriptive words included "extreme simplicity," "lines," "sanitary," "durable," "compact," and "unencumbered," and they outlined how modern had come to "reflect the spirit of our age." They dedicated more than twenty pages to specific colors, fabrics, textiles, and furniture that could be used to decorate in the modern style, making modern useful, practical, reasonable, and, without specifically saying so, their accepted choice.[26]

Given that most women decorated their own homes, the expert's advice helped them define their own space, even as it was a subtle reminder that the proper place of a woman, even in these modern times, was in the home. The definition of women's roles and the validity of their work outside the home was an issue under considerable debate during the Depression. Although advances had been made, the economic decline gave voice to those who advised young women to reconsider careers, even as the number of women working outside the home was steadily increasing. In the summary of President Hoover's study on recent social trends in 1931–1933 designed for high school and college use, the section discussing women pointed out that although the numbers of working women increased, "the tradition lingers that [a] woman's place is in the home, and the social philosophy regarding her status" was linked to this traditional outlook.[27] More married women than ever before were working outside the home, which was raising concerns about the family. Margaret Collins, writing in *Scribner's* in 1937, chastised society at large for its role in convincing women that they could "simultaneously bring up a family and have a full-time career outside the home." The "damage" was "ruining the children" and "poisoning" the image of those women who chose to stay at home. The conflict among women between career and motherhood adversely affected the individual woman, her family, and the larger society. Critics wondered whether a woman could balance a career with home and family. Traditionalists agreed that the only true career for a woman was marriage and children, whereas modernists advocated for the self-satisfaction of a career with a successful home life. This division was played out in the larger society, with 82 percent of Americans polled in 1936 agreeing that women should stay at home to create more job opportunities for men. Of the women polled, 75 percent agreed. States and localities, mirroring the federal government's 1932 Economy Act, which allowed for married female personnel to be laid off first and made it difficult for them to qualify for jobs, implemented similar laws and policies. The social pressure only further divided women about their role in the private sector or the quality of their skills. A *Ladies' Home Journal* poll from 1939 pointed out that only 38 percent of the women polled believed a woman surgeon was as competent as a man, and only 17 percent felt a woman engineer was as skilled as a man.[28]

By taking on the responsibility of decorating their own homes, women could, according to Frances McMullen in 1932, answer their "calling," at least as society proscribed. The hard times called for women to use their skills to domesticate the tension of the modern era by restoring the home to "an enviable and estimable place in the human scale, [so as to] make the world safe. . . . For when homes in general are run with skill, tact, economy and efficiency, producing their full quota of comfort and progeny . . . who then will dare lift a voice against the sex, no matter what else it elects to attempt." For McMullen, like many women who read her books and articles, succeeding at managing the home was one way to do their part and "prove still an asset of no mean economic value" to society.[29]

The key to their contribution lay in recognizing that they were living in an entirely new era. In a 1936 issue dedicated to modern home designs, the editors of the *American Magazine of Art* informed its readers that "the times in which we live inevitably shape us [and] . . . inevitably take the shape in the things we produce." Modern interior designs were being developed and manufactured and to not appropriate them meant a woman fell short of her role in creating and maintaining a comfortable and modern home. Writing in 1933, *Modern Interiors* dedicated twenty-eight pages of text and photographs to the "simple lines, and some of the effects of dynamic symmetry" that modern designers had introduced. Fully aware of the fear many women had regarding modern designs, they avoided terms such as "functional, mechanistic, bakelite, [and] chromium" and instead used softer terms such as "orderly, efficient, [and] economical." And most significant, the editors promoted modern designs because they had "won a place in the hearts of men."[30]

The famous decorator Winnifred Fales advised American women that since the onset of the Depression, new fabrics, colors, and designs had become affordable, useful, efficient, orderly, and exciting. She laced her prose with positive words such as "new," "exciting," "revolution," and "change," and she took great pains to point out how the modern styles consciously broke from the past. Modern women needed their home spaces to reflect their "new-found independence" by incorporating the best of the new styles to showcase her family's adoption of the modern outlook. Her positive and confident prose read like a testament to modernism, where virtually all things new had both utilitarian and ideological value. When writing about the importance of lighting in the home—because "good light is *becoming* light"—she argued that to not modernize would lead to eyestrain, "shadows which deepen every suspicion of a wrinkle into a furrow," and a generally unhealthy room. With proper lighting, "nerves and muscles relax," allowing everyone in the room to experience better "health and safety."[31]

Fales was convinced that by incorporating modernism into the home, a whole new change in attitude would ensue. This shift in consciousness brought with it a new appreciation for the inherent beauty of wood, linoleum, tile, wall coverings, paints, and draperies. Rather than make household decorating a task in masking what furniture or tables looked like, Fales advised her readers to celebrate that "birch is birch" and not an imitation of something else. Truth in fabrics and furniture identified both the beauty and honesty of modern American living. Women needed to make their homes harmonious, which meant making the rooms open, simple, and clean.[32]

By the middle of the 1930s, the promotion of modern designs by interior decorators dominated mainstream media through numerous advice books and magazine articles. Usually written by women in a conversational tone, as if taking place over coffee, at the beauty salon, or at the department store where many of the designs might be on display, they detailed the efficiency, ease, simplicity, and utility of modern designs in the home, using reasoned and straightforward language. Psychologists such as J. C. Flugel and Joan Riviere had written about style, fashion, and taste among women in the early part of the decade, suggesting that through their acquisition of fashionable commodities they built a sense of equality and identity. A woman's freedom, it seemed to them, came in large measure from their ability to use consumer items as part of their own definition process. Perhaps the women who wrote the interior decorator advice books and columns understood this, for their tone was not unlike those 1920s-era advertising copywriters Roland Marchand labeled as "prophets of modernity," singing the praises of modernist design, furniture, and appliances. In renowned decorator-cum-educator Gladys Miller's textbook/manual, she outlined the advantages and utility in these designs. The plethora of new materials—Bakelite, chromium, rayon, linoleum, Plexiglas, neon, safety glass—developed by chemists and other scientists were necessary for modern interior decorating. "Decorators have been ingenious in finding new ways of using the materials scientific laboratories have made available," she wrote, and women have created a new and modern sense of decoration where efficiency of design, organization, and a "unity of thought and then unity of action" dominated. In 1936 Elizabeth Otey pointed out in *Good Housekeeping* that the "new order" of interior decorating confirmed her belief that beauty "serves a purpose" and that by understanding and applying the design concept that "lines must be simple and clear," a functional and modern living space resulted. For more genteel women, Sarah Lockwood suggested they consider the advantages of this new style. "We are wrong," she wrote, to not accept this "renaissance" in decorating even as it was still developing its basic design schemes. Although her book dedicated scant space to specific modern decoration, she admired the new "spirit bold enough to express itself freely and without hypocrisy" and recognized that the times were changing and that the "new generation is alive and kicking."[33]

"This book is not concerned with old mansions or museums of Europe," wrote Thelma Burrows proudly in 1938, but is intended to serve as a "guidebook of style, balance, color, and design to meet the versatile requirements of the American house and apartment." As a well-known decorator, consultant, and former head of the Georgiana Studio of Design in New York City, she wanted to write a book to instruct American women on the basics of modern living and decoration. She focused on the newer designs, which she linked to the American spirit of practicality, simplicity, and common sense, which had created a "style of furniture which is not only beautiful but significant . . . [called] Modern." Designed as functional and easy to use and apply, Burrows opined that the new housewares were the harbinger of the future and would usher in a new era of beautiful homes and interiors. The simplicity of the designs encouraged "the Modern idea . . . to harmonize an object with its purpose," and by extension, to define the home as the haven for the family.[34]

Helen Koues, director of the *Good Housekeeping* Studio, wrote in much the same authoritative tone in 1939 to suggest that modern interior decoration needed "sweeping horizontal lines" to achieve a "feeling of freedom and space," as exemplified on p. 135. She pointed out that its features—simplicity in form and space, harmony in design, and contrast in light and feel—were influenced by modern architecture, and that the more extreme features of the earlier moderne home design prevalent in the 1920s "have

"Images of Modern." From Florence B. Terhune, Decorating for You (New York: M. Barrows, 1944), 53.

disappeared and Modern . . . introduces only the most simple and pleasing forms." Through ten chapters she reminded her readers, whom she made no secret in identifying as women, that a well-decorated, modern home was the keystone to happy and successful family life.[35]

Anna Hong Rutt wrote both a text for students and a practical handbook for homemakers interested in redecorating their houses. The result, *Home Furnishing* (1935), provided a plethora of suggestions for the modern American woman. "Almost every woman has some natural ability to recognize beauty and suitability in houses and their furnishings," she wrote, but they had to learn how to determine beauty as an aesthetic and apply it with the proper design elements and expressiveness. Modernism, one of the four basic expressive themes she introduced (along with formal, informal, and natural), once was reserved for "young, courageous" people "interested in a style . . . expressive of their own day." But the new idea of modernism, and she was clear that this term be used when describing the design theme, was now accessible to every woman because it affirmed the basic modernist tenets of the new era. It was, she wrote, "based on that creation of man which is now the dominant one in his life—the machine." She told her readers that modernism was a new way of seeing the world as part of a "broad new culture" of honesty, simplicity, efficiency, and functionalism in the home.[36]

Modernism in the home became a permanent part of the American mindset, as the social and cultural influence of the machine and its human foundation outlined the consciousness of a modern society. Virginia Hamill, writing in the *Woman's Home Companion* in 1938, described the new woman Rutt was writing for. As a "trim dark-eyed up to the minute young woman" who saw the value in utilizing every "bit of space" and making certain that "every article of furniture [had] a definite reason for being," this new woman understood modernism's simplicity and utility and favored materials such as pressed wood, plastic, metal, glass, and brick, which did not hide their inherent use, for "function determines form." Rutt and Hamill believed that the decorator needed to adhere to the organic nature of the home and plan the furniture, wall colors, lights, draperies, carpets, heat, appliances, tables, and chairs to flow naturally into one another, while breaking down traditional barriers to rooms and their uses. Past interior decor was cluttered and divisive, creating separation within the home and family. The modernist decorator broke these divisions down and created open and utilitarian living space. "Modern furnishings," Rutt wrote, "should always be fresh, original, and stimulating," expressing the "self-confidence and directness of youth."[37]

A nonprofit agency called the Leisure League of America published a slim volume in 1934 dedicated to interior decorating. Written by well-known decorator Helen Daggett, the book, which sold for twenty-five cents, advocated for new and modern means of organizing and designing the interior of a house while warning women to avoid the more extreme art deco forms. She advised women that like other traditionally feminine tasks, using reason and planning meant that decorating could be done without spending too much money. The key was to understand how decorating worked, based on "certain principles of action" that came from organization and experience to create "an atmosphere of charm and harmony in the home." The modern application was guaranteed to please everyone and improved the family's social status. Daggett wrote that women needed to break free from the cumbersome and ornate decorating past, because with modern designs and proper planning, reason, and organization, any woman could create a modern, comfortable family home. She used action words such as "determined," "informed," "interpreted," "training," and "studies" to suggest to her female readers that decorating was a skill that necessitated applying expert advice. She knew that many women were hard pressed to understand the significant changes going on in the world of interior decorating, as "new generations are always introducing new ideas," so she informed them of the "very simple" modernist home decorating, which was "beautiful [in] its simplified expression."[38]

For Daggett, several rooms demanded modernist interior decorating. One such room was the girl's room. How could any mother, the section began, imagine sending their daughter to live in the city after graduation without exposing and training her in the ways of modern decorating? The young woman might move to the city and find that because her room was so "uninteresting," she would not "feel that life is worth living." The instruction process required little preparation, just the focus and desire necessary to educate her in the positive values of planning, the efficient use of space, and the necessity of organization. Another central room for modern design was the bathroom, where Daggett asked her readers to "resist the thousand and one accessories" available and instead focus on making it "efficient in design, harmonious in color, and washable." Throughout the booklet, Daggett strongly advocated for modernism and recognized that its focus on organization, efficiency, and reason made for excellent interior decorating. The leveling effect of mass production made it easier to decorate one's home with furniture and other accessories that a few years before "only the wealthy could have" afforded. To her, modernism meant making available all the stylistic periods so that individuals applied their own taste to define a room, say, in the Edwardian style, although still utilizing modernist planning, organization, and reason. For her, the form didn't much matter, but making sure that the function of the room was utilized in the proper manner was at the heart of Daggett's advice. Modernism in interior decorating did not mean one design or period but was open to all previous periods if applied correctly.[39]

But the central location of a woman's power, nearly all the decorators agreed, was the kitchen. The "modern kitchen" needed to follow the basic lines of efficient use of space and work to blend modern technology into the flow of the room, therefore ensuring both practicality and artistry. *Ladies' Home Journal* advised women in 1938 to modernize their kitchens to make the "preparation of meals a pleasure," which would benefit the entire family. The efficiency and simple arrangement of utilities, combined with the labor-saving devices introduced by modern industrial designers, made this room equal in terms of decorating purpose to the rest of the house. As if to reinforce the text and photos with reality, a full-page ad followed the article advocating modern electric cooking as a means of liberating women from the "dark ages."[40] In a straightforward manner, Elizabeth Burris-Meyers's *Decorating Livable Homes* (1938) put the modern ideal into its rational context by writing that the kitchen, "with all its machinery, is really a laboratory for the preparation of foods," which Dorothy Draper wrote should now resemble "models of sparkling efficiency." At the 1939 New York World's Fair, a regular feature sponsored by an appliance manufacturer pitted the organized, efficient, and well-kept Mrs. Modern (who used all of the most recent male-designed items in her kitchen) against the flustered, overworked, and weary Mrs. Drudge, who refused to change the way she did her kitchen work. The message was plain to all who watched the show: women who could control the technology would tame the kitchen in the World of Tomorrow; or, as the editors of *Vogue* wrote, the woman of tomorrow should be a "perfectly working machine . . . [whose] mind will work clearly, unfogged; with cold logic and warm sympathy."[41]

Decorator Lydia Powel focused her advice to women on a budget on the complex task of making their home modern, attractive, and up to date. Through plentiful practical tips on everything from draperies to floor coverings, she guided her reader through the basics of home decoration and ended with an encouragement to adopt a modern style. Comparing the acceptance of modernism in the home to women's clothing fashions, where no woman would wear clothing from the early part of the century, modernism grew out of a desire to eliminate the "fussy" household littered with "too many ornaments . . . draperies . . . [and] heavily stuffed furniture." In the new world order that followed World War I, she wrote, people wanted basic, practical, and useful furnishings purchased at low cost. Designers saw "beauty in simple forms" and began making everything from beds to dishes in this utilitarian and functional form, with the hope of converting people's "homes into machines for the living." Powel recognized that women might revert to the safety of their mother's or grandmother's style, but if they tried the modern style "they will end by liking it better than the old ways." She implored her readers to seek out free information from the federal government, for their agencies knew "more than anybody in the world about homemaking and house cleaning," and that as proponents of modernity, women could "trust the advice the government experts" provided.[42]

Powel's book, like many others, tried to convert her readers to the modern style by connecting it to the traditional feminine ideal of family. Beginning with the living room, the home decorator needed to make sure to give the right impression, as visitors "judge you by" what your living room says to them. A modern woman must think, learn, research, and design this most important room in order to encourage healthy family time. A cold living room drove family members away to other rooms in the house or even out of the house to "hang around the drugstore or the tavern." When the living room was made warm with the newest modern designs, families stayed home together and encouraged friends and neighbors to visit, even leading to job opportunities or suitors. The checklist for making a warm room ranged from installing modern heating, insulation, and windows, to using light colors on the walls, comfortable furniture, and draperies that let the light in but block the cold out. The next most significant room for the family was the kitchen. Powel told her readers that "there are no set rules" anymore, and with modern inventions such as linoleum and the plethora of other devices brought into the home through science, "by the end of your life, there will be not one hard job left to do with your fingers in your kitchen. It will be done for you by some clever and cheap machine." The days of looking at the kitchen as the source of drudgery and fear were over, as it became a place of comfort and beauty where the modern woman used her skills to make the room efficient, organized, and filled with appliances free of meaningless "ornaments and frills." The kitchen should present itself in clean, organized lines designed to reduce the needless and inefficient movement that identified premodern kitchens. With the new inventions, and by recognizing and utilizing space in a rational manner, the modern kitchen and the preparation of food would ensure a happy and satisfied family.[43]

Emily Post, famous for her homemaking and decorating advice in *Ladies' Home Journal* and in syndicated newspaper columns, wrote *The Personality of a House* to help women better understand how to make or remake their houses into more beautiful and charming homes. She was critical of modern designs, suggesting they more closely resembled "coffins," "cemetery monuments," "asylum[s]," "machine shops and boiler factories," and "hospital operating room[s]." For her, the style was too overtly "masculine" for American women and nearly impossible to make warm and personable. Her rejection of modern design reflected her association with what she labeled more "mature" styling, free from the faddishness of the market. Modern decoration wanted to separate from the past, which Post feared would cause decorating to lose its center. "To many of us," she wrote, "'Home' is something more than an experimental laboratory or a parade-ground for the eccentricities of fashion." However, she recognized that many younger women might want to adopt the new decorating style, and so she outlined several ways to utilize the modern styles, straining at every stage not to insert some condescending term into the prose. Many things "have so radically changed in the last few years that some expression of this change is inevitable," she wrote, and the modern aesthetic of "utility, suitability, form, line, scale, harmony, distinction, and sincerity of purpose . . . are immutable."[44]

Gladys Miller argued in 1939 that "decoration cannot be divorced from the society, economics, or science" of the era that spawned it. She traced the history of decorating back to the 1500s, outlining how each specific style emerged and their current applications. Her section on the twentieth century specifically called for the acceptance of modern interior home designs, which she connected to an "evolving style" driven by the "breathtaking" speed at which society advanced in the years leading up to the Depression era. She observed how modernism in art, music, literature, architecture, and other areas broke "away from tradition [and] awakened interest in the future." Innovations and ideas from architects and designers could open decorators' eyes to new ways of seeing and living in the world, where new materials such as linoleum and plastics could mix with traditional materials such as steel and wood to transform women's homes and their furnishings. "The standards of living have changed," she asserted, and the modern woman needed to realize the "social importance as well as the economic implications" of the modern world. There was a general consensus among government and business leaders that one of the causes for the economic crash was underconsumption, and that a better job needed to be done to convince the public to buy. In fact, their ability to consume became intertwined with the salvation of democracy and defined not only their social position but also their identity as citizens of the United States. All women, regardless of their socioeconomic class, needed to see the advantages, beauty, and utility in modern designs and purchase them for their homes. "Decorators have been ingenious in finding new ways of using the materials scientific laboratories have made available," she wrote, and women need to create a new and modern sense of decoration where efficiency of design, organization, and a "unity of thought and then unity of action" dominated. Modernist designers were iconoclasts focused on simple, good decoration to "make living easier, more comfortable, more pleasant and more worthwhile."[45]

Winnifred Fales had made a national reputation for herself in 1923 with the publication of *A Simple Course in Home Decorating* affirming the use of traditional decorating styles. Her attitude had changed by 1936 when she published *What's New In Home Decorating* detailing how to incorporate modern designs into the home. "The new design movement is revitalizing and transforming every phase" of the home, she wrote, encouraging decorators to follow the path laid by designers, advertisers, and so many others. Modernism drew its ideas from "machinery, skyscrapers, airplanes, shipping, bridges, Coney Island, cotton picking, and the American landscape . . . which more truly express the quickened tempo of our harder working, harder playing, complex modern lives." The average American woman needed to take advantage of the newer fabrics, colors, and designs that had come to the fore since the onset of the Depression. They were affordable, useful, efficient, orderly, and exciting. She laced her prose with positive words such as "new," "exciting," "revolution," and "change," and she took great pains to point out how the modern styles consciously broke from the past. The woman's home of the 1930s should reflect her "new-found independence" and incorporate the best of the new styles to showcase her family's adoption of the modern outlook. Fales's positive and confident prose reads like a testament to modernism, where virtually all things new had both utilitarian and ideological value. "What it boils down to," she wrote, "is that the designers of our homes and their furnishings are interpreting the Spirit of *our* Times, rather than invoking the ghosts of a dead past"; yet it was up to women to embrace the power of their decoration as "*adapting* rather than too docilely *adopting*."[46]

Nowhere was this idea of adaptation more evident than when Fales discussed the use of color and technology in the kitchen. Traditional designers were afraid to use "pure color" in the kitchen because its naturalness and simplicity suggested an unremarkable ordinariness. Modern women inverted this reasoning, arguing that these paint colors were inexpensive and easy to clean and they wanted them in their kitchens. With names that invited images of "delicacies," these new colors reminded one of the naturalness of the forest, plains, or desert and were used to create a warm, inviting, and hygienic cooking environment. The constant invention and promotion of "new gadgets for a new age" was approached with the same reasoning, for not every kitchen tool designed was necessary. Because most women were on a tight budget, if an item did not have multiple uses a woman needed to reconsider its worth and value to the home. With so much to choose from in "this astounding New Age," and with inventions such as the electric grill, waffle iron, and chafing dish making it increasingly easy "to cook and serve a meal right on the table," women needed to stay informed and educated to guarantee that each purchase was a necessity. If the kitchen held items that harked back to the "days before coordinated equipment was even dreamed of," then the time for redecoration and modernization was at hand. The modern kitchen needed to be clean and hygienic with bright colors and distinct lines for the efficient movement of both the cook and the guests. Modern appliances made for efficient and healthy meals; refrigeration guaranteed freshness; and stoves and ovens ensured proper cooking to preserve the vitamins and nutrients in the food. The most "outstanding feature of the kitchen," Fales believed, was that it was "smooth and easy to keep clean as the proverbial china dish. No dirt-harboring cracks; no rough or porous surfaces that demand frequent scrubbing; nothing that will ever be injured by grease, smoke, or grime." She advised her readers that the modern kitchen gave women the best opportunity to appropriate, adapt, and domesticate modern designs.[47]

The Depression era challenged the nation's women to accept and make modern decoration part of the family home, which signified the hope for a brighter future. The styles developed primarily by male designers were appropriated by women, often through the advice of women decorators, and were transformed by them into zones of identity and empowerment available in virtually all price ranges, and they represented the tone of a new generation of American women. Although the art deco or moderne of the 1920s left many women cold, the new modernism of the 1930s had an "easy, rhythmic swiftness" conducive for any American home. Modernism was tied to the inclusiveness of the era, shredding the elitist suggestions of the earlier decorating periods. This "lack of pretense," which Fales labeled "functional modern," came with four basic attributes: comfort, simplicity, sincerity, and beauty. Comfort was obvious, and Fales defined simplicity as continuous lines "with long, sweeping curves replacing the customary sharp angles." She made certain to connect the functional style to streamlining, which had already begun to dominate kitchen appliances, and pointed out how it was appearing more frequently in household furniture. For sincerity, it was the "absence of ornament" that allowed the customer to view the craftsmanship of the piece, as "materials are chosen for suitability" and faking, which she attributed to the ornamental tendencies of earlier designs, was not tolerated. What one saw, in essence, was what one got.[48]

As influential as the advice these decorators gave American women may have been, the influence of modernist decoration was not left just to them, because the organizers of the six world's fairs and expositions during the era (Chicago, San Diego, Cleveland, Dallas, San Francisco, and New York City) made certain to incorporate modern homes and their furnishings in their testaments to the modern future. At Chicago's Century of Progress Exposition in 1933, one of the more popular features, which was replicated at the other expos, reinforced the home as the traditional place for women and presented displays promoting the ease and wonders of the modern home. Gilbert Rohde's "Design for Living" exhibit outlined the advantages of home modernism to the fairgoers, blending traditional features into modern decor. The exposition featured eleven model modern homes designed to educate women on the advantages of modernity and how the new designs and technologies would make their home comfortable and a haven for the family. The modern homes and their interior decor as presented at the expo helped normalize and make legitimate American modernism in the home. And because the home laid the foundation for the greater society, modern rational design and decorating came to define the new American way.[49]

For only a quarter, visitors to San Diego's 1936 California Pacific International Exposition received the *Official Guide and Souvenir Program* that outlined all the wonderful things to see and visit. Among those earmarked as essential for women to visit was the miniature village, Modeltown and Modernization Magic, sponsored by the Federal Housing Administration. The three-foot-high models changed from broken-down houses to modern, efficient, and clean homes "by clever mechanical devices." Each modern home was designed by a southern California architect and came with an exact price for construction. Modernization Magic used before-and-after techniques to show how run-down neighborhoods could be transformed through modern technology and promised a future where homes, like the rest of society, would be organized and planned to maximize space and time to ensure greater pleasure.[50]

By far the most comprehensive display came at the end of the decade at the New York World's Fair. Heralded as the World of Tomorrow, it promised a future that could be realized in the here and now of 1939 if only the people, and in this case women, believed. Through its food and housewares exhibits, the fair visually confronted women concerning their attitudes regarding their work in the kitchen. How they prepared meals and cleaned up afterward was the focus of these exhibits, encouraging them to replace the antiquated practices and technology of the past with the modernist techniques and appliances of the present. In 1940, when the fair opened the America at Home Pavilion, it presented sixteen modernist interiors as the future vision of America's homes. Still gendered in its separation of space and work, the decor nonetheless displayed women in control of their environments and the activities that took place within them. The interiors were modern, with all the newest technology and designs, but the masculine tendencies of the male designers were tempered by the use of color, fabric, and placement to make the rooms warm, comfortable, and resplendent with the touch of a woman.[51]

The modernist appropriation by the nation's women, as instructed by female experts, was part of a larger trend toward a new style of urban and suburban housing. Earlier in the decade, Catherine Bauer published her epic *Modern Housing*, which looked at modernist European housing trends and projected them onto her American reading audience. The future of housing meant an entirely new way of thinking about the home, one that put function at the forefront, and community units, where "light, air, spaciousness, the sense of urgent and pleasant use" were the markers. Although this new style of house first took form in the Northeast, it was in the West and South where it found its most modern representation. New migrants and new housing developments with lots of sun and space helped the modern ranch-style home become the perfect vehicle for the modern American future. In these homes, modern appliances and furniture were not bound by housing designs of earlier eras and could flourish and create a distinct and new American style—a modern style. It was in these new modern homes that decorators encouraged women to accept modernity as the way to create familial harmony and maintain the home as the preserve of modernist values. It was up to women decorators, along with advertisers, to spread the good news and inform a generation of American women about the values of modernity. Most accepted wholeheartedly, and a new way of being in the home took hold and came to identify the postwar generation.[52]

The story of these decorators and the advice they gave to America's women opens another window into understanding the perceived role and social function of women during the Depression era. For example, one of the more interesting questions involves the relative dearth of women as designers of the furniture and fixtures that dominated women's advice books and columns. Although women as decorators seemed to be a given, there were significant hurdles for women to enter the more masculine world of design. Numerous scholars have outlined the difficulties educated women faced and the tactics they utilized to carve out a space within the male professional world of early twentieth-century America. As new professions arose and opportunities increased, so too did the barriers for entrance defined by education or other licensing requirements. These criteria helped enforce the separate professional, and by association personal, spheres between men and women. As they developed, women found it nearly impossible to be taken seriously in science and engineering, just as they found roadblocks to their desire to be architects or designers. In order to operate in this gendered professional work world, they had to feminize their skills, as in the case of Lillian Gilbreth, who, despite her expertise as an industrial engineer, found that after her husband's death she had to promote herself and her work within the realm of *domestic* science. Within this dichotomy of work roles, women were placed in the role of "interior decorating," a term subjugating them to a soft, almost intuitive role compared to the hard, scientific, and calculated male-directed term "interior designer."[53]

A clear divide existed between the decorative arts associated with the feminine and the practical or industrial designs associated with the masculine. So entrenched were these conceptions that even though many women attended specific schools such as the Philadelphia School of Design for Women (founded in 1848), the New York School of Design for Women (founded in 1852 and merged to form the Cooper Union in 1859), and the Western Reserve School of Design for Women in Cleveland (founded in 1882), and later in the early twentieth century at coeducational schools such as the Rhode Island School of Design, the Parsons School, CalArts, and the Pratt Institute, they were still viewed within the nineteenth-century cult of domesticity and relegated to "occupations associated with the 'feminine.'" When they graduated from these programs, employment within the industry for women was limited to fashion, interior decoration, and general illustration.[54]

Their circumscribed role solidified as America's industrial and commercial revolutions transformed the social landscape. One response to these changes in the early twentieth century came in the form of the arts and crafts movement, in which designers, many of whom were women, sought to reclaim the handiwork of the decorative and fine arts, to celebrate those things handcrafted, and to cultivate and preserve honesty in construction, materials, and design. Even as women played a central role in this movement, they quickly found themselves, as Wendy Kaplan argues, "limited to areas associated with domesticity . . . [and] confined to 'women's work.'"[55] This did not mean their contributions were insignificant, but in fact just the opposite, as they helped define and identify the movement.

What it does signify, however, is the rigid sexual division of labor that was the design industry on the eve of the Depression era. There were women professionally trained to be designers, and a few were given opportunities to design as their training directed, such as Ilonka Karasz, Bertha Schaefer, Virginia Connor, and Florence Knoll, but they labored under what Edward S. Cooke has labeled "the dominant male power structure." When a woman such as Belle Kagan, for example, tried to navigate the divide between the contested world of the male designer and the feminine world of decoration, she was met with resistance. Kagan remembers an instance during the 1930s when an appliance company invited her to their factory to consult on new designs, thinking her a man named Bell. When she arrived they rescinded their offer because they did not feel comfortable working with a woman.[56]

The US Department of Labor statistics bear out this division. In 1910 there were 2,603 women identified as designers, compared with 11,788 men; by 1940 the numbers for men grew to 23,614, whereas the number for women rose to only 8,871. Add draftsmen and architects, who were often charged with designing furniture, fabrics, materials, and accessories, and the gender divide becomes even wider.[57] In the early 1950s the Society for Industrial Designers had only one woman member, the wife of noted designer Gilbert Rhode, Peggy Ann, who took over his company after his death.[58] Men were viewed as the designers working in the world of engineering, mathematics, and science, whereas women provided the aesthetics, beauty, and that quality that would make it acceptable for home consumption.[59] Most studies of modern designers during the interwar period find few women mentioned; one such study includes ninety-seven men in the biographical section with zero women.[60]

Those women who were able to break through and compete with men in the interior design world of the 1930s were pressured to conform to society's view of their gender, which often limited them to the softer arts such as decorating. Does this suggest that women were passive receptacles who advocated for and utilized male-created modern designs to simply satisfy their men or provide a haven in the modern mold of the cult of domesticity for their families? In her feminist critique of architecture, urban planning, public space, and the home, architect Leslie Kanes Weisman argues that "men own and 'rule' domestic space, while women are confined to and maintain it," suggesting that women were indeed passive in their acceptance of the masculine environments called "home" and only worked to operate them as domestic spaces in line with the cult of domesticity.[61]

However, her assessment ignores the power of women to both appropriate and transform home interior designs to fit their identity. If the home was where traditional gender identities were enforced, they also became, as Christopher Reed convincingly argues, the "staging ground for rebellion against these norms." Because they were generally "excluded" from the creation process, they used their power as consumers to control the space they were socially encouraged to decorate.[62] Although men dominated the design and construction of the home, and in this way defined it as space, women asserted their control over how the space was to appear through the extensive advice books and articles they wrote as part of their emergence as professional interior decorators during the Depression era. In this way they altered the relationship set out by the masculine design as their female readers, trusting the advice provided by expert women, transformed their homes to meet their needs and desires. Home decorating, especially through the utilization of modernist designs, "provided women with new opportunities for self-expression."[63] Women were not passive in accepting what men designed, whether in the overall structure of the home, or the furniture, carpet, appliances, and other accessories that went in it. They were active agents in the negotiation process, as the expert advice givers encouraged them to reject some modern elements as too masculine, or suggested repurposing them to make them fit into *their* understanding of space. Women interior decorators played a primary role in this process, serving as a mediator between the masculine creations of the designers and the feminine applications in their interiors.

Design historian Penny Sparke labels women decorators as pioneers of female control and identity who played an "important role in introducing women to modernity." She uses the career of Elsie de Wolfe as a case study of this process, pointing out how her decorating advice book, *The House in Good Taste* (1913), brought together the domesticity of the Victorian home ideal with the more modern conception of space and identity. De Wolfe's goal was clear: the home was the woman's purview, not as a subservient but as the definer of place, and in many ways, a representation of self. Far from simply replicating images designed to satisfy their traditional roles as wives, mothers, and lovers, the professionalization of interior decorators and the advice they provided in magazines created, according to Susan Fraiman, a "language of feminine pleasure, self-expression, and autonomy." Women readers accepted the decorating advice provided by professional women during the 1930s because they recognized that not only were they fulfilling the traditional consumerist demands placed on them as housewives, but in their ownership of the interior of the house, decorating served as an outlet for discontent and challenged the male-dominated world they navigated. It was their conversion to modernity.[64]

The Depression era challenged the nation's women to accept and make modernism part of the family home. Many hoped the lack of financial resources would encourage families to find ways to spend time together in the home listening to the radio, playing board games, gardening, or simply being with each other. The home and family became central to the hope for a brighter future, and it needed to be comfortable, warm, and inviting. Women were charged with making the home the center of the family's existence, for although the divorce rate was low, perhaps because people could not afford the costs, desertion rates soared and many men suffered emotional depression due to their inability to maintain the economic health of the family. Out of work or working for wages and salaries cut drastically, many men felt inadequate, leaving it to the woman to help assuage the husband's negative self-image by making do with the resources available, creating other means to augment the family pantry, and decorating in a way that was inexpensive, functional, and warm. The styles introduced by male designers utilized modernist ideals as they were convinced that these new interior designs would make the home efficient, warm, and cost-effective. Women designers, who had once shied away from the alternative modernist designs in the earlier era, now saw them as key to America's salvation, for they appealed to all price ranges, were stylish, and represented the tone of its generation.

Florence B. Terhune in *Decorating for You* informed her readers that modern decorating was "really a state of mind" connected to the same features as "sky travel and . . . the Boulder Dam." The earlier versions of this style, with its exaggerated patterns and chrome outlines, had given way to a more "functional efficiency," one that "parades a sophisticated simplicity and mobility that is as arresting as it is livable." Terhune's promotion of modern design comes in 1944, later than the other decorators discussed here, and was designed to help women plan for the postwar, because "Tomorrow Should Be Wonderful." Her optimism about the future of interior design is laid at the feet of modernity, because through the work of "eminent scientists" and others, the advances of the day will only increase exponentially, forcing the consumer to "pinch our ears to make sure we are still rational." Modern planning, organization, and rational thought would define, this decorator advised her readers, the future.[65]

In the years after World War II, modern design in furniture, housing, and other aspects of interior decorating would increase, reaching its peak, at least in the opinion of designers Gordon Lippincott and Walter Margulies, in the middle of the 1950s. But it was the women of the Depression era who began this "good trend" in modern decorating, as they came to appropriate modernist thought, through interior decoration advice, in their American homes.[66]

SOUNDS FOR THE MODERN AGE

MUSIC AS CELEBRATION OF MODERNITY

5

Echoing the lyric from Sam Lewis and Victor Young's 1932 song "Street of Dreams," the generation experiencing the Great Depression believed that "yesterday's gone, tomorrow is near." Their belief that a new day was coming was both liberating and exhilarating, and they hoped to distance themselves from the failures of the past and create a new world order. In an era where everything seemed uncertain, many turned to music for what musician Alexander Richardson called "spiritual fortification." The ideals of the past were broken and new dreams were vital to speak to and for the Depression-era generation "distracted by the worries and uncertainties of the times." But even as they imagined the future, they pined for the "good old days" to root their optimism. They were cautious in their modernist enthusiasm, not wanting to discredit the entire past, but to pick and choose to celebrate some aspects while ignoring others. This blending of organized, planned, and scientifically efficient society with selected memories of the past defined their understanding of their time and place and allowed them to hope and believe that a new and better world lay within their grasp.[1]

Music played a central role in the acceptance and dissemination of modernity as herald of the future. The varieties of cultivated and vernacular music formed a bond with their listeners and brought people together to listen, dance, sing along, or even learn how to play an instrument. This collective behavior made music during the era of special significance, and when coupled with the modernist technology of radio, film, and records, music offered a sense of unity and brought people together. There were few songs that praised rational thought or scientific methodology, for in the popular realm songs remained focused on the time-honored themes of love, romance, and heartbreak. But these traditional themes were addressed in a manner that spoke to the modern generation by recalling an imagined past using specific phrases, references, and images transmitted via modernist technology of records, jukeboxes, or radios. Performers and bands altered and cultivated images and identities that spoke to and for this modern generation by adapting their sound, voice, or lyrics to new mediums. In the cultivated realm, the federal government created a program to provide "good" music to the masses, whereas composers, emerging out of the more dissonant sounds of the 1920s, began blending traditional American musical forms into their works to better speak to a larger and more diverse audience. In these ways, and in many others such as dance (modern or popular) or Broadway musicals, music provided the sounds that gave definition to the modernist America that was the 1930s.

Music and musicians had the potential to free people from their temporal situations and uplift them. In the difficult times of the Depression era, music played this crucial role, using both sound and lyric to release people from their day-to-day worries and provide some hope and cheer in the unity that came with their participation. Artists and musicians during the 1930s, as LeRoy Campbell observed, stood ready to assume the role of "prophet who sense the coming of a new era" in a time that demanded their social responsibility. Music needed to serve the interests of the people; new times necessitated new music, and the day's listeners were "imbued with its spiritual message" as it became "physically a part" of them.[2]

During the 1930s, music was everywhere. The continued growth and expansion of the radio and record industry, temporarily stalled after the crash, grew by leaps and bounds as the Depression wore on. Radio networks CBS and NBC Red and Blue were drawing more than 42 million listeners daily by 1932, and by the end of the decade 81 percent of homes had at least one radio, with Americans tuning in for more than six hours a day. The majority of the programming on the air was music, accounting for more than 60 percent of all broadcasting, and by 1939, 75 percent of the songs heard were classified as popular music. The reception of music over the radio was divided generally by class, as numerous studies pointed out that the higher the economic level, the greater likelihood the listener would favor classical sounds. Popular music found its greatest audience among the middle and working classes, as well as those in the twenty- to forty-year-old age ranges. By the middle of the decade radio was ubiquitous in the American household and making headway in automobiles, as nearly a quarter of all cars had them by 1939. The record industry grew apace after suffering a major slump until 1932, after which sales increased for the next dozen years by 500 percent. Between 40 and 70 percent of the records released went into the more than 350,000 jukeboxes dotting the country's drugstores, soda shops, barrooms, and any other place where people congregated. The types of music played over the air and purchased were as eclectic as the American population, ranging from classical orchestra and opera to folk, blues, hillbilly, and jazz.[3]

The audiences for these media included people from all socioeconomic classes and age groups, but it was the target audience of those under twenty-five to which radio's songs most appealed. The 1930s nurtured the parents of the much-heralded baby boom that came after World War II, representing 40 percent of the country's population under the age of 30. And largely because of their presence in the marketplace, radio programming featured music that could be consumed by this new demographic. The 1934 Lundberg study of the leisure activities of suburban Westchester County (north of New York City) found that listening to the radio accounted for 17 to 30 percent of this age group's leisure time, with music being their most preferred program. This tendency was confirmed later in the decade by the Lynds' *Middletown Revisited* study that focused on the middle- and working-class community of Muncie, Indiana. The influence of this new medium had sociological implications, for as Lundberg suggested, radio had "revolutionized both the amount and kind of music to be heard in homes." Observers of the day also recognized the significance of this trend, linking it with "creating new art forms and altering the basis of old ones," especially in music.[4]

Listening to the popular music of the 1930s hardly resembles something transitory or potentially transformative by today's listeners' ears. The lyrics resound in sugarcoated paeans to love or hark back to a bucolic past, but they do so using language and imagery unique to the era. If the music of the Depression era sounds old-fashioned and somewhat dated to present-day listeners, to its generation it was modern compared to the music of the earlier part of the century, which was old-fashioned, tired, and nearly irrelevant. Music consumers wanted sounds that spoke to them using the modern mediums that gave their songs a different sound than songs from an earlier era. For example, the popularity of a new singing style called "crooning," where the singer whispered or sang very softly into the microphone, which was first introduced in the latter part of the 1920s, owed its success in understanding the sonic limitations and capabilities of the microphone and how the sound was transmitted over the radio and record player. During the 1930s, numerous crooners achieved radio popularity, the most famous being Rudy Vallée and Bing Crosby, as they used their smooth voices and rhythmic articulation to attract primarily female listeners. Their voices were sensual, and their songs seemed to pulsate over the airwaves. Most significant, this was modernist music, for only with the microphone and the radio was this sound possible and popular, and as Allison McCracken argues, it brought about a shift from "visible, stage singing, to an aural, electronically reproduced sound that was marked by the singer's emotionalism" and the imposition of the voice into the home space. In this way, music became new and modern and appealed to the American people.[5]

Another example involves the compilation of song titles from the listing of number-one songs from the popular radio program *Your Hit Parade* between 1935 and 1939, where nearly half refer to a lost past or a dream for the future. "Soon" we will no longer be "Chasing Shadows," for "Life Is a Song" where "Once in a While" "These Foolish Things" will provide "That Old Feeling." Maybe it was just "Over the Rainbow" or "East of the Sun," but the songs that were played over the airwaves gave the listener a sense that "Heaven Can Wait," and that "Wishing" did not bring "Pennies from Heaven." The real focus was on the here and now, and although they may have felt "Alone" and "Lost," "These Foolish Things" would pass and with their "Pocket Full of Dreams" they would be "A Little Bit Independent." Stringing together song titles, of course, does not provide the full force of the songs, but it does convey in an obvious manner, because these were the number-one songs aired over the radio, the general mood of the people. The titles of these songs suggest how the writers presented their stories and how they reflected back on situations in the hope of a better future.[6]

Modernity, at its core, was ambivalent to the rational, urban, modern world. As rapidly as things were changing, there was a strong desire to retain a connection with the way things had been in order to differentiate the authentic from artifice. As society became more integrated and interconnected through the variety of systems that rational planning and industrial organization demanded, there was a sense of lost identity as older connections disappeared in the wake of progress. Modernist society was still developing and creating new patterns of communication, education, politics, economics, and living space. Virtually every aspect of American society was, in one way or another, undergoing a transformation. As the modernist identity was being defined, in large measure through the ideals of scientific planning, reason, and organization, a tension between those things lost and those things born expressed an aspect of the modernist moment.

In many ways, modernism owed much of its definition to a reliance on nostalgia. As Svetlana Boym reminds us in *The Future of Nostalgia*, it is not a desire for a return to a place that prefigures nostalgia but rather a "yearning for a different time," one that is no longer fixed but imagined. Linda Hutcheon goes one step farther by suggesting that those who actually do go back (in literature) to what they thought they wanted end up disappointed because they confused place with time. It was their youth or some moment of exuberance they wanted to revisit, but try as they might, the physical space where they returned simply could not conjure the same feeling. As literary theorist Tammy Clewell has argued, modernism was unable to "abandon epistemological foundations" completely and maintained a "productive engagement with the past."[7] This suggests that as modernism was being appropriated during the Depression era, and as music played a central role in this process, there was a conscious and deliberate negotiation with the past. There needed to be a recognition of those things that were passing in order to appropriate modern symbols, meanings, and ideas. The reliance on the past helped reflect modernity, as it referenced an understanding that not only were things changing, but that there was a past. In this way, the modernists manipulated the image of the past in order to better understand the present. This nostalgia—the desire to return to some particular place or time—revealed the paradox of modernity and its fundamental role in the reformation to modernism's tenets. Everywhere one looked there were reminders of the past, whether it be in FDR's speeches and his references to his pastoral upbringing or other aspects of the country's shared past, the desire of the CCC to get young men back in touch with nature (and, by extension, all citizens by encouraging them to visit the parks), the documentary photography of the Farm Security Administration, films such as *Gone with the Wind*, advertising (especially food products), or the whole back-to-roots movement that was so much a part of the Depression era, reflecting the desire to reject the past as old-fashioned while at the same time upholding its values and images.[8]

Modernity meant bridging the gap, as Jeffrey Meikle has suggested, between the "past, present, and future," and few manifestations of this leap were as obvious as music.[9] In the 1930s the airwaves and record players were dominated by sentimental songs, often concerning unrequited love or the pining for an absent lover. Even those songs that spoke directly to an existing relationship dripped with the traditional attributes of Tin Pan Alley sentimentality, and although these have their place within the pantheon of modernist hymns, they are not necessarily nostalgic in the modernist sense. The pastoral modernist song broadcast over the airwaves came from Nashville, Atlanta, or even Chicago or Los Angeles in the form of hillbilly and western music, later to be coined "country music." The technological advances in radio and phonograph records in the 1930s helped give rise to artists as wide ranging as Gene Autry, Jimmie Rodgers, Roy Acuff, Bob Wills, and even marginally Woody Guthrie as an example of a folk musician's connection to this phenomenon, who captured the imagination of the American public in their harking back to the good old days.

Given their present situation during the Depression, many Americans found solace in the lyrical and musical imagery presented by these types of artists via the Grand Ole Opry, the National Barn Dance, or WSB in

Atlanta, the South's first radio station. Many of the songs heard over these and other stations and programs throughout the country spoke to the difficulties of the modern world and reminded listeners of bygone days back on the farm. These were the homespun songs like those from the Carter Family, who retained their Virginia rural identity even as they achieved commercial success with their record sales and radio appearances. Their songs, such as "In the Shadow of Clinch Mountain," "Worried Man Blues," "My Dixie Darling," "Lonesome Homesick Blues," and so many others, reflected the image of a simpler time when families sat around the hearth, worked the land on their own time, and held their faith in God close to their heart. Jimmie Rodgers also made his career, cut short by his early death in 1933, on these types of songs. Known as the Singing Brakeman, he yodeled his way through songs that resonated with the realities of the present mixed with the longing for the past. In "Waiting for a Train" (1928) he laments his lack of money and being "a thousand miles" from home. In "Mississippi Moon" (1932) he asks his absent sweetheart to return with him to that "spot in memory" where they fell in love, for he longed for "the world I used to know." In what would become a standard in the country music repertoire, "Roll Along Kentucky Moon" (1932), Rodgers painted a similar picture, complaining that he was forced to live on "memories and dreams" far away from his bluegrass home.

Many of these songs used traditional musical arrangements, melodies people could quickly recognize, and contemporary lyrics. The Carter Family's songs were often modifications of folk ballads using melodies from church services. This was not unique to either them or to this genre of music: union songs and other popular songs recycled recognizable melodies, often from Christian hymns, because they were easy to play and well known to the listener. Woody Guthrie's "Do Re Mi" and "I Ain't Got No Home," for example, used melodies from traditional rural hymns adjusted to modern lyrics. The same can be said for Roy Acuff's 1937 hit, "Great Speckled Bird," whose lyrics were written by Reverend Guy Smith in the 1920s. Acuff's use of a traditional melody gave the song a certain authenticity while it underscored his lamentation that his listeners needed to reconnect to the true God, even in the "presence of all the despisers." These songs, and many more like them, were of the same sort used for camp-meeting religious revivals. Choruses sung at these meetings offered an invitation for union and, after a brief reminder of the sins of man, outlined the guarantee of salvation. One only had to trust and be faithful to the heritage of their beliefs in order to be saved. Even as temptation waited around every corner and nonbelievers courted doom, the songs extolled the virtues of the past in order to achieve salvation in the present.[10]

Probably the most popular nostalgic songs of the 1930s came from cowboys. They first appeared over the radio, like those heard on the National Barn Dance singing about wide-open spaces, roping dogies, and the joys of being a cowboy. It wasn't long until Hollywood saw the potential of this character, the singing cowboy. Hollywood studios had used the West and westerns as a touchstone formula since they began, and by the Depression era the western serial represented a key aspect of the Hollywood movie industry. Stars such as Tom Mix, Hoot Gibson, Charles Starrett, Ken Maynard, and others were near guarantees at the box office, with legions of fans from nearly all age groups paying their nickels to see the most recent episode. These action movies, where honesty was rewarded and corruption was revealed and dismantled, were Depression-era staples, but with Gene Autry's starring roles in first *The Phantom Empire* and then *Tumbling Tumbleweeds* (both 1935), a new type of hero emerged—one that, in a way, became the lead voice in the modern chorus.

Autry came to movies based on his radio and touring popularity. He wasn't an actor, and as Peter Stanfield has written, he never played anyone but himself, yet he was among the leaders at the box office throughout the decade. And he sang. He had developed a strong fan base through his radio exposure, especially among female listeners, and this carried over into the forty-five films he made through 1940. His appeal transcended gender lines as men and boys also flooded to his pictures, for his representation spoke to a "partnership with, rather than set apart from, his audience." His presence on the screen reassured audiences that although times were hard, by working together to identify and ameliorate the problems around them, they could and would make things better. As Autry himself said when referring to his cowboy songs and by extension his movies, "It's not exactly a negative philosophy, because in expressing dissatisfaction with sad things there is a natural approval of happier moods."[11]

Many of the songs that made him famous during the era represented this modernist duality. The cowboy Autry wanted to go back to the days when he rode the range, hung out with his buddies in the bunkhouse, and sang pretty songs to local girls in "Take Me Back to My Boots and Saddle" (1935). But the song was also a lament, for the singer was far removed from this pastoral scene and had to rely on the memories of "the ranch where I was born." His signature or brand-name song, "Back in the Saddle" (1939), recounted the glory days of being out where a "friend is a friend" and had a purpose. Yet this cowboy way of life that was no longer accessible could only be kept alive if the singer held firmly to the simple yet true rhetoric of the past. In "Old Faithful" (1936), he reassured his horse that even though his days were numbered, the years of loyal service and this one last ride ensured the animal "pastures white with clover." In "The Last Roundup" (1933) it was the cowboy's turn, as he rode toward greener pastures aboard his trusty Old Paint. Death and mourning played a dual role in most cowboy lyrics: on the one hand, they lamented the passing of a loved one, but on the other hand, they celebrated the life that was and will be. In Autry's first big hit, "Silver-Haired Daddy of Mine" (1935), which was recorded by dozens of singers during the 1930s, he longed for his father's forgiveness as his youthful zeal caused him to abandon the "vine-covered shack in the mountains" where he grew up and where his father remained. But he could not "turn back the pages of time"; his father had passed into the loving arms of his wife in heaven. The future was painted as heaven, or "A Gold Mine in the Sky" (1937), where old friends met up under a flawless blue sky and finally had the time to just "watch the world roll by."

Bob Nolan of the classic western cowboy band the Sons of the Pioneers wrote one of Autry's more famous songs, "Tumbling Tumbleweeds." He had composed a variety of songs for the silver screen heroes to sing, first for Autry and later for former Pioneer bandmate Roy Rogers. Nolan's songs held a special place in the imagery of modernity as he characterized the emptiness of the desert and the wide-open spaces of the West as mystically transformative. In "Tumbling Tumbleweeds," Nolan outlined the hardships of finding meaning in the fast-changing world of the 1930s, forcing him to drift along like the ever-present, yet somehow because of its pervasiveness invisible, tumbleweed, reflecting his nostalgic ambiguous understanding of modernity. The hero was "Travelling with the Sun" (1936) to find the "Open Range Ahead" (1937) in the hopes of quenching his thirst with "Cool Water" (1936). But the devil tempted good men with mirages of peace and happiness, and only through commitment and faith could one remain true. If the wanderer and his horse could stay on the straight and narrow path and avoid the modern temptations, salvation awaited under the "that big green tree, where the [cool] water's runnin' free, and it's waitin' there for me and you."[12]

Nolan's songs underscored the basic formula that cowboy singers utilized, namely, the reality of salvation. The genre's constant focus on joining up with lost friends and animals, dreaming of homesteads, or not being fenced in by the social restrictions of the day resonated with the ideals of modernity. The cowboy singers were not out of touch with the modern world and did not really believe in the nostalgic past they sang about, but they used this contradiction to justify the comfort and guilt they felt in the present. They sang for those making the transition from the hard life of rural America to the relative luxury of modern urban society who felt guilty because of their perceived abandonment of the imagined life they left behind. The struggle to make it in the modern world, although at first alien to them, was quickly accommodated as they measured their success by the hope of buying a comfortable home, sending their children to school beyond their own experience, and laying the foundation for what came to be identified during the era as the American dream. Working in the auto plant, steel mill, or rubber factory was difficult (and different work from what their ancestors did), but the results brought modern happiness mixed with the fear that they might forget their roots. This modern shift in consciousness demanded they retain an understanding of where they came from, whether mythical or real, in much the same manner as countless immigrants from eastern and southern Europe maintained their language and customs long after their integration into America. Even as the cowboys sang about the past or relished the artificial freedom that came with rootlessness, the popularity of their songs documented the power of modernism and served as atonement for the acceptance of the new faith by holding up the past as fundamental for their salvation.

The rapidity of change that marked the Depression era brought forth a slew of nostalgic cultural manifestations. The impetus began earlier in the century, as the forces of modernization encouraged the preservation of past building techniques in the arts and crafts movement, the celebration of America's past in Henry Ford's Deerfield Village, or the recasting of colonial Williamsburg. During the 1930s, a variety of government-sponsored activities collected and preserved Americana, including national historic sites, the Federal Writers' Project guidebooks, Farm Security Administration photographs of migrants, and a host of others. All of them featured the idea that to accept modernity there needed to be an appreciation or adoration of those people and things that were sacrificed for the potential of the present. The cowboy and his way of life were also a part of this tendency, evolving from the Wild West shows of the late nineteenth century through the artistic explosion of serious western art by Wister or Remington to the pulp fiction of Zane Grey and Louis L'Amour. Elizabeth Outka described this as "commodified authentic," where consumers are connected to the perception of authenticity by their understanding of the past, which thus justifies their modernity. Cowboy songs were part of this search for authenticity, stimulated not only through the singing cowboys but also through the intercession of folklorists, anthropologists, and others who wanted to preserve this American way of life. Leading this mission was John A. Lomax, beginning with *Cowboy Songs and Other Frontier Ballads* (1910), *Songs of the Cattle Trail and Cow Camp* (1919), and *American Ballads and Folk Songs* (1935), who, along with Charles Seeger's work with the Resettlement Administration, wanted to make certain that America's folk songs would, as Beulah Charmley wrote in 1935, "stand as an authentic historic and artistic record of the period."[13]

The championing of the West, its peoples, and its history also resonated with American composers of cultivated music who were still searching for authentic American musical forms. At the turn of the twentieth century, Arthur Farwell promoted the belief that the American West held the most authentic sounds and stories for composers to utilize—not only through his own compositions but also through transcriptions he published in his *Wa-Wan Press* (1901–1911). Charles Wakeman Cadman took up Farwell's clarion call and used his arrangements to outline the tension between the traditional and emerging modern society in *Four American Indian Songs* (1914) or *Shanewis* (1918). By the 1930s, composers such as Virgil Thomson, Roy Harris, and Aaron Copland combined the western pastoral with the populist vision of the common man to announce the emergence of distinct American modern art music, as well as celebrate the authenticity of the past. Thomson's music for Pare Lorentz's *Plow That Broke the Plains* (1935) and *The River* (1938) blended a variety of American vernacular melodies, including hymns, into complex symphonic arrangements. Roy Harris, who was perhaps the most celebrated American composer in this vein because of his western birthright, used its symbolism more overtly in *Farewell to Pioneers* (1935) and his *Symphony No. 3* (1938). All of these composers, plus many others, used the imagined West as a means to reach American audiences by blending classical arrangements with vernacular melodies. This led to the creation of a whole series of modernist classical compositions by these composers, including Aaron Copland, the son of Russian-Jewish immigrants raised in New York City. They all used the authenticity and nostalgia of the West in much the same manner as the singing cowboy, by suggesting that one way of life was being replaced with another, and that through creative sampling, the ideals and symbols of this past were woven into the fabric of modernity. "However, it remains to be seen," wrote Roy Harris in 1934, whether this blending of the past with modernity "will prove to be the dying echo of an overconfident hope, or the prophecy of strong voices arising from the lives of millions of Americans."[14]

There were other ways in which the songs and sounds of the Depression era spoke to their generation. Popular music in the years leading up to the Depression era displayed a certain unity of language, symbols, and sounds that were challenged by contemporary songwriters and musicians during the era. The prior limitations of recording technology, combined with the emphasis on sheet music sales as markers for popularity, created both conformity in the material and a loss of control as to its usage. Although the themes of courtship and love remained constant in the lyrics, each generation tied their understanding of these ideas to their own sonic and visual cues, whether occurring in specific words, images, media presentation, costumes, dancing, or types of music. This construction was conscious by those both creating and receiving these cues or signs, and through this exchange they developed a system of understanding and communication. Those not part of this heteroglossia were often confounded and confused by the signs, words, and symbols, because they challenged the unitary understanding of their definition of similar terms. To those born and raised in the early part of the twentieth century, for example, love often meant marriage, family, and work. For adolescents and young adults in the 1930s, love had other meanings, for the economic limitations often meant they had to forgo marriage, family, and even the idea of work. "Life Is Just a Bowl of Cherries" (1931) is a good example of this as singer Ethel Merman chastised those who saved their money for the future as foolish, suggesting instead that they "live and laugh at it all" in the moment. This advice would have had less receptivity in the earlier era, but given the situation of the Depression, the unpredictable nature of work and money reinforced her notion of spending it while you have it and found a home in the hearts and minds of modern Americans.[15]

This modernist generation sought out songs, sounds, and images that reflected an understanding of their world. In general, lyrics and music should not be taken literally but symbolically, because they reveal not only the rhetorical structure of language but also the complex relationship between the musician and his or her audience. So when Ozzie Davis reflected on the racial atmosphere during the 1930s, he recalled the music of Duke Ellington, which advised young black people to "struggle against it," even though there were no specific songs he could point to. It was the presence and importance of Ellington, his band, the music, their unwillingness to sacrifice their identity as African Americans, and their generational acceptance by the dominant society that signified Davis's admiration. His understanding of the complex relationship between race and music was exemplified by the fact that by the end of the decade many white swing bands were integrated, and jazz, from which swing derived, became increasingly accepted as multiracial. Popular music helps define the lived experiences of its listeners, joining them together in what they hear in the sounds with what they see and experience in their daily lives. In this way, what Davis recalled was not unusual from what many experienced. Change was endemic during the 1930s, and new patterns of existence were being matched by the music these listeners consumed.[16]

Swing, as both music and an idea, reflected the modernist urban tone. Many musicians in the bands learned to play their instruments by listening to the radio or via records. The music was mythically born in 1935 by the "King of Swing," Benny Goodman, and unleashed a consumer frenzy that lasted through World War II. The naming and defining of the music itself revealed its modernist identity, as they sought to define it outside of jazz: "Jazz comes out of a man's horn, and swing is the *feeling*," said alto saxophonist Benny Carter. In general, both the musician and the audience believed that the music was "the tempo of our times" and agreed that the music was different from earlier forms of jazz, identifying the development of complex arrangements utilizing larger bands and built-in solos that demanded greater precision and, combined with the influence of the recording engineer, producer, and radio sponsor, was quicker in getting its musical point across. The tempo was fast, immediate, and premeditated. "You must hear their music to know what it is," *Vogue*'s Wilder Hobson wrote in 1936, and many in his generation agreed that it was "America's present-day folk music."[17]

Swing spoke to and for its generation in a manner that separated it from earlier jazz or any other musical forms. It also challenged the accepted ideals of society and music, offending some members of the earlier generation, who believed the new sounds were "transforming the decadent and sophisticated youth into a ruthless barbarian, thumping his feet and waving his arms in some primitive dance of obscene and cruel rites."[18] The duality expressed by sixteen-year-old music student Dorothy Bergman underscored the coded division between generations, for on the one hand, she worried that her generation's music lacked the transcendent beauty of earlier cultivated music, but she also recognized that it was the "only modern music that expresses any side of our side of life."[19] The utilization of professional arrangements combined with radio exposure and records signified its modernity, breaking free from the sounds and traditions of the past and becoming increasingly new and experimental. Frank Norris wrote a piece for the *Saturday Evening Post* on Benny Goodman in 1938 that discussed his unique sound, work ethic, and generational appeal, and he suggested that the new music was already "trying for new and freer uses of its instruments." Further, he likened the scene of a live Goodman performance to a "camp meeting," quoting a noted New York University psychologist who described the concert scene where a "combination of circumstances have made them one-minded and their inhibitory checks have broken down."[20] William Roberts Tilford, writing for the staid magazine *The Etude*, also drew a connection between the performance of jazz and swing to "the old fashioned southern colored camp meeting," where the "wild blares and screeches of the trumpets and clarinets . . . sounded like profane 'Hallelujahs' and 'Amens.'"[21]

Swing revealed its modernist identity in other ways as well. Bands would often remake classics as jazz tunes, which detractors saw as a desecration and signified a disrespect for the past. Reed Dickerson, writing in *Harper's Monthly*, tried to educate the noninitiated into the musical vernacular of "hot" jazz, but he wondered how anyone could explain the cacophony of sounds that was jazz. Certainly there was rhythm, polyrhythm, and blue notes, but how these were joined together in syncopation was a bit of a mystery to him. He even noted the unique words and phrases musicians and their supporters used to describe the music, like "riffing," "getting off," or "going to town."[22] His analysis points to another aspect of modernism, namely, the use of specific words and language to describe their music and performers. These new terms made their elders shake their heads. This "hepster" lingo identified those who were in the know from those who were square and became a symbol of unity for modernists. Cab Calloway was one of the prophets of this new language, eventually publishing a dictionary in 1938. Among the terms he outlined and young people used with regularity were "cat" for a swing musician, "chick" for a hip girl, "cop" to acquire, "dillinger" for a particularly swinging song, "got your boots on" to signify hipness, "icky" as non-hip, "kill me" for having a good time, "lick" for a great musical phrase within a song, "righteous" for doing someone a good turn, "sailing" for being high or drunk, "solid" for righteous, "viper" for those who smoked "weed" or "reefers," and many more. Words that meant one thing to one generation meant something else to the modern "jitter bug" (swing fan). The *Hepcat's Jive Talk Dictionary* (1946) included hundreds of words and phrases that challenged the unitary language of the dominant society and identified the generational subculture.[23]

Most young people did not use these terms in everyday conversation, but they were conscious of their usage and meanings, particularly as they often appeared in the songs of the day. And even if these hepcat words did not appear, traditional terms such as "love," "marriage," and "the future" took on new meaning as a result of their modernist connotations. The language and the tone of how specific terms were used in songs spoke to young people in a manner different from the generation before. "Stompin' at the Savoy," with music by Benny Goodman, Chick Webb, and Edgar Sampson, documented not just a "swingin' band" but a tone and ambiance where dancers can find happiness, joy, and "romance," whereas the eponymous Duke Ellington song "It Don't Mean a Thing (If It Ain't Got That Swing)" defined this mood, whether "sweet or hot," as the rhythm of the moment. Cole Porter's "Night and Day" from 1932 was recorded by numerous bands during the era. It used a syncopated "tick tick tock" of a clock to document the passing of time until lovers could be together again, but the wait seemed endless. The music had to have "a kick in it," Jack Leonard sang with Tommy Dorsey in 1936, to create "a dancing mood." Benny Goodman's theme song, "Let's Dance," was both a sonic and lyrical testament to the abandon of swing dancing and the modern arena of courtship—the dance floor. Perhaps the most evident of how music and lyrics presented the modern tone was Cab Calloway, Irving Mills, and Clarence Gaskill's "Minnie the Moocher," with its call-and-response moments, hepster slang, and evocative lyrics of sexuality and an exotic lifestyle. Calloway's performance in the many film shorts of the song, and even in a 1932 Betty Boop cartoon, blended the traditional African American cakewalk into the bluesy song. In the end, what many of the songs of the era suggested was that it "'Tain't What You Do" that counted, but how you swing it. "If you try too hard," the Trummy Young and Sy Oliver song from 1939 intoned, then you just didn't get it.[24]

In much the same manner that cowboy songs harked back to the past to better understand the present, much of the popular music of the 1930s, "sweet" or "hot" in swing vernacular, used nostalgia as the lyrical hook to get the listener's attention. "Homesick, tired, [and] alone in the big city," the singer longs for the simple life back home in the South. "When It's Sleepy Time Down South," which became Louis Armstrong's theme song for many years, sounded like a dream that painted the Old South with a romantic patina while ignoring the less-than-glamorous reality. Many nostalgic songs used this fantasy-like approach to blend the past to the present, commenting "was it only yesterday / My, how time can fly," in "Throw Another Log on the Fire," or the definitive "Thanks for the memory / Of sentimental verse, nothing in my purse." In "Star Dust" Hoagy Carmichael pines for a past lover while "dreaming of a song" whose "melody haunts" him, knowing that a reunion was a "fairy tale, a paradise" unlikely to be realized. The song "Yesterdays" has the singer vacillating between the happiness of recalling his "gay youth" and sadness that these days were gone and live only in his dreams. When one was "up in the world" the longing for the imagined stability of the past resonated, even if it meant going back to the "tumbled down shack by an old railroad track" in "Old Shanty Town." But the "Old Spinning Wheel" only used dreams from the past "covered with dust and forgotten," for life was in the here and now.[25]

The opening line from the classic 1933 song "Stormy Weather" outlined another aspect of this looking back to situate the present: "Don't know why there's no sun up in the sky . . ." The sadness brought on by the constant rain and "gloom and mis'ry" was tolerated by the hope that one day he/she would "walk in the sun." There was optimism amidst the sadness and recognition that the past was not all wine and roses, but the melancholy feelings on the problems of the present day laid the foundation. "The ghost of you clings," but reality reminds the listener that these were "Foolish Things" best kept as memories. In "Sophisticated Lady" the singer grieved that the flame of love "flickered one day and died away," and that the lesson learned led to a more temporal level of commitment—no more "thinking of tomorrow." But in the quiet of her own moments, she longed for the lost love of youth. Sometimes days brought hardship and sadness along the "Boulevard of Broken Dreams," where one walked "along the street of sorrow" among their "broken dreams" and "scattered schemes."[26]

The dream metaphor was used throughout the era as a way to break from the past. One could "Wrap Your Troubles in Dreams," or "trade in your old dreams for new" on the "Street of Dreams." Many of the songs reaffirmed the reality of the day, assuring the listener that "This Is No Dream" and that the disappointment they felt about their outlook was normal, as every dream was "made to be shatter'd just to build them anew." In the classic Depression-era song "Brother, Can You Spare a Dime," Yip Harburg laments how once "they" said the people were "building a dream," which underscored the illusion of pie-in-the-sky promises and reminded people that only by working together could their dreams be realized. One could spend their time "Day Dreaming," or "With My Eyes Wide Open [I'm Dreaming]," or even be "In the Middle of a Dream," but it was made clear in these songs that people controlled their own future. "It's my universe," sang Bing Crosby in the Burke and Monaco song "I've Got a Pocketful of Dreams," and "even with an empty purse" he remained hopeful. Even if dreams were "made of imagination," the future lay firmly in the hands of those willing to make it their "own creation," wrote Hart and Rodgers in 1932's "Isn't It Romantic." The modern times would "blow away the past" and lead to a better place "Beyond the Blue Horizon." Although the lyrics of these types of nostalgia and dream songs paint an elegiac picture, when combined with the deliberate rhythm and melody, the music helped create a dreamlike state that encouraged dancers to hold each other close and sway to the music.[27]

The past was made present in these songs, which were reminders of the visible failures and the faith that tomorrow would bring respite. "Dreamers tell us dreams come true," sang Ray Eberle with the Glenn Miller Orchestra in 1939, but only if one's resolve was "strong enough" to maintain the faith necessary to build the better tomorrow. The sense of hopefulness came through in the tone of many of these romantic and nostalgic songs, performed with an upbeat tempo that projected a more hopeful mood. Although "nothing's what it once used to be," conversion meant that "somewhere over the rainbow, skies are blue," and with a little faith and trust in the ideas and formulas of the day, soon "Happy days [would certainly be] . . . here again." Everyone was searching for a better day, looking forward because they were unsatisfied with the present situation. "It's a wonderful world . . . [to] talk of heaven on earth," for "yesterday things were gloomy," but there was a new hope in the "New Sun in the Sky."[28]

Most of these songs were recorded by a variety of singers and bands and appeared on the charts many times throughout the era. Except for when the song was featured by a crooner such as Bing Crosby, or even a western singer such as Gene Autry, the focus was more on the music and melody than on the actual lyrics. The question as to how much of the actual lyrics people heard or understood has been long debated; however, when those in the 1930s listened to these songs over the radio, on jukeboxes, at home on their record players, or perhaps even at a live performance, audiences were transported through the tempo, tone, and spirit of the music. And, given multiple recordings and the technological ability to play and replay any song, the songs of the era resonated with the people and spoke to them like hymns of modernity.[29]

The influence of modernity resonated through more than lyrics and melodies, as new technology challenged and often replaced traditional methods of how people learned to play an instrument. In the not-so-distant past, many young people were introduced to music and given rudimentary lessons in their churches, synagogues, schools, or even urban settlement houses. With the proliferation of music over the radio and increased record sales, many began turning to these mediums to learn how to sing or play an instrument. The Lundberg study confirmed that the radio and record player had "revolutionized" the role of music in the home, and it seemed only natural that these modern devices would aid in musical education. Howard Hanson, one of America's leading composers and director of the Eastman School of Music, recognized that musicians and audiences should not fear the influence of the machine on music, because it could both increase musical appreciation and instill in young people the desire to play an instrument. "The creative field of music has never been more promising," he concluded. His enthusiasm was not misplaced, as it was reported by 1938 that radio programming was responsible for a 300 percent increase in piano sales. The president of the Baldwin Piano Company believed that once people were exposed to the "spiritual and intellectual benefits" of music heard over the radio, their desire to learn to play an instrument increased exponentially. Pitts Sanborn, director of the Radio Institute of the Audible Arts, believed that radio had the revolutionary power to transform listeners' understanding and appreciation of quality music, and that people wanted to be kept abreast of the latest music in their "swiftly moving world." Radio was the key.[30]

For some, the radio or record player was their teacher. Many nascent jazz and swing musicians listened to their favorites over the radio to glean musical tips or to hear the latest hot standards. The sounds emanating from this machine made many want to become musicians, and they used the radio to learn how to play their instruments. Jazz/swing guitarist Tiny Grimes stayed up late to hear Duke Ellington and others on his radio and played along with what he heard, trying to blend his guitar into the swing music that was being broadcast. Bandleader and trumpet player Erskine Hawkins used the radio to develop his musical style in a manner like Grimes, by blending his horn into the songs he heard and considering ways to change them to fit his desire. Joe Williams, Charles Thompson, Maxine Sullivan, and many more used the radio to practice their singing, to work on phrasing and/or breathing, and more significantly, because they were either far removed from or lacked the means to attend live performances, to tap into modern sounds. They wanted to be part of the choir of the airwaves. Recordings played a similar role. It is accepted lore that aspiring white musicians in the late 1920s and 1930s used the records of jazz greats to learn their "chops." Wingy Manone, Art Hodes, Dick McPartland, Bud Freeman, and many more admitted they used records to learn the licks perfected by the likes of Armstrong, Oliver, Beiderbecke, and Ellington. They slowed the record down with their finger to catch each note and then replicate it as best they could. They also went to live performances and watched how the musicians were playing and from these experiences learned how to play many jazz standards. Budd Johnson called this process his school and through records mimicked many of the best saxophone solos by his jazz idols. The impact and influence of records on musicians cannot be understated, for like radio, they served to both introduce new sounds and invite membership into the modern sound. Bandleader Woody Herman, who grew up in a Polish-German family in Milwaukee, said that it was only through records that he was exposed to Ellington, Goodman, and others. Through modern technology he connected to his generation and used this introduction to become a leader in the music industry. Even folk/blues guitarist Huddie Ledbetter

("Leadbelly"), who, according to his promoter, John Lomax, utilized only his natural ability to play and sing, admitted he learned much through "listening to other singers off phonograph records."[31]

But it was the radio as teacher that transformed the nature and meaning of music. When students heard the electronic transmission of their instruments over the radio, they tried to copy that sound rather than the live sound. The radio broadcast altered the perception of sound, as it had with singers like the crooners, and students now modeled what they played after what the machine produced. Of course, the many radio music courses encouraged lesson books to aid the students, but these only revealed the notes and timing. The sound they sought to replicate came from the radio.

The radio was seen by many as the savior in the pursuit of training young people to play "better" music. Given the medium's vast listenership, music educators believed that by introducing listeners to the basics of music appreciation, their acceptance of cultivated music would grow. Part of this process involved teaching the hundreds of thousands of listeners the rudiments of playing an instrument through the "magic of radio." A program on NBC Red called "Fun in Music" offered lessons over the air while the same network also broadcast the "Home Symphony" show that encouraged listeners to play along with the studio orchestra. The titles of the songs were announced in advance, and interested listeners could, for a small fee, have a music booklet sent to them. The "Fun in Music" program for children developed as an offshoot of University of Michigan professor of music Dr. Joseph Maddy's experimental radio musical education programs begun in the latter part of the 1920s. Designed to reach into rural areas that did not have musical education programs, the program's success encouraged NBC Red in 1937 to include the show on its coast-to-coast network lineup. Like the "Home Orchestra" program, booklets were ordered in advance of the lessons; as a sign of its success, during its first year as a national program between 200,000 and 500,000 booklets were ordered. Maddy encouraged his listeners to share the lesson books, meaning that nearly a million youngsters used his program and lesson books to learn how to play music. The success of these programs led to others, including Olin Downes's "Music Is My Hobby" program, also broadcast by NBC, where nonprofessional musicians were featured over the air as part of the "orchestra."[32]

Given this success, some educators began to advocate, as had Maddy, for using radio in the classroom in order to teach children to play and appreciate "better" music. The appeal of the radio challenged "educators to develop techniques. . . by experiment and research" to create musical education programs that could be used in the classroom. A study carried out by the University of Wisconsin in 1931 tested the viability of radio musical education versus traditional instruction. Twenty-five schools used the radio to teach basic music education and appreciation to sixth-, seventh-, and eighth-grade students. The researchers measured the students' ability to play and their overall participation to suggest that the "radio lessons were highly successful in teaching music" when measured by the general progress of the students. The results were more conclusive for students living in rural areas or without established music programs. Marguerite Hood, a music teacher in Montana, had similar success in bringing musical education to the far-flung reaches of her state over station KGVO's Montana School of the Air program. She used her influence to promote network musical programming that was beneficial to her students, like NBC's "Music Appreciation Hour" hosted by Walter Damrosch. But when NBC changed the time of his program in 1937 so that it was broadcast at noon in Montana and the local affiliates chose to broadcast other, more profitable programming instead, Hood began her own radio musical broadcast to reach all of that state's schoolchildren. Creating a network of four stations, she presented a thirty-minute lesson every Wednesday that reached an estimated 10,000 students in Montana and North Dakota.[33]

The modern radio brought modern music into the homes and consciousness of its listeners. Not that music self-identified as modern, except in those few instances when truly modern compositions were played over the air (much to the disappointment of many in the radio audience), but the manner of presentation and reception set the tone and temper of modernity. The music coming through the radio set was different in tone, texture, resonance, pitch, and a host of other technical ways. It was also different in how it was received, appropriated, and utilized. People now worked while listening to cultivated music, women did their chores while whistling along with the most popular tunes of the day, and young and not-so-young people used the medium to perform, create, and become part of what they heard over the radio. Places of worship that were once the central location for nonprofessional musicians to learn how to play and to perform were displaced by the radio, and even recitals, which in the past were reserved for churches and other local facilities, were overshadowed by the power and reach of the radio. With this modern technology, the student was "assured an audience made up of listeners from all over . . . the world, [who] will be listening in large numbers."[34]

Radio also redefined how performers approached their craft. There were new techniques, guided by the modern technology that demanded change. Singers, for example, had to alter their tone and volume because of the tonal qualities of the microphone. "Many artists," *Popular Mechanics* wrote in 1935, "have been forced to change their technique entirely" because of the radio microphone. No longer did the voice go from singer to listener; now it was filtered through a transmitter, then an amplifier, and then transformed electronically into sound waves sent out to receivers that reconstructed them into music coming out of the radio. The singer had to understand "the equation between the amount of voice used and the distance . . . from the microphone." Musicians also had to alter their presentation to meet the needs of the microphone, making certain that individual instruments did not overwhelm the recording amplifier. A band of four or a swing band of twenty-five had to consciously work with the radio sound engineer to make certain that the proper tone and volume was achieved. This sometimes meant a different band setup from a public performance, as certain instruments overwhelmed the controls, like the drums, and often had to be muted or placed farther away from the radio microphone. The advance of modernity altered the tone and texture of the music, and for those who listened to these new sounds on the radio or from records, it played a significant role in their acceptance of these new, modern musics.[35]

The same held true for composers of cultivated music. Leopold Stokowski, the esteemed conductor of the Philadelphia Orchestra throughout the Depression era and the guest conductor of the NBC Symphony Orchestra, described in great detail the ways in which radio broadcasting altered a composer's work. He outlined how the transmission of musical sound was dependent on a variety of modern nonmusical factors. For example, the sound that was picked up and broadcast was to a large degree controlled by the size of the studio, the arrangement and quality of the microphones, the acoustics in the room, and the general setup of the orchestra itself. Making the issue even more complex was the fact that most receiving equipment, namely, the radios in most people's homes, lacked the proper frequency range to accurately reflect the music. "The scientific explanation can be simply stated. The characteristic or quality of tone in music is mainly due to harmonics or overtones. At present, many of these cannot be and are not transmitted and received by the radio." As a result, what the listener heard was neither what was composed nor being played, but served as a representation of the music. Stokowski described in technical detail how the frequency range of the radio, set at 5,000 cycles per second, is nearly 8,000 cycles less than what is necessary to capture the live sound of music. He also pointed out that radio's intensity range, or the distance between soft and loud tones used by composers to convey emotion, was set at about thirty decibels, whereas live performances utilize at least an eighty-five-decibel intensity range. The radio engineer compressed all the sounds coming from the orchestra into the thirty-decibel range with a basic volume control, making sure there was no sound overload during loud parts and that the quiet parts were made audible. The sounds heard by the listener were also modified by the microphone itself, for unlike the human ear with its multiple means of receiving sound, the microphone captured sound as a "*single* ear attached to a *single* circuit." What was transmitted was a monotone rush of sounds absorbed simultaneously by the listener, and like the frequency and decibel range, the microphone compressed the sound into one unit.[36]

Stokowski was not negative toward the radio, but he wanted the industry to improve through what later came to be called cable radio hookup and stereo sound. He believed, like many others, that the radio held tremendous potential for creating and disseminating new music to a vast and compliant audience. They were open to the modern sounds heard over the radio, for unlike Stokowski, most were unaware of the sonic limitations and accepted as authentic what the radio played. As Stokowski suggested, the composer and musician increasingly had to adapt to the studio and work with the sound engineer. The tonal attributes of specific instruments also had to be moderated in order for the microphone to accurately pick up the sound, ensuring that the modern musician approach his or her art with a scientific mindset. Through multiple takes the engineer made certain that the correct sound was being broadcast or recorded, experimenting with microphone placement and other tactics to better capture the appropriate sound. Without the joint effort of the musician and engineer, "sounds that either do not exist or that would not exist" were made audible.[37]

Central to the discussion of the sonic qualities of the music heard over the radio was its potential for social uplift. If what was heard could improve society, then the necessary cost and energies were justified. Music had long been used in various celebrations to bring people together; likewise, the modern songs of the 1930s were part of the general promise of salvation being offered, whether over the radio, on records, or at live performances. Contributing to this promise under the umbrella of the Works Progress Administration and Federal Art Project One was the Federal Music Project (FMP). Its central purpose, aside from the employment of skilled musicians, was to bring cultivated music to the masses. To do this, FMP orchestras played virtually anywhere in order to serve communities by "helping to provide some form of spiritual sustenance" in the form of music. Under the directorship of Nikolai Sokoloff, the FMP used extensive live performances, radio broadcasts, and educational activities to expose and convert the people to, to his mind, better music than the popular tunes they preferred.[38]

The FMP orchestras brought music to Americans wherever they could set up a stage and provided educational opportunities for children and adults. From its inception in the summer of 1935 through early 1941, FMP orchestras in all forty-eight states employed more than 25,000 musicians and gave 249,000 performances to more than 158 million Americans. The orchestras were of various sizes and generally made up of American citizens in both the pit and at the conductor's podium. They organized for special, often patriotic, occasions and gave free concerts at festivals, veterans' homes, hospitals, schools, parking lot openings, public parks—virtually anywhere they were invited. FMP administrators believed that music needed to play a primary role in the "social transition" of the Depression era. They cited "recent scientific investigations" that described the positive effects of music on people's ability to handle the "demands of contemporary life." The FMP also gave many concerts in schools and used these appearances to encourage music lessons. Over the period of its existence, the FMP taught 1.5 million classes to 17 million students. Given that music was one of the first cuts made to education budgets, the FMP educational units played a central role in maintaining the primacy of music in many children's lives. Numerous educators wrote to Sokoloff or regional directors thanking them for their tireless efforts. These letters went directly to the project's publicity office, operated by Harry Hewes, who altered them to portray the redemptive qualities of music and how the FMP was actually helping save people.[39]

The FMP, perhaps more than any other New Deal agency, utilized the radio to sing the praises of the New Deal and the emerging new America. Sokoloff believed that the FMP was ushering in a new age for American music, a "new spiritual and cultural awakening" for which radio played a central role. In 1938 alone, the project produced 2,800 radio broadcasts and began a program of recording the best orchestral performances and sending them out to rural communities throughout the country. By 1941 the FMP gave more than 8,000 radio performances to millions of listeners. They produced specific programs linking the positive aspects of the WPA to their musical selections or to patriotic events such as Washington's birthday, National Music Week, and the seventy-fifth anniversary of the Battle of Gettysburg. Their broadcasts regularly featured American composers long ignored by private orchestras, who favored the European masters. The FMP hoped to stimulate a new era of cultivated music appreciation among the citizenry by using compositions by American composers who utilized American themes and tones. "The dawn of a music culture, identifiably America's own," announced American composer and conductor Ferde Grofé in 1938, meant that future "generations of Americans" will know and appreciate their own music. This musical nationalism was closely linked to the nostalgic themes inherent in the compositions, using "our own ideals, history, and folk-habits" to create a music that spoke to and for Americans. Through April 1939, the FMP performed 6,772 American compositions from 2,034 American composers, and helped create the Index of American Composers in the Library of Congress with 7,300 titles from 2,258 composers.[40]

One of the more interesting forays made by the FMP that spoke directly to the issues surrounding modernism was its sponsorship and high hopes for a 1937 short opera titled *The Romance of Robot*. It was brought to the attention of the FMP in New York City in the summer of 1936, with a libretto by Tillman Breiseth and score by Frederic Hart, and after nearly a year of rehearsals it premiered on April 12, 1937. It also closed that day. The opera was about a scientist named Electro who set out to create the "perfect man . . . whose operating costs" were low and "whose energy knows no limits." The scientist employed a bevy of "Electro-lysed" women with names such as Whistle, Klaxon, and Wheel to oil and take care of the man of steel. They had renounced the "silly past times" and dedicated themselves to the robot, singing, "We adore you, man of steel / We admire the way you feel / Humbly at your feet we kneel / We adore you, man of steel." But all was not what it seemed, for these same women protested the robot's lack of emotion and their loss of free will. So Electro created a female robot named Cylindra—a "perfect modern beauty" with "steel-cut headdress . . . copper bodice . . . [and] hydraulic pumps"—and gives her the soul from one of the electro-lysed ladies-in-waiting so that she might know love. Of course, Electro falls for her, but given his human limitations, he transferred his soul to the robot to be with his love. Once given a soul and the power of love, the robot rejected Cylindra for a songbird named Philomena who was really a beautiful woman trapped until the love of the robot freed her. The robot denounced his machine-age identity and accepted the limitations of humanity, and as he and Philomena pledged their undying love, Electro wandered aimlessly, regretting that he put his faith in the machine at the expense of humanity: "My soul is gone, my source of strength / I must confess I feel a frightful emptiness."[41]

That the opera failed is of little surprise given the strained metaphors in the libretto and the lack of originality in the score. What makes *Romance* interesting was the investment that the FMP placed in its potential. Something about the theme intrigued New York City's regional director, Lee Pattison, who believed that a modern operetta focusing on the complexity of modernism would resonate with New York City's citizens and perhaps the nation. He hoped that *Romance* would be performed by FMP units throughout the country and be broadcast nationally over the radio. The principal character, Electro, outlined the dark side of modernity without an appropriate counterbalance. This simplistic formula had been used beforehand in a variety a ways, from films such as *Metropolis*

(1927) and *Modern Times* (1936), or even Huxley's novel *Brave New World* (1931). Of course, there were many concerned with the negative effects of the machine age, particularly as it related to employment, but by the time of *Romance*, most people had come to accept the tenets of modernism and incorporated them into their daily lives, consciously or otherwise. The strict dichotomy outlined in the failed opera no longer existed, and the modernity on display and consumed in the Depression era tempered the harsh and cold machine-age dictums of the past. *Romance* failed because it spoke to the past, and the contemporary audience that viewed it, as well as theater and music critics, saw through its obvious dated criticism of the modern era.

By the time of *Romance*, considerable discussions concerning the positive role of technology, science, and other attributes linked to modernism had taken place. As radio and recording technology improved and affected daily life, inventors, scientists, and social psychologists began to explore other uses and effects of music, and in this way they suggested the power of music beyond entertainment and into science. Electricians and inventors had long experimented with the possibilities of capturing music with electric currents. This was closely linked to the development of "talkies" in film and, later, the creation of magnetic tape to capture and record sound. As scientists sought to harness the magic of electricity to produce the "untouched possibilities" of electronic music, they knew that using electric current to amplify sound was only the first step. The real challenge was how to develop ways in which science could improve or even replace existing instruments. For example, a microphone could only pick up a small range of tones and sounds coming from a piano or violin; yet an electronic version of these same instruments, reduced to their electric frequencies, could replicate all the subtle tones and nuances of the performance. By using an electronic resonator to pick up the sound and then send these impulses through an amplifier with a variety of volume and tonal controls, a more pure and natural sound could be produced. Harnessing the power of electricity for musical production offered "unlimited tonal quality, unlimited range and unlimited volume" for those willing to accept this new technology. The "Music of the Future," *Popular Mechanics* announced, was "now a reality." Ordinary citizens could witness this power by augmenting their radio sets with something called the Telecolor, which projected colors into the home interpreting the tones of the music. Using "thyratron tubes," the device utilized the basic colors red, blue, and green mixed with neutral white light to bring visual electronic magic into the homes of the consumer. The listener could now not only hear the music but also, through the projection and blending of the colors, see how the music feels.[42]

Music affected the listener. Songs and music created a sense of unity and togetherness, an identity of belief. Given the pervasiveness of music during the Depression era, psychologists and other scientists dedicated significant study to the effects of music on the human psyche. Some, such as C. E. Seashore, explained how the tonal qualities of sound could be used to better educate and understand the effect of music on both the performer and the listener. The question of why a certain student could or could not perform certain pieces had always focused on natural talent, but modern science went beyond nature to analyze the effects of sound waves, frequencies, and tonal representations, in combination with "scientific measurements" of inheritance, guidance, racial makeup, training, and a host of other variables, to better explain and develop training methods. Other scientists examined the psychological features of the modern song as it related to the power of syncopation and sales. The effect of rhythm so prevalent in modern music was seen as a primal link to human cohesion, as well as desire for community and social connection. The sales of sheet music were closely tied to the exposure songs received over the radio, as people tended to purchase songs they heard regularly over those heard less frequently. However, the research also indicated that songwriters were less able to predict which types of songs would sell regardless of radio play. In other words, just because something was heard did not mean it would sell more sheet music. In the end, the variable determining the "purchase of sheet music is a phenomenon of social pressure rather than selective judgment by the radio audience."[43]

Music, in the modern sense of the word and ideal, was a necessary component of Depression-era America. It improved work, increased morale, unified, built solidarity, and helped inspire the people in a time of transition to a new way of being. The 1930s was an era of change, and this was reflected by the proliferation and acceptance of the varieties of modernist music. Maya Angelou remembers during the Depression when traveling blues performers came through her grandmother's country store in rural Arkansas. Her "grandmother would say, 'Sister, come away from that. That's worldly music.' And it was worldly music in the best sense of the word." Angelou loved what these blues singers were singing and heard in their songs a unity of consciousness that was not the same as her grandmother's.[44] Noted country music scholar Bill C. Malone relates how while his mother was in church singing the hymns of his faith, his father and other men were outside trading stories. The sacred and the profane—women on the inside asked for their God's guidance in the troubled times, while men wondered how long they could hold on to their failing cotton farms against the encroachment of modernity. Both sides were fearful but excited, for any liberation from the closed and limited society in which they labored in poverty had to be better. And from where did they get the good news for which they both rejoiced and feared: music over the radio. "The remarkable confrontation of rural folkways with urban-industrial technology" provided what came to be called country music its foundation, its root. The music of the Depression era served as social hymns, uniting diverse peoples through radio, jukeboxes, records, and live performances. Those who listened and sang along, tapped their feet or fingers to the music, danced, learned to play or played along with what they heard, or even those who just sat back and enjoyed—all of them participated in the sonic awakening that was 1930s America. All facets of what music wrought were altered, transformed, and made modern even as music sampled the past and used traditional sounds and techniques. The influence of science, technology, and modernist ideology made the music of the era generational, speaking to and for its listeners. These modern songs helped to build unity and transcend temporal identity—to take the believers away from this place and project their consciousness toward salvation and acceptance. Through the radio, phonograph records, and live performances, many Americans wanted songs that provided what Malone called the "capacity for deliverance." These were the songs of modernity that traced individual lives throughout the Depression era and transcended musical categorizations of cowboy, country, jazz, swing, Tin

Pan Alley, or classical, for all of these were part of the concord of modern music.[45]

All songs and music are sacred in their way, as they speak to each generation or cohort from whom they spring, documenting those ideas, symbols, sounds, or words most revered. The belief that songs and melodies join believers together was not reserved for the 1930s but is a constant in human history. In the years leading up to the Depression era, music was used by slaves working the fields, by industrial workers in virtually every enterprise and in their quest for justice, by women on porches and in dining rooms sewing and proclaiming their right to equality, and of course by children playing games and learning the basics of counting and spelling. Music, songs, and melodies play a central role in human development and consciousness. While these songs were different types of commodities than the popular or cultivated songs written, produced, and consumed during the Depression era, they were no less desirous of an audience, of a listener, of someone who might get some joy or solace from the melody, the music, or the words. But one thing is clear: the songs, music, and melodies of the 1930s spoke to their generation, and in doing so they served as a connection to modernity, not unlike hymns. Society was turned upside down during these years, and in the search for new ideals and identities, music played an instrumental role in the acceptance of modernity. Whether it came via the unity of lyrical imagery and language, the construction of new sounds, the projection of music through new technology, the innovation required to utilize these new technologies, or simply by the composition of songs and melodies that sampled the perceived authentic texture of the American experience, music provided the chorus for its generation. Eduardo de la Fuente used Max Weber's "sociology of religious types" to argue that some modernist composers easily fit into his categorization of prophet, whereas others better fit Weber's typology of priest, whose "true function . . . is to live in the present" and present the good news to the congregation. His analysis also applies to Autry, Ellington, Mercer, Lerner, Goodman, Crosby, and a host of popular performers who used their musical abilities no less than those with traditional cultivated musical training to encourage people to grasp "the Absolute."[46]

EPILOGUE
NEW DIRECTIONS AND CHALLENGES
THE POSTWAR DIVIDE

In a 2014 *Harper's* magazine article, writer Adolph Reed, Jr., laments the demise of American liberalism and the increasing abandonment of ideals rooted in the early twentieth century that sought to regulate capital and organize the social and economic affairs of the state to best serve the majority. He rightfully places the peak of this ideology during the Roosevelt era, especially in the announcement in 1944 of the "second Bill of Rights." The article accurately delineates the slow decline of these ideals, culminating in the shift right by the Democratic Party in the latter part of the 1980s and early 1990s. By the time of the new century there was, as the article is titled, "Nothing Left."[1]

Reed's observations are spot on, for in the period after 1945, when World War II's demand for central planning and mobilization gave way to other desires, there began a slow turn away from the Depression era's commitment to modernity. *Modernity and the Great Depression* provides several examples of the appropriation and acceptance of modernity during the 1930s, which carried over through most of the 1940s, but its influence permeated nearly every aspect of American social and cultural life during this era of crisis. It is important to remember that while society in this century takes as a given the complexities and nuances of modernity and it effects, to the Depression-era generations, many of these issues were still very new. Electricity, for example, while nearly omnipresent to Americans today, was for many during the Depression a new technology. By 1939, 90 percent of those living in rural areas were without electricity, only a 15 percent improvement over the 1930 number of 75 percent. Nearly one-third of the homes in the country lacked an indoor toilet. Hollywood's commitment to talkies was still in its early stages, and the proliferation of network radio broadcasts, while increasing at an explosive rate during the decade, represented an innovation that was still undergoing widespread investigation as to its positive or negative effects. In the 1936 film *The Petrified Forest*, starring Humphrey Bogart, Bette Davis, and Leslie Howard, and written by future FDR speechwriter Robert Sherwood, the story line explores the demise of the individualist ethos of the earlier generations and the acceptance, albeit with some trepidation, of the modernist way of being.[2]

The acceptance of modernity was transformative for many Americans, but it was also very new, which explains in a way why the dissemination as detailed here led to its apotheosis. While the chapter on interior decorators, for example, places these home interior experts at the center of informing primarily white women of the advantages of modern home fixtures, similar work has been done to examine how male industrial designers worked actively to incorporate modernist ideology into their concepts. The same holds true for the chapter on the CCC and NYA, for there are countless examples of how the New Deal adopted and promoted modernist thought—order, planning, and reason—into its programs, including the Agricultural Adjustment Administration, the Farm Security Administration, the Works Progress Administration, and the Federal Security Administration. These examples are not merely liberal policy adaptations but entirely new ways of addressing the complex issues of modern America. The chapters on the world's fairs and music can be viewed from another side that also illuminates the attraction and acceptance of modernity, primarily through advertising, radio, and film industries that pointed to advantages of the promotion of modernity. There was no turning back, only forward. Literature of the day discussed these same tendencies, whether through nostalgic looks back or social realism. What this all suggests is that modernity permeated nearly all aspects of society, and while certainly there were many who resisted its tendencies and were perhaps even unaware of their acceptance to this new way of being, the ontology, both symbolic and real, of modernity as defined in the Depression era was transformative.[3]

Yet its time was marked. "Today modernism is exhausted," wrote Daniel Bell in his 1976 *The Cultural Contradictions of Capitalism*, but his observation reflected an evolving process begun during the ascendancy of modernity that only came to a head after several decades of its tenets being challenged by various quarters.[4] Modernity had always had multiple interpretations, each taking on a slightly different meaning to reinforce Joseph Singall's description of the many-windowed and many-faceted room. In many ways it depended on which way one looked. For some, modernism held that by using reason the problems plaguing American society could be solved. Others saw modernity as the key to a reasonable transformation of humanity through logic and scientific methodology. Still others saw in the many manifestations of modernity the liberation of the individual from the superstitions of the past and the dawn of a new way of being.

In all of these ways of seeing modernity, and smaller schisms within each, humanity was at the forefront of a new world where salvation was direct, tangible, and democratic. Many appropriated modernist icons to define themselves within this new world, as a testament to their identity and faith in the progress. However, within this faithfulness always lay some doubt, oftentimes manifested in the modernist ambiguity, a tension between the limitations of the past, the uncertainty of the present, and the hope of the future. All believed that modernity in all its forms had transformed the American consciousness, creating a new belief system tied to a faith that a better world awaited: one free from the problems and designs of the past; one no longer limited by superstition or the multisocial constructions of identity; one open to the reality of human progress. World War II tested the resolve of these ideals and this new consciousness, pitting a future based on equalitarianism against the failed notions of nationalism and aggression. The Cold War also demanded that a modernist consensus, rooted in American exceptionalism, continue to transform American society and, through active foreign and economic policy, spread the good news of the American way. Domestic or foreign crises were handled with modernist logic and reason, oftentimes blind to the emotional or even human element of their actions.

This complete faith in the potential of modernity encouraged a whole generation to rise up and challenge its most basic assumption, namely, that through reason and planning a better world could be created. Where was this better world, many in the 1960s and 1970s asked? How had modernity made life better for minorities, women, homosexuals, and the poor? Where was that General Motors city of the future that was so clean and efficient? How had modernity reduced the need for war or lessened the fears of catastrophic annihilation? The challenges to modernity came from those same liberals that Reed laments no longer exists, for the reasonable and logical challenges to civil rights, the war in Vietnam, and the unequal distribution of capital and power, were all by-products of the faith instilled in this generation by their elders. Many began questioning the logic behind the faith born in the Depression and called for a new way, reverting in some quarters to naturalistic romanticism, which would congeal into the conservative revolution of the past forty years or more.

The questions raised in the latter part of the century hark back to the Depression era's complexity. Even while modernity was being disseminated and appropriated, Wendy Wall argues that a small group of politicians, business and advertising leaders, and other "cultural elites" conspired to "further their own political and social agendas" through the propagation of something they labeled the "American Way." The naming of their ideals suggests that those who did not follow were being misled, and the "ensuing battle—pitting 'democracy' against 'freedom,' mutualism against individualism, and a progressive ethos against interclass unity—presaged contests that would continue into the postwar era." While her focus centers on the tension within the post-1945 American consensus and the complexity of collective identity, she details its roots in the New Deal era as organizations such as the National Association of Manufacturers, the Liberty League, and corporations such as General Motors and DuPont appropriated modernist techniques, via the radio, advertising, and the creation of rhetoric, to challenge the beliefs inherent to the inclusive tendencies of 1930s-era modernity. In many ways World War II served as both the high point for modernity and the opening for these elites, as the US government found itself in many ways allied to their agenda in order to win the war. But the American Way proponents' lack of organization, the proliferation of rival ideologies, and the power of the modernist-pluralistic message slowed its development until after World War II.[5]

In the aftermath of World War II, the devastating emotional toll encouraged many Americans to reevaluate their future and choices. The numbers of men killed in action or wounded meant that those who did come back sought the complacency of normality: job, home, wife, and children. The means to acquire this stability resided in the vestiges of modernity, namely, the triumvirate of government, industry, and labor and the commitment to a planned and organized economy. However, the aftermath of the war witnessed an explosion of consumption aided in large measure by pent-up demand from the combination of the Depression and war and through the careful demobilization of the millions of soldiers. This postwar competition for jobs, money, and residency undermined the ideals of modernity, as planning and reasonable solutions to these problems and other problems revealed huge gaps, which those promoting the American Way would exploit, revealing the limitations of modernity to deal with the new, modern problems.

This postwar version of modernism found itself embroiled in a schism between the ideals of the high modernists and those who held a more romantic notion of modernity. Robert Genter's *Late Modernism: Art, Culture, and Politics in Cold War America* describes the tension between high modernists who sought to "separate art from the detritus of daily existence" and the romantics who held firm to the more sacred ideals of aesthetics and art that had founded the movement in the latter part of the nineteenth century. Both used their influence in art, literature, and other media to promote their version of modernism and used their rhetoric to apply their definitions to the past. One side felt that modernism's commitment to pluralism and planning lessened the power of individuality and had created a weak and wholly middlebrow culture lacking a critical base. The other side saw tremendous potential in the liberating effects of modernity, allowing for the participation of a greater number of people that would enhance the genius of *homo Americanus*. This division within modernism, an ambiguity inherent from the start, had been held in relative check because of the immediate crises during the Depression era, but in the postwar world both sides felt free to express their version without reservation. Now that the crises were over, they seemed to believe that the time had come to purge modernity of its heresies, as both sides advocated for their version of modernist orthodoxy.[6]

Perhaps one unusual place where this modernist schism was exposed was in science, particularly as it related to the nation's nuclear program. On one hand, the atomic bomb helped end the war and with the emerging Cold War seemed necessary to prevent catastrophe. Scientists of all stripes now saw, as they had during the war, their service and intellect as necessary for national security. They were encouraged by the new Department of Defense to develop new ideas, based on the principles of the reformation that would help maintain American preeminence and prevent the spread of Soviet totalitarianism. On the other hand, many of these same scientists were concerned that the military's appropriation of their ideas was counter to their beliefs. Many were investigated and some were brought before House and Senate committees, or their security status was revoked because of their real or perceived political alliances. The 1950 revelation that nuclear scientists Klaus Fuchs and Julius and Ethel Rosenberg conspired to reveal secrets brought heightened security and control by the military and government, forcing science to conform to the stricture of politics. In 1954 Robert Oppenheimer, one of those whose loyalty had once been unquestioned, found himself embroiled in a loyalty issue (he opposed the development of the hydrogen bomb) that ended with his security clearance being revoked due to his flirtation as a youth with socialist ideas.

Oppenheimer's story was not unique, as the postwar red scare affected all aspects of society and led to the enforcement of a type of modernist ideology not present during the 1930s. It seemed as though the varied structures of modernity were changing, adapting to the issues that faced a newer, modern America. While many of the forms of the earlier incarnation remained, their function had changed, leading many to challenge the foundation on which modernity had been founded. Richard Abrams's *America Transformed* describes the period after 1941 as "revolutionary," owing its influence, in agreement with Wall, to "the work of relatively small groups of leaders" and the prosperity of the postwar period. Science was responsible to a large degree for this prosperity, allowing for cheaper foods as a result of bio-engineering, medicines, and other health-related advances that allowed for longer, healthy lifespans, or even the development of more efficient mass-production techniques; but these same advances led to an increased polarization between rich and poor, environmental crises, concern over the use of hormones in foods, new diseases, and a general sense of what President Carter called "malaise" or a weakening of the spirit.[7]

The unprecedented material progress made in the decades after 1945, accomplished largely under the auspices of union-negotiated contracts tied to cost of living, suburbanization (more than half of those considered working class lived outside cities by the middle of the 1960s), and even the proliferation of television (which encouraged people to stay home) helped erode the social solidarity that was closely connected to the modernist tenets of the Depression era and reinforced during World War II. The end result, even with the activism of the 1960s, was a turn toward the cultural politics of the individual over the more structural ideologies of social justice, unity, and a belief in centralized planning that guaranteed everyone access to the bounty that is America. In many ways the very success of modernity helped spur its decline, leading to what Abrams labels a "full-blown counterrevolution."[8]

The period after the war became the crucible, to borrow from Arthur Miller, of American modernity. Numerous commentators, critics, and scholars joined with Miller to better understand the ramifications of the modernist transformation. William Whye's 1956 *The Organization Man* painted a portrait of a society where individual thought was often subsumed by the desires of the many; further, because of this group-think mentality, many leaders in business and industry preferred not to make difficult decisions in the hope that the system itself would correct any larger problem or issue. His study augmented the findings made earlier in 1950 by sociologists David Riesman, Nathan Glazer, and Reuel Denny, who suggested that consumption, status, and the approval of others working within the system had created a society based on other-directedness and, in an ironic title, *The Lonely Crowd*. Many of these same themes, such as commitment to organizations and the consensus so much a part of the consciousness promoted by modernity, were challenged and attacked in the artistic community as conformist and stultifying. Beat writers such as Lawrence Ferlinghetti, Allen Ginsberg, Kenneth Rexroth, Jack Kerouac, Gary Snyder, and many more saw in the organizational structure, so logically defined and utilized during the apogee of modernity, a trap designed to weaken the individual for the good of the group.

These were some of the romantic moderns that Genter describes, who would serve as prophets of sorts, along with philosophers C. Wright Mills, Herbert Marcuse, and Paul Goodman, for the next generation in the New Left and the counterculture. Antiheroes such as James Dean, Marlon Brando, Elvis Presley, and Little Richard combined with fictional creations from Tennessee Williams, Edward Albee, and Arthur Miller to present a society out of balance, a tyranny of sorts, where not fitting in led to neurosis, alcoholism, and, inevitably, suicide. Rock music in particular picked up this theme by the mid-1960s, challenging the scriptures of the youths' modernist parents for their conformity and willingness to trust the experts over their own intuition. The mantra of never trusting anyone over thirty resonated as an attack on modernity, even as they operated and profited from the very system they felt alienated from.

At the same time, by 1960 church membership had risen to more than 63 percent and through television reached millions more. Billy Graham and Monsignor Fulton Sheen delivered the message of personal salvation and laid the groundwork for future televangelists Jerry Falwell, Jim Bakker, and the host of those dominating the Christian Broadcast Network in the 1970s. In the 1950s an amazing 86 percent declared the Bible to be the word of God and used their faith as a means to illuminate their loyalty to the American Way. To not believe opened oneself to suspicion from others, clearly something to be avoided.

Fear, more than anything else, helped lay the foundation for the challenge to modernity. Worries about the bomb, about communists outside the borders and those within, about civil rights, about making enough to buy the new house outside the city, to gas up the car, to pay for insurance, to build the patio, to send the kids off to school—it seemed like an endless list of things for concern, and as the country entered the 1960s, the sense of panic and fear only heightened. From the assassination of President Kennedy to the election of Richard Nixon, the country was, as Theodore

Roszak wrote in 1969, coming apart at the seams. This constant barrage savaged modernist beliefs and was taken up by those forces described by Wendy Walls and repurposed to fit their definition of the American way. Even something as phenomenal as the NASA space program, which seemed in so many ways to be pulled right out of the Futurama exhibit at the 1939 New York World's Fair, failed to counter the rising opposition to the modernist, or as Matthew Tribbe labels it, the "rationalist" mindset that helped put Americans on the moon in 1969. This event, and the subsequent moon missions afterward, was the perfect realization of the modernist credo that people could accomplish anything through reason, organization, and a commitment to scientific methodology. However, after 1972's Apollo 17 moon landing, the next three planned missions were scrapped due largely to public disinterest and a growing distrust of the rationalist ideology that had created unprecedented abundance, but also contributed to growing social alienation, increased insecurity tied to nuclear proliferation, social unrest, and even the war in southeast Asia. Subsequently, many people turned inward, and the 1970s "saw the rise of more spiritual worldviews that challenged the dominance of secular rationalism" in both New Age and traditional religious denominations.[9]

As Daniel Rodgers argues in *Age of Fracture*, "The key to the age was the conscious efforts of conservative intellectuals and their institutional sponsors to reshape not only the terms of political debate but the mechanics of intellectual production itself." He layers his analysis as a battle between the ideas developed in the 1930s and those that rose up in the years afterward, using an excellent 1955 quote from President Eisenhower that serves to pinpoint the larger context of the debate: "At issue is the nature of man. Either man is a creature whom the Psalmist described as 'a little lower than the angels' . . . or man is a soulless, animated machine to be enslaved, used, and consumed by the state for its own gratification."[10] By the 1970s those who challenged modernity became the majority on both the left and the right, as Democratic president Jimmy Carter admonished the American people for turning away from basic Christian beliefs and challenged the concept that government could solve the problems facing the country. The individual, he suggested, needed to be the instrument of change. Writer Tom Wolfe observed in the mid-1970s that the United States was in the midst "of a third great religious wave in American history, one that historians will likely term the Third Great Awakening." Driven in large measure by policies and scandals within the government over the previous fifteen years and compounded by the protests, riots, and general disaffection that many felt as a result, he traces the reactive need for this awakening back to the 1930s, when "visionaries" created ideas and designs for a modern world stripped of excess and where reason would solve social problems. However, society as a whole began to reject this reasonable universe in favor of one based in "sheer faith [for] something, anything (even holy rolling) to believe in." This turning away from the rational modernist salvation toward the more mystical and spiritual permeated all aspects of society, he suggests, and was driven by diverse groups ranging from fundamental Christians and politicians, to hippies, the New Left, and a host of New Age movements promising heightened awareness and inner peace.[11]

This inward turn had ramifications all through society, but most obviously within the consciousness of what had once been the working class, now rebranded as the laboring middle class. Jefferson Cowie traces the "swan song" of American labor during the latter part of the 1970s, through the combined effect of failed organizing efforts, political fragmentation, a decline in solidarity in the face of market initiatives, and the general deindustrialization of the nation's industrial heartland that signified an end to "the unified notion of a 'working class'" that had come to the fore primarily during the Depression era. In effect the labor movement failed because those who were in it no longer believed in its power, utility, or message.[12] The modernist social contract between society and science, between individuals and the greater good of the group brought about by organizational planning and development for which Roosevelt became in many ways the symbolic prophet of the gospel of modernity, was formally challenged from 1980 to 1992 by the Reagan and Bush administrations, which advocated for market liberation and individualism and a return to an earlier form of normalcy that relied on the difficult-to-define American spirit. It became, as Rodgers asserts, "the efforts to recover the agency of history's common folk fragmented" and were given over to the "management of symbolic politics." Words, not ideas, became the loci of power.[13]

Modernism seemed to have the right answers to the Depression era's ills. It suggested that together the American people, using reason, order, and planning, could and would make the country even greater than it had been before the economic and social collapse. It was more than just an intellectual or cultural idea; it was a social phenomenon that many, including John Dewey, identified as foundational to the salvation of the United States. Its desire for shared goals and norms, the understanding of the individual's contribution to the group and the inherent desire to identify with that group, along with the acceptance of a hierarchical system where the individual feels camaraderie with others, laid the foundation for a modern American society. Those who accepted this new social system of modernity shared their enthusiasm through their daily activities, oftentimes linked to consumption, in order to detail the positive advantages of order, planning, and reason. In addition, they understood that this version of modernity also meant sacrificing individual needs for the betterment of the group, which not only led to greater solidarity but also connected them to the ideals and experiences of the Founding Fathers, the Revolutionary era, and those of the Civil War generation. Any of FDR's speeches in his administration reveal these connections and ideals, and the programs that he initiated and their fundamental social goals pointed to the need to get the people to accept a new way of seeing themselves, their communities, and their government. But it was not only with FDR that these goals and ideals were promoted, for as this volume attests, one can see the promotion and proliferation of modernism during the 1930s in a wide variety of ideas, events, or activities. To ignore them and view them as simply part of the era without suggesting that something more was part of the process is to ignore the underlying and significant meaning modernism had throughout American society.[14]

NOTES

Introduction. Order, Planning, and Reason

1. See Arthur M. Schlesinger, Jr., *The Coming of the New Deal* (Boston: Houghton Mifflin, 1959), 1–23. This evocation of FDR would continue through much of his four terms. For a different take on his ascension to the White House, see Matthew Avery Sutton, *American Apocalypse: A History of Modern Evangelicalism* (Cambridge, MA: Harvard University Press, 2014); and Matthew Avery Sutton, "Was FDR the Antichrist? The Birth of Fundamentalist Antiliberalism in a Global Age," *Journal of American History* 98 (March 2012): 1052–1074.

2. *The Plow That Broke the Plains*, directed and written by Pare Lorentz, music by Virgil Thomson, cinematography by Leo Hurwitz, Ralph Steiner, Paul Strand, and Paul Ivano, produced and distributed by the Resettlement Administration (RA), 1936. Lorentz also wrote and directed another RA documentary with the same tone titled *The River* in 1937.

3. John Dewey, *A Common Faith* (New Haven, CT: Yale University Press, 1934), 87.

4. Susan Stanford Friedman, "Definitional Excursions: The Meanings of *Modern/Modernity/Modernism*," *Modernism/modernity* 8, no. 3 (2001): 500, 501, 505. For overviews on this discussion as they apply to the United States, see David A. Hollinger, "The Knower and the Artificer," *American Quarterly* 39, no. 1 (Spring 1987): 37–55; Daniel Joseph Singal, "Towards a Definition of American Modernism," *American Quarterly* 39, no. 1 (Spring 1987): 7–26; James Naremore and Patrick Brantlinger, eds., *Modernity and Mass Culture* (Bloomington: Indiana University Press, 1991), esp. 1–23; Andreas Huyssen, *After the Great Divide: Modernism, Mass Culture, and Postmodernism* (Bloomington: Indiana University Press, 1986). The "AHR Roundtable: Historians and the Question of 'Modernity'" in *American Historical Review* 116, no. 3 (June 2011), included the following articles: Zvi Ben-Dor Benite, "Modernity: The Sphinx and the Historian," 638–652; Gurminder K. Bhambra, "Historical Sociology, Modernity, and Postcolonial Critique," 653–662; Dipesh Chakrabarty, "The Muddle of Modernity," 663–675; Carol Gluck, "The End of Elsewhere: Writing Modernity Now," 676–687; Mark Roseman, "National Socialism and the End of Modernity," 688–701; Dorothy Ross, "American Modernities, Past and Present," 702–714; Carol Symes, "When We Talk About Modernity," 715–726; Lynn M. Thomas, "Modernity's Failings, Political Claims, and Intermediate Concepts," 727–740; and Richard Wolin, "Modernity: The Peregrinations of

a Contested Historiographical Concept," 741–751. See also Daniel Lord Smail and Andrew Shryock, "AHR Forum: History and the 'Pre,'" *American Historical Review* 118, no. 3 (June 2013): 709–737.

5. Daniel J. Singal, "Film, Popular Entertainment, and the Melting Pot through the Lens of Modernist Culture," *Modern Intellectual History* 10 (2013): 491–492.

6. Terry Smith, *Making the Modern: Industry, Art, and Design in America* (Chicago: University of Chicago Press, 1993), 159–161.

7. Christina Cogdell, *Eugenic Design: Streamlining America in the 1930s* (Philadelphia: University of Pennsylvania Press, 2004), 203.

8. Ástráedhur Eysteinsson, *The Concept of Modernism* (Ithaca, NY: Cornell University Press, 1990), 1–50; Christopher Wilk, "What Is Modernism?" in *Modernism: Designing a New World, 1914–1939*, ed. Christopher Wilk (London: V&A Publishing, 2006), 14; Jeffrey L. Meikle, "Domesticating Modernity: Ambivalence and Appropriation, 1920–40," in *Domesticating Modernity: The Arts of Reform and Persuasion, 1885–1945*, ed. Wendy Kaplan (New York: Thames & Hudson, 1995), 144. Meikle has made similar arguments in *American Plastic: A Cultural History* (New Brunswick, NJ: Rutgers University Press, 1995) and *Twentieth Century Limited: Industrial Design in America, 1925–1939* (Philadelphia: Temple University Press, 1979).

9. Smith, *Making the Modern*. The literature and debate concerning modernity and its definitional meaning is extensive; some examples include Marshall Berman's excellent *All That Is Solid Melts into Air: The Experience of Modernity* (London: Verso, 1982); Michael Saler, "Modernity and Enchantment: A Historiographic Review," *American Historical Review* 111, no. 3 (June 2006): 692–716. Paul Forman has convincingly argued that the primacy of science on modernity's principal theorist allowed for scientists to view technology as the engine for positive social change and how a reversal in the order (technology as the leader of science) becomes a demarcation of the postmodern. See "The Primacy of Science in Modernity, or Technology in Postmodernity, and the Ideology in the History of Technology," *History and Technology* 23 (May/June 2007): 1–152. See also Fredric Jameson, *Postmodernism, or, The Cultural Logic of Late Capitalism* (Durham, NC: Duke University Press, 1991), esp. 302–323.

10. George Richards, *Beyond Fundamentalism and Modernism: The Gospel of God* (New York: C. Scribners's Sons, 1934), 67.

11. Franklin D. Roosevelt, "New Deal Speech before the Democratic National Convention," July 2, 1932, in *My Friends: Twenty-Eight History Making Speeches by Franklin Delano Roosevelt*, ed. Edward H. Kavinoky and Julian Park (Buffalo, NY: Foster & Stewart, 1945), 143.

12. Roger Babson, *A Revival Is Coming* (New York: Fleming H. Revell, 1936), 35.

13. The Great Awakenings of the eighteenth and nineteenth centuries involved a mixture of secular and spiritual ideals, much like what was being asked for by some religious leaders during the Great Depression. Other evangelical and early fundamentalist churches saw in the crisis the moment for revival, which in a way set the stage for the secular ideals of modernity. See Thomas S. Kidd, *The Great Awakening: The Roots of Evangelical Christianity in Colonial America* (New Haven, CT: Yale University Press, 2007); Patricia U. Bonomi, *Under the Cope of Heaven: Religion, Society, and Politics in Colonial America*, updated ed. (New York: Oxford University Press, 2003); Peter W. Williams, *America's Religions: From Their Origins to the Twenty-First Century* (Urbana: University of Illinois Press, 1990, 2008); Stewart J. Brown and Timothy Tackett, eds., *The Cambridge History of Christianity*, Vol. 7, *Enlightenment, Reawakening, and Revolution, 1660–1815* (New York: Cambridge University Press, 2006). For an interesting connection to more modern manifestations of the ideals of the Awakenings, see David L. Chappell, *A Stone of Hope: Prophetic Religion and the Death of Jim Crow* (Chapel Hill: University of North Carolina Press, 2004); Garry Wills, *Head and Heart: American Christianities* (New York: Penguin, 2007); Ellis Sandoz, *Republicanism, Religion, and the Soul of America* (Columbia: University of Missouri Press, 2006); Barry Hankins, *The Second Great Awakening and the Transcendentalists* (Westport, CT: Greenwood, 2004); Jackson Lears, *Rebirth of a Nation: The Making of Modern America, 1877–1920* (New York: Harper Collins, 2009); Quentin J. Schultze, "Evangelical Radio and the Rise of the Electronic Church, 1921–1948," *Journal of Broadcasting and Electronic Media* 32 (Summer 1988): 289–306; Joel A. Carpenter, "Fundamentalist Institutions and the Rise of Evangelical Protestantism, 1929–1942," *Church History* 49 (March 1980): 62–75; Jerma A. Jackson, *Singing in My Soul: Black Gospel Music in a Secular Age* (Chapel Hill: University of North Carolina Press, 2004).

14. Robert T. Handy, "The American Religious Depression, 1925–1935," in *Religion in American History*, ed. Jon Butler and Harry S. Stout (New York: Oxford University Press, 1998), 380. See also William R. Hutchison, *The Modernist Impulse in American Protestantism* (Cambridge, MA: Harvard University Press, 1976). One result of this apparent decline during the 1930s was American fundamentalism's subsequent rise to prominence by the 1950s. See Joel Carpenter, "Fundamentalist Institutions and the Rise of Evangelical Protestantism, 1929–1942," *Church History*, March 1980, 62–75.

15. Richards, *Beyond Fundamentalism*, 69.

16. Malcolm Cowley, *The Dream of the Golden Mountains* (New York: Viking, 1980), 13.

17. John Dewey, *Liberalism and Social Action* (New York: Pedigree, 1935), 54.

18. For a discussion of the idea of civil religion, see Robert Bellah, "Civil Religion in America," *Daedalus* 96 (Winter 1967): 1–21.

19. Charles A. Beard, "The Ideal of Progress," in Beard, ed., *A Century of Progress* (New York: Harper & Brothers in cooperation with the Century of Progress Exposition, 1933), 3.

20. Franklin D. Roosevelt, "The Right to a More Abundant Life," Address to the Federal Council of Churches, December 6, 1933, in *My Friends*, 25.

21. Stuart Hall, "Cultural Studies: Two Paradigms," in *Media, Culture, and Society: A Critical Reader*, ed. Richard Collins (London: Sage, 1986), 33.

22. Kenneth Saunders, "What Is the Modern Mind?" *Saturday Review of Literature*, August 22, 1931, 66.

23. FDR Addressing the Critics, June 28, 1934, Fireside Chat #5, available at http://www.presidency.ucsb.edu/fireside.php (accessed August 1, 2016).

Chapter 1. The End of Times

1. William Thomas Walsh, "What Does 'Modern' Mean?" *Catholic World*, November 1930, 129.

2. Ibid., 131. See also "The New Modernism," *Christian Century*, March 4, 1936, 351–353.

3. Peter Gay, *Modernism: The Lure of Heresy from Baudelaire to Beckett and Beyond* (New York: Norton, 2008), 1–6.

4. Robert M. Crunden, *American Salons: Encounters with European Modernism, 1885–1917* (New York: Oxford University Press, 1993), xiv.

5. Richard Pells, *Modernist America: Art, Music, Movies, and the Globalization of American Culture* (New Haven, CT: Yale University Press, 2011), 19.

6. Quoted in Leo P. Ribuffo, *The Old Christian Right: The Protestant Far Right from the Great Depression to the Cold War* (Philadelphia: Temple University Press, 1983), xi–25. Although I refrain from following him down the path of psychohistory and his examination of extremism, it is important to note that his understanding that during the 1930s the division over the nature of religion and society in many ways outlines the ascendency of modernity at the expense of traditional or fundamental Christianity. See also "Finds Church Dazed by 'Era of Frenzy,'" *New York Times*, September 29, 1932, 15.

7. Babson, *Revival Is Coming*, 15, 47, 17, 6, 35. Babson also published *How to Increase Church Attendance* (New York: Fleming H. Revell, 1936).

8. "Another Challenge to Modernism," *Literary Digest*, September 18, 1934, 26; Darrell Jadock, "The Modernist Crisis," in *Catholicism Contending with Modernity: Roman Catholic Modernism and Anti-Modernism in Historical* Context, ed. Darrell

Jadock (New York: Cambridge University Press, 2000), 1–29. For an excellent overview of what "modernism" meant with reference to scriptures, see Herbert Leslie Stewart, *Modernism, Past and Present* (London: John Murray, 1932).

9. Edwin Ewart Aubrey, "What Is Modernism," *Journal of Religion* 15 (October 1935): 426–447.

10. "Scores Modernist God," *New York Times*, March 9, 1936, 11.

11. Allison N. Trice and Charles H. Robertson, *Bible vs. Modernism: A Compendium of Sundry Critical Hypotheses and Their Refutation* (Nashville: Rock City, 1935), 105, 99, 108.

12. Demetrius Zema, *The Thoughtlessness of Modern Thought: Concerning the Ideas of Civilization, Culture, Science, and Progress, Fordham University Conferences, Fall Session, 1933* (New York: Fordham University Press, 1934), 2–3, 5, 7, 34, 1.

13. Walsh, "What Does 'Modern' Mean?" 132, 133, 134.

14. "Dr. Myers Wants Stronger Clergy," *New York Times*, September 18, 1933, 15.

15. Dan Gilbert, *Our Retreat from Modernism* (San Diego, CA: Danielle Publishers, 1939), 6, 73, 100, 12, 14, 169.

16. Ibid., 169.

17. "Lesson for October 9: Spiritual Worship," *Negro Star* (Wichita, KS), October 10, 1938, 2; "Lesson for December 4: The Sin of Lying," *Negro Star* (Wichita, KS), December 12, 1938, 2.

18. Harry Emerson Fosdick, "Beyond Modernism: A Sermon," *Christian Century*, December 4, 1935, 1549; "Dr. Fosdick Upholds Old-Time Religion," *New York Times*, January 18, 1932, 13; "Dr. Fosdick Shifts the Emphasis," *Christian Century*, November 20, 1935, 1481; "Protestants Seen at Mercy of Foes," *New York Times*, March 22, 1937, 15; "Catholics Warned of Peril in 'Isms,'" *New York Times*, June 17, 1935, 11.

19. Shailer Mathews, "Unrepentant Liberalism," *American Scholar*, July 1938, 296.

20. Ibid., 302–303, 306.

21. Horace E. Orr, "Liberalism and Youth," *Christian Century*, August 15, 1934, 1045.

22. Henry P. Van Dusen, "The Sickness of Liberal Religion," *World Tomorrow*, August 1931, 257–258.

23. "The Waning Belief in Heaven and Hell," *Literary Digest*, March 3, 1934, 20.

24. Herbert Leslie Stewart, *Modernism, Past and Present*, 3.

25. Richards, *Beyond Fundamentalism and Modernism*, x, 63, 259.

26. Kenneth J. Heineman, *A Catholic New Deal: Religion and Reform in Depression Pittsburgh* (University Park: Pennsylvania State University Press, 1999).

27. "Catholics Urged to Heed President," *New York Times*, June 13, 1935, 14; Hogan quoted in Alison Collis Greene, "The End of 'The Protestant Era,'" *Church History* 80 (September 2011): 601.

28. Sutton, "Was FDR the Antichrist?" 1052, 1062. For an extended examination, see Sutton's *American Apocalypse*.

29. Monroe Billington and Cal Clark, "Clergy Reaction to the New Deal: A Comparative Study," *Historian* 48 (August 1986): 509–524.

30. "Niebuhr Questions the Vitality of the Protestant Religion," *Newsweek*, April 29, 1933, 28; Reinhold Niebuhr, *Reflections on the End of an Era* (New York: Charles Scribner's Sons, 1934), 83, 321.

31. Reinhold Niebuhr, "Modern Utopias," *Scribner's*, September 1936, 142–145; Reinhold Niebuhr, "The Church and Political Action," *Christian Century*, August 1, 1934, 993; Reinhold Niebuhr, "The Fellowship of Socialist Christians," *World Tomorrow*, June 14, 1934, 297; *The Essential Reinhold Niebuhr: Selected Essays and Addresses*, ed. Robert McAfee Brown (New Haven, CT: Yale University Press, 1986), xii; Niebuhr, *Reflections*, 28–29, 13, 32.

32. Reinhold Niebuhr, "Our Romantic Radicals," *Christian Century*, April 10, 1935, 474, 476; Reinhold Niebuhr, "When Will Christians Stop Fooling Themselves," *Christian Century*, May 16, 1934, 658–660; Niebuhr, *Reflections*, 238.

33. Brinkerhoff Jackson, "Modernism in Architecture," *Sewanee Review* 44 (April–June 1936): 183–184.

34. "Liberalism as a Faith," *New York Times*, July 2, 1934, 22.

35. Bryan Wilson, "Secularization: The Inherited Model," in *The Sacred in the Secular Age: Toward Revisionism in the Scientific Study of Religion*, ed. Philip E. Hammond (Berkeley and Los Angeles: University of California Press, 1985), 9–20.

36. Handy, "American Religious Depression," 380. See also Hutchison, *Modernist Impulse in American Protestantism*.

37. Works that express this pre-crash optimism include Stuart Chase, *Men and Machines* (New York: Macmillan, 1929); Michael Pupin, *Romance of the Machine* (New York: Charles Scribner's Sons, 1930); John Herman Randall, *Our Changing Civilization* (New York: Frederick Stokes, 1929); Edward Filene, *Successful Living in This Machine Age* (New York: Simon & Schuster, 1931); Henry Ford, "Machinery, The New Messiah," *Forum* 79 (March 1928), 359–364. For excellent overviews, see Cecilia Tichi, *Shifting Gears: Technology, Literature, Culture* (Chapel Hill: University of North Carolina Press, 1987); Richard Guy Wilson et al., *The Machine Age in America* (New York: Brooklyn Museum in association with Harry N. Abrams, 1986).

38. Samuel C. Kincheloe, *Research Memorandum on Religion in the Depression, Bulletin #33* (New York: Social Science Research Council, 1937), 45–107.

39. Lloyd Cassel Douglas, "Hearts in Tune," in *Music and Religion*, ed. Stanley Armstrong Hunter (New York: Abingdon Press, 1930), 57, 58, 62.

40. Kincheloe, *Research Memorandum*. See also Beth Wenger, "Synagogues and the 'Spiritual Depression' in the 1930s," in *Perspectives on American Religion and Culture*, ed. Peter W. Williams (New York: Blackwell, 1999), 124–139; Martin E. Marty, *Modern American Religion*, vol. 2 (Chicago: University of Chicago Press, 1991), 250–259. For an excellent exploration of documentary photography and American religion in the 1930s as seen through Farm Security Administration and other New Deal agency photographers, see Colleen McDannell, *Picturing Faith: Photography and the Great Depression* (New Haven, CT: Yale University Press, 2004).

41. Robert S. Lynd and Helen Merrell Lynd, *Middletown in Transition: A Study in Cultural Conflicts* (New York: Harcourt, Brace & World, 1937), 295, 301, 302, 305, 306, 299; George A. Lundberg, Mirra Komarovsky, and Mary Alice McInerny, *Leisure: A Suburban Study* (New York: Columbia University Press, 1934), 194.

42. Lynd and Lynd, *Middletown in Transition*, 300–311; Lundberg et al., *Leisure*, 205.

43. John Dewey, "Intelligence and Power," *New Republic*, April 25, 1934, 306.

44. Alan Ryan, *John Dewey and the High Tide of American Liberalism* (New York: Norton, 1995), 21.

45. John Dewey, "A God of the God," *Christian Century*, February 8, 1933, 194–195.

46. John Dewey, *Art as Experience* (New York: Milton, Balch, 1934); Victoria Grieve, *The Federal Art Project and the Creation of Middlebrow Culture* (Urbana: University of Illinois Press, 2009), 30.

47. Dewey, *Common Faith*, 84. For an excellent contemporary review, see Henry Nelson Wieman, "John Dewey's Common Faith," *Christian Century*, November 14, 1934, 1450–1452.

48. John Dewey, "The Liberation of Modern Religion," *Yale Review* 23 (June 1934): 767.

49. Dewey, *Common Faith* (based on the lectures given at Yale in 1934 from which the above article is derived), 1, 9–10, 32.

50. Dewey, *Common Faith*, 49, 60, 87. As an aside, Dewey's ideas of the social connection to intellect closely mirror those of Maurice Halbwach's theories on the social construct of memory written in the same era. See Halbwach, *On Collective Memory*, ed. and trans. Lewis A. Coser (Chicago: University of Chicago Press, 1992).

51. Dewey, *Liberalism and Social Action*, 26.

52. Herbert Hoover, *American Individualism* (New York: Doubleday, Page, 1922), 9.

53. Dewey, *Liberalism and Social Action*, 26, 45, 55, 93. Dewey expounds on the historical nature of liberalism and its effects in "Authority and Resistance to Social Change," *School and Society*, October 10, 1936, 457–466.

54. John Dewey, "Education and New Social Ideals," radio broadcast over WEVD, January 14, 1936, published in *Vital Speeches*, February 24, 1936, 327–328.

55. Katherine Glover in conversation with John Dewey, "Tomorrow May Be Too Late," *Good Housekeeping*, March 1934, 20–21, 222–225; John Dewey, "Education, the Foundation for Social Organization," *Journal of the National Education Association* 25 (December 1936): 274. See also Saunders, "What Is the Modern Mind," 66.

56. Adolph Berle and Gardiner Means, *The Modern Corporation and Private Property* (New York: Macmillan, 1932); Stuart Chase, *A New Deal* (New York: Macmillan, 1932); Richard Pells, *Radical Visions and American Dreams: Culture and Social Thought in the Depression Years* (Middletown, CT: Wesleyan, 1973), 43–95. I am not referring to the attraction of Americanized Marxist or socialist ideas, but to the way in which the ideas of planning, order, and efficiency were written about as testimonials of the modern way of thinking. For an excellent overview of the Americanization of Marxist thought in the 1930s, see Michael Denning, *The Cultural Front: The Laboring of American Culture in the Twentieth Century* (New York: Verso, 1996), 423–462.

57. Charles Beard, "The Idea of Progress," in *Century of Progress*, 3, 15.

58. Ernest Minor Patterson, "Economic Adjustment in a Machine Age," *Proceedings of the American Philosophical Society* 70 (1931): 272.

59. John T. Greenan, *American Civilization Today: A Summary of Recent Social Trends* (New York: McGraw-Hill, 1934), 6, 137, 138.

60. William E. Akin, *Technocracy and the American Dream: The Technocrat Movement, 1900–1941* (Berkeley: University of California Press, 1977), x. For its background leading to the 1930s, see 1–26. The rest of the volume outlines its agenda and effect, albeit limited, during the era.

61. Stuart Chase, *Technocracy: An Interpretation* (New York: John Day, 1933), 11.

62. Lewis Mumford, *Technics and Civilization* (New York: Harcourt, Brace, 1934), 279. For an excellent contemporary review of the work, see Rosalind Williams, "Lewis Mumford's *Technics and Civilization*," *Technology and Culture* 43 (January 2002): 139–149. An excellent biography is Donald L. Miller, *Mumford: A Life* (New York: Weidenfeld & Nicolson, 1989). Mumford himself later reviewed his work in "An Appraisal of Lewis Mumford's *Technics and Civilization*," *Daedalus* 88 (Summer 1959): 527–536.

63. Mumford, *Technics*, 7, 31, 45.

64. Ibid., 109, 169, 158, 215, 217, 267.

65. Mumford, "Appraisal," 533.

66. Mumford, *Technics*, 326.

67. "The New Modernism," *Christian Century*, March 4, 1936, 352. See also James Davison Hunter, *American Evangelicalism: Conservative Religion and the Problem of Modernity* (New Brunswick, NJ: Rutgers University Press, 1983), 15–55; Cleanth Brooks, Jr., "The Christianity of Modernism," *American Review* 6 (February 1936): 435–446; Harold Bosley, "Is Liberal Protestantism a Religion?" *Christian Century*, June 1936, 898–900.

68. Fredric Jameson, *Postmodernism, or, The Cultural Logic of Late Capitalism* (Durham, NC: Duke University Press, 1991), 389.

69. Smith, *Making the Modern*, 2–10, 427; Miles Orvell, *The Real Thing: Imitation and Authenticity in American Culture, 1880–1940* (Chapel Hill: University of North Carolina Press, 1989), x–xv, 154–155; Tammy Clewell, *Mourning, Modernism, Postmodernism* (New York: Palgrave Macmillan, 2009), 2–17; Robert Genter, *Late Modernism: Art, Culture, and Politics in Cold War America* (Philadelphia: University of Pennsylvania Press, 2010).

Chapter 2. A New Model Army

1. FDR, First Inaugural Address, March 4, 1933, in *My Friends*, 1–6.

2. FDR, "Radio Address to the Forum on Current Affairs," October 5, 1937, in *The Public Papers and Addresses of Franklin D. Roosevelt*, vol. 6 (New York: Macmillan, 1941), 412–413.

3. "Radio Address for the Mobilization for Human Needs," FDR radio speech, October 13, 1938, http://www.fdrlibrary.marist.edu/cgi-bin/htsearch (accessed August 1, 2016).

4. Ronald L. Johnstone, *Religion in Society: A Sociology of Religion* (Englewood Cliffs, NJ: Prentice Hall, 1992), 35–66.

5. Percy R. Hayward, *The Dream Power of Youth: Young People Today and the Religion of Jesus* (New York: Harper & Brothers, 1930), 88; *New York Times*, May 7, 1934.

6. Franklin D. Roosevelt, Executive Order 6101 Starting the Civilian Conservation Corps, April 5, 1933. From John T. Woolley and Gerhard Peters, The American Presidency Project, University of California at Santa Barbara, http://www.presidency.ucsb.edu/ws/?pid=14609 (accessed August 4, 2016).

7. Franklin D. Roosevelt, "As the President Sees It," in *The New America: The Spirit of the Civilian Conservation Corps*, ed. Alfred C. Oliver and Harold M. Dudley (New York: Longmans, Green, 1937), xix; Kenneth Holland and Frank Ernest Hill, *Youth in the CCC* (New York: Arno, 1942, 1974).

8. Franklin D. Roosevelt, "Three Essentials for Unemployment Relief," March 21, 1933, in *The Public Papers and Addresses of Franklin D. Roosevelt*, Vol. 2, *The Year of*

Crisis, 1933 (New York: Random House, 1938), 80; Franklin D. Roosevelt, *On Our Way* (New York: John Day, 1934), 40–43.

9. Phoebe Cutler, *The Public Landscape of the New Deal* (New Haven, CT: Yale University Press, 1985), 66.

10. Virginia Kendall Reserve State Park Historic District, National Register of Historical Places Registration Form, US Department of the Interior, prepared by Jeffrey Winstel, National Park Service, 1995, 41–42 (hereafter referred to as NRHP). For a detailed account of the Virginia Kendall Reserve, see Kenneth J. Bindas, ed., *The Civilian Conservation Corps and the Construction of the Virginia Kendall Reserve, 1933–1939* (Kent, OH: Kent State University Press, 2013).

11. John C. Paige, *The Civilian Conservation Corps and the National Park Service, 1933–1945: An Administrative History*, National Park Service, US Department of the Interior study (Washington, DC: US Government Printing Office, 1985), 9–34.

12. Carroll Aust, interviewed by Donna Sinclair, January 22, 2001, in Donna Sinclair and Richard McClure, eds., "No Goldbricking Here: Oral Histories of the CCC in the Columbia National Forest, 1933–1942," Heritage Program, Gifford Pinchot National Forest and History Department, Portland State University, http://www.ccrh.org/oral/ccc%20book_all.pdf (accessed August 5, 2016); Clinton Harris Dean, interviewed by Kenneth Steeber, October 1, 1995, Shenandoah National Park, Luray, Virginia, original manuscript on deposit at Shenandoah National Park Archives; Edward Mokan, interviewed by Carrie Janey, September 25, 1999, Skyland Conference Hall 66th Reunion of the Shenandoah Chapter of the Civilian Conservation Corps, Shenandoah National Park, Luray, Virginia, original manuscript on deposit at Shenandoah National Park Archives, both at http://www.nps.gov/shen/historyculture/upload/ccc_oral_history_dean_clinton.pdf (accessed August 5, 2016); Robert Gonyeau, interviewed by Mary Kasamatsu, July 19, 1987, Woodsmoke Productions and Vermont Historical Society, "Fighting the Depression: The C.C.C.," *Green Mountain Chronicles* radio broadcast and background information, original broadcast 1988–1989, available at http://vermonthistory.org/research/research-resources-online/green-mountain-chronicles/fighting-the-depression-the-c-c-c-1933 (accessed August 5, 2016).

13. Robert Fechner, "A Short Story of the CCC," in Oliver and Dudley, *New America*, 23, 24, 28; Paige, *Civilian Conservation Corps*, 9–34; Elden B. Sessions, "Educational Work of the Civilian Conservation Corps Camps in Ohio" (PhD diss., Ohio State University, 1937), 1–10; Stanley Cohen, *The Tree Army: A Pictorial History of the Civilian Conservation Corps, 1933–1942* (Missoula, MT: Pictorial Histories, 1980), 6–15.

14. Interview with Jack Pollari, May 7, 2002, in Sinclair and McClure, "No

Goldbricking Here"; *Annual Report of the Civilian Conservation Corps: Fiscal Year Ended June 30, 1938* (Washington, DC: US Government Printing Office, 1938), 5–11, 91–95; Walter Davenport, "Thy Woods and Templed Hills," *Collier's*, September 9, 1933, 10–12; "Report Shows 31,000 Race Men Enrolled in CCC Camps," *Capital Plain Dealer* (Topeka, KS), January 3, 1937, 2.

15. The example used here was replicated throughout the United States during the CCC's years of existence. But given the breadth of their reach, it seemed more reasonable to focus on one such CCC camp and project to serve as an example of the larger goals and successes of the Corps. For studies of other projects, see, for example, Cynthia Brandimarte with Angela Reed, *Texas State Parks and the CCC: The Legacy of the Civilian Conservation Corps* (College Station: Texas A&M University Press, 2013); Harley E. Jolley, *"That Magnificent Army of Youth and Peace": The Civilian Conservation Corps in North Carolina, 1933–1942* (Raleigh, NC: Office of Archives and History, 2007); Olen Cole, *The African American Experience in the Civilian Conservation Corps* (Tallahassee: University Press of Florida, 1999); Tara Mitchell Mielnik, *New Deal, New Landscape: The Civilian Conservation Corps and South Carolina's State Parks* (Columbia: University of South Carolina Press, 2011); Robert Pasquill, Jr., *The Civilian Conservation Corps in Alabama, 1933–1942: A Great and Lasting Good* (Tuscaloosa: University of Alabama Press, 2008). This is a selected list as the number of articles, books, and websites dedicated to the CCC on the local and state level is vast.

16. Narrative Report of CCC Accomplishments, submitted by Forrest E. Smith, Project Supervisor for Ohio S.P. 5, CCC Co. 576, Peninsula, Summit County, Ohio, 1, in CCC Reports, 1935–1936, CVVA 15294, Container #3, Folder #12, Cuyahoga Valley National Park Archives (hereafter referred to as CCC Reports, 1935–1936); NRHP, 29.

17. NRHP, 32.

18. Wagner to G. C. Harman, Inspector, Second District, State Park Emergency Conservation Work Office, January 31, 1934; Wagner to Harman, January 11, 1934, both in CVVA; Joseph Stahl, "A Brief History of the Virginia Kendall State Park," *The Kendallite*, typescript, CCC newspaper, January 17, 1936, 2, NRHP; letter from A. H. Good to Wagner, February 14, 1934, in H. S. Wagner, NPS Copies of Correspondence related to CCC, 1934–1942. CVVA 15294, Container #3, Folder #21 (hereafter referred to as Wagner Letters, CVVA).

19. Wagner to Harman, June 14, 1935; Wagner to Herbert Evison, Regional Officer, Region One, Branch of Planning and State Cooperation, Attn: K. C. McCarter, Technical Coordinator, September 18, 1936; Wagner to R. F. Wirsching, Inspector, District D—Region One, Branch of Planning and State Cooperation, NPS, February 19, 1937; Wagner to Conrad L. Wirth, Supervisor of Recreation and

Land Planning, NPS, US Department of Interior, August 30, 1938, all in Wagner Letters, CVVA.

20. NRHP, 28–29; Nick Scrattish, *Historic Resource Study: Cuyahoga Valley National Recreation Area* (Denver, CO: US Department of the Interior, National Park Service, 1985), 240–242; Wagner to NPS, September 9, 1938; Wagner to Wirth, February 4, 1936; Wagner to Evison, June 23, 1938; quotation from Wagner to Wirsching, February 19, 1937.

21. NRHP, 29–30.

22. Smith, *Making the Modern*, 8; Forrest E. Smith, Superintendent, CCC Unit #576, Narrative Report of CCC Accomplishments, March 31, 1936, listings. NPN, in CCC Reports, 1935–1936.

23. James R. Lyons, "FDR and Environmental Leadership," in *FDR and the Environment*, ed. Harry L. Henderson and David B. Woolner (New York: Palgrave, 2005), 195–218; Robert Fechner, "My Hopes for the CCC," *American Forests: The Magazine of the American Forestry Association* (January 1939): 1.

24. Franklin D. Roosevelt, "A Radio Address on the Third Anniversary of C.C.C.," April 17, 1936, reprinted in *The Public Papers and Addresses of Franklin D. Roosevelt*, vol. 5 (New York: Random House, 1938), 170; *Annual Report of the Director of the Civilian Conservation Corps, Fiscal Year Ended June 30, 1941* (Washington, DC: US Government Printing Office, 1941), 13.

25. *Reforestation by the CCC* (Washington, DC: US Government Printing Office, 1941), 9; Section V. Roosevelt's Emergency Programs: 1933–1935, 1–13; Walter Rogers, *The Professional Practice of Landscape Architecture: A Complete Guide* (New York: Wiley, 1997), 1–21.

26. Albert H. Good, *Park and Recreation Structures* (US Department of the Interior, National Park Service, 1938; New York: Princeton Architectural Press, 1999), 5. Wagner's recommendation of Good found in Wagner's letter to Ickes, December 1, 1933, as cited in Scrattish, *Historic Resource Study*, 238n92, 255.

27. Sarah T. Phillips, *This Land, This Nation: Conservation, Rural America, and the New Deal* (New York: Cambridge University Press, 2007), provides an excellent discussion of the role and meaning of New Deal policies and their effect on the environment and the conservation movement; see esp. 1–74. See also A. Dan Tarlock, "Rediscovering the New Deal's Environmental Legacy," in *FDR and the Environment*, 155–176; quotation from NRHP, 45, 47. See also Linda Flint McClelland, *Building the National Parks: Historic Landscape Design and Construction* (Baltimore, MD: Johns Hopkins University Press, 1998), especially ch. 10, "A New Deal for State Parks," 381–424.

28. *CCC Annual Report*, 1938, 70–72; Sessions, "Educational Work of the CCC,"

41–58. Sessions also asked the six hundred workers their future vocational expectations, and although nearly half chose "uncertain," a majority of those who picked an occupation selected mechanic, factory worker, clerk, farmer, trucker, or welder (63).

29. Helen M. Walker, *The CCC through the Eyes of 272 Boys: A Summary of a Group Study of the Reactions of 272 Cleveland Boys to Their Experience in the Civilian Conservation Corps* (Cleveland, OH: Western Reserve University Press, 1938), 7–25. Much of what Walker writes about the generational division within the families of enrollees is similar to Lizabeth Cohen's *Making a New Deal: Industrial Workers in Chicago, 1919–1939* (New York: Cambridge University Press, 1990), esp. 53–98.

30. Interview with Paul Grooms, May 1, 2002, in Sinclair and McClure, "No Goldbricking Here"; Charles Lord-Stowe, interview by Woodsmoke Productions, July 19, 1987 (see n. 12); John Kochan, interview by John Amberson, September 25, 1999, at Skyland Conference Hall (see n. 12); interview with Ben Marshall, October 24, 2001, in Sinclair and McClure, "No Goldbricking Here."

31. Roosevelt quote from *Reforestation by the CCC*, 13; Neil M. Maher, *Nature's New Deal: The Civilian Conservation Corps and the Roots of the American Environmental Movement* (New York: Oxford University Press, 2008), 6.

32. James Wilson, "Community, Civility, and Citizenship: Theatre and Indoctrination in the Civilian Conservation Corps of the 1930s," *Theatre History Studies* 23 (June 2003): 77; the entire article is a valuable discussion of the role and influence of theater on unity and the success of the CCC.

33. *The CCC at Work: A Story of 2,500,000 Young Men* (Washington, DC: FSA/CCC, 1941), 94, 102.

34. Walker, *CCC*, 46–50; Lurtie McDonald, interview by John Amberson, September 25, 1999, at Skyland Conference Hall (see n. 12).

35. Captain A. W. Belden, "Editorial," *The Kendallite*, July 19, 1935, 2.

36. Wagner, letter to G. C. Harman, Inspector, Second District, March 6, 1934, Cuyahoga Valley National Park Archives.

37. "Letters to the Voice of Experience," *The Kendallite*, March 13, 1936, 4.

38. Sessions, "Educational Work of the CCC," 158–160, 172–174, 196.

39. *A Manual for Instructors in the Civilian Conservation Corps Camps* (Washington, DC: US Government Printing Office, 1935), 1–4, 51; Charles Lord-Stowe, interview by Mary Kasamatsu for Woodsmoke Productions (see n. 12).

40. Folklife Archives, Manuscripts, "Interview with Gilbert Sanders Regarding CCC (FA 81)" (1987), FA Oral Histories, Paper 11, http://digitalcommons.wku.edu/dlsc_fa_oral_hist/11 (accessed August 5, 2016); Carroll Aust interview (see n. 12); Charles Wagner, interview by Norman Taylor, August 28, 1991, Shenandoah

National Park, Luray, Virginia, original manuscript on deposit at Shenandoah National Park Archives; A. W. Belden, "Editorial," *The Kendallite*, December 6, 1935, 2.

41. Maher, *Nature's New Deal*, 96; for a more detailed examination, see 77–113.

42. Jeffrey Ryan Suzik, "Building Better Men: The CCC Boy and the Changing Social Ideal of Manliness," *Men and Masculinity* 2 (October 1999): 166.

43. Walker, *CCC*, 29–31, 81–83.

44. FDR, "A Radio Address on the Third Anniversary of the CCC," April 17, 1936, in *Public Papers and Addresses*, 5:170; Tulloch quote from NRHP, 6, 33–34; "Editorial," *The Kendallite*, August 30, 1935, 2; Robert Fechner, frontispiece, *CCC in Ohio* (Columbus, OH: Federal Writers' Project Publication, 1938), 1.

45. Walker, *CCC*, 50–53, 70–71.

46. Paige, "Civilian Conservation Corps," 93–95; Dwayne Mack, "May the Work I've Done Speak for Me: African American Civilian Corps Enrollees in Montana, 1933–1934," *Western Journal of Black Studies* 27 (2003): 236–245; Walker, *CCC*, 74–75, 88.

47. "What of the CCC Worker?" *Kansas Whip*, October 30, 1936, 8; "Report Shows 31,000 Race Men Enrolled in CCC Camps," *Capital Plain Dealer*, January 3, 1937, 2; "CCC Camp Advisors," *Cleveland Gazette*, April 6, 1935, 1; "Negro: Illinois, Michigan," *Cleveland Gazette*, September 28, 1935, 2; Folklife Archives, Manuscripts, "Interview with George Childress Regarding CCC (FA 81)" (1987), FA Oral Histories, Paper 8, http://digitalcommons.wku.edu/dlsc_fa_oral_hist/8 (accessed August 5, 2016).

48. Maher, *Nature's New Deal*, 90–96; quotation from Howard W. Oxley, "Inducting CCC Enrollees into Citizenship," *School Life*, April 1938, 286; Howard W. Oxley, "Enrollees Become Better Citizens," *School Life*, March 1937, 215–216.

49. Richard Baker, Sr., "The Forest Camps of America," *Contemporary Review*, June 1935, 715–720; Maher, *Nature's New Deal*, Flechner quoted on 103, McEntee quoted on 154.

50. Holland and Hill, *Youth in the CCC*, 237; Walker, *CCC*, 73; Albert Cabell Ritchie, "Which Way America?" *Vital Speeches of the Day*, August 12, 1935, Vol. 1, 723–725.

51. Tulloch, oral history, NRHP, 10–11; Maher, *Nature's New Deal*, 54; Conrad Wirth, *Civilian Conservation Corps Program of the United States Department of the Interior*, March 1933 to June 30, 1943, A Report to Harold L. Ickes, Secretary of the Interior (Washington, DC: US Government Printing Office, January 1944), 2–5.

52. *Final Report on the WPA Program, 1935–1943* (Washington, DC: US Government Printing Office, 1946), 3–10; Nick Taylor, *American-Made: The Enduring Legacy*

of the WPA: When FDR Put the Nation to Work (New York: Bantam, 2008), 95–202. There are many great books that explore the meaning and legacy of the New Deal and WPA, beginning with Arthur M. Schlesinger, Jr., *The Politics of Upheaval* (Boston: Houghton Mifflin, 1960) and William E. Leuchtenberg, *Franklin D. Roosevelt and the New Deal* (New York: Harper & Row, 1963), and continuing through Robert S. McElvaine, *The Great Depression, America, 1929–1941* (New York: Random House, 1984), Alan Brinkley, *The End of Reform* (New York: Vintage, 1995), and David M. Kennedy, *Freedom from Fear: The American People in Depression and War, 1929–1945* (New York: Oxford University Press, 1999), to name just a few. Critics and some historians have pointed out the political patronage potential in the creation of the WPA and other alphabet agencies, and although the Democrats' political motivation to help create long-term alliances (much akin to their support of the 1935 Wagner Act) cannot be disproven, the focus here is to suggest their connection to modernity.

53. Quotation from *Workers' Handbook, WPA* (Washington, DC: US Government Printing Office, 1936), 12; June Hopkins, "The American Way to Welfare: Harry Hopkins and New Deal Work Relief," in *The New Deal and Public Policy*, ed. Byron W. Daynes, William D. Pederson, and Michael P. Riccards (New York: St. Martin's, 1998), 215–243; Marta Gutman, "Race, Place, and Play: Robert Moses and the WPA Swimming Pools in New York City," *Journal of the Society of Architectural Historians* 67 (December 2008): 532, 553; Skelton quoted in Kenneth J. Bindas, *Remembering the Great Depression in the Rural South* (Gainesville: University Press of Florida, 2007), 54.

54. Statement on the National Youth Administration, FDR speech, June 26, 1935, in *Administrative and Program Operation of the National Youth Administration, June 26, 1935–January 1, 1937* (Washington, DC: US Government Printing Office, 1937), 1–3.

55. Only with the onset of defense contracts in late 1940 and 1941 did the unemployment rate for young people begin to decline. *Final Report of the National Youth Administration, Fiscal Years 1936–1943* (Washington, DC: US Government Printing Office, 1944), 9–25; *The Purpose and Progress of the National Youth Administration in Ohio* (Columbus, OH: National Youth Administration, 1936), 1–30.

56. Charles Taussig, foreword to Betty Lindley and Ernest K. Lindley, *A New Deal for Youth: The Story of the National Youth Administration* (New York: Viking, 1938), vii–viii.

57. Palmer O. Johnson and Oswald L. Harvey, *The National Youth Administration* (Washington, DC: US Government Printing Office, 1938), 1–6, 15–22.

58. Ibid., 32.

59. Ibid., 88–89.

60. *Final Report of the NYA*, 43–62, 233–235; W. Thacher Winslow, *Youth: A World Problem: A Study in World Perspective of Youth Conditions, Movements and Programs* (Washington, DC: US Government Printing Office, 1937), 90–95; *The Tenth Youth* (Washington, DC: US Government Printing Office, 1940), 1–5; Lewis L. Lorwin, *Youth Work Program: Problems and Policies* (Washington, DC: American Council on Education, 1941), 1–21.

61. *Final Report of the NYA*, vii.

62. Aubrey Williams, address delivered in Pittsburgh, October 22, 1936, and Philadelphia, May 1, 1936, quoted in Mary Rodgers Lindsay, *Youth Gets Its Chance: A Study of NYA Workers in New York City* (New York City: National Youth Administration, 1938), iii.

63. Richard A. Reiman, *The New Deal and American Youth* (Athens: University of Georgia Press, 1992), 5, 6; Taussig quoted in Lindsay, *Youth Gets Its Chance*, 41.

64. Lindsay, *Youth Gets Its Chance*, 1–178, 188–202.

65. Lindley and Lindley, *New Deal for Youth*, photos following page 3; Taussig, foreword to Lindley and Lindley, viii.

66. Lindley and Lindley, *New Deal for Youth*, 17, 21.

67. Ibid., 131, 134, 147, 150.

68. Ibid., 84, 85, 195, 198, 107.

69. William Levy, "The Ohio NYA Enriched Work Experience Program" (PhD diss., Ohio State University, 1945), 65, 2, 74, 134, 135, 138.

70. Gerson B. Chertoff, *Development of Interest in Social Problems, Evaluation Studies Report #2* (Columbus: National Youth Administration in Ohio, 1937), 1, 2, 8, 9.

71. Ibid., 17, 36.

72. Lindley and Lindley, *New Deal for Youth*, 255, 293; "National Youth Administration in District #11," pamphlet produced by Federal Writers' Project WPA in Ohio, n.d.; S. Burns Weston quoted in *Off-Campus Projects in Ohio Colleges and Universities* (Columbus: National Youth Administration in Ohio, 1937), ii, 1.

73. Elizabeth Louise Feigenbutz, "Service Rating in the National Youth Administration of Ohio" (MA thesis, Ohio State University, 1941), 10, 11; Mary Jane Corbett, "Youth in Relief Families: A Social Survey" (MA thesis, Ohio State University, 1936), 3, 48, 49.

74. Mary Jane Corbett and Donald J. McNassor, *The Morale of Youth Workers: A Report on the Development of Morale of 1000 Youth Employed on Work Projects of the National Youth Administration in Ohio*, Division of Research in Program Evaluation, Report #3, January 15, 1938 (Columbus, OH: National Youth Administration, 1938), 17.

75. Franklin Delano Roosevelt speech, "Radio Address for the Mobilization for Human Needs," October 14, 1938, from John T. Woolley and Gerhard Peters, The American Presidency Project, http://www.presidency.ucsb.edu/ws/?pid=15549

(accessed August 5, 2016); Radio Address, April 14, 1936, http://www.fdrlibrary.marist.edu/cgi-bin/htsearch (accessed August 5, 2016).

76. Paul Weaver, "Youth and Religion," *American Academy of Political and Social Science* 236 (November 1944): 152, 157.

Chapter 3. Salvation Awaits

1. Robert W. Rydell, "Introduction: Making America (More) Modern: America's Depression-Era World's Fairs," in *Designing Tomorrow: America's World's Fairs of the 1930s*, ed. Robert W. Rydell and Laura Burd Schiavo (New Haven, CT: Yale University Press, 2010), 1. Robert Rydell in *World of Fairs: The Century of Progress Expositions* (Chicago: University of Chicago Press, 1993) discusses various aspects of world's fairs and expositions and is the natural starting point for anyone reading or researching these phenomena. See esp. 1–11 (quotation on 5); 61–91.

2. Rydell, "Introduction," 8.

3. Warren Susman, "The People's Fair: Cultural Contradictions of a Consumer Society," in *Culture as History: The Transformation of American Society in the Twentieth Century* (New York: Pantheon, 1984), 211–229; Lauren Rabinovitz, *Electric Dreamland: Amusement Parks, Movies, and American Modernity* (New York: Columbia University Press, 2012), 1–65.

4. Christina Cogdell, *Eugenic Design: Streamlining America in the 1930s* (Philadelphia: University of Pennsylvania Press, 2004), 85.

5. Grover Whalen quoted in Smith, *Making the Modern*, 405.

6. Gerald Wendt, *Science for the World of Tomorrow* (New York: Norton, 1939), 307. In fact, in the introduction to their study *Fair America: World's Fairs in the United States* (Washington, DC: Smithsonian Institution Press, 2000), editors Robert W. Rydell, John E. Findling, and Kimberly D. Pelle outline six schools of thought concerning the analysis of world's fairs as they apply to the United States, including how they reinforced the dominant culture, how they were "read" by the participants in response, how they were used to exploit minorities and racist fears, how they were modern versions of "potlatches," how they were visions of technological or architectural expos, and how fairs have captured popular memory in a variety of academic and nonacademic mediums. Their book places the fairs within the context of post–Civil War political, cultural, and economic reconstruction efforts. See the introduction, 5–13, and "Fairs in an Age of Industrialism's Advance," 14–44.

7. Daniel J. Kevles, "Physicists and the Revolt against Science in the 1930s," *Physics Today* 31 (February 1978): 23–30; John C. Burnham, "Introduction," in *Science in America: Historical Selections*, ed. John C. Burnham (New York: Holt, Rinehart & Winston, 1971), 252–259. See also the remainder of that section, 260–348.

8. Glen Scott Allen, *Master Mechanics and Wicked Wizards: Images of the American Scientist as Hero and Villain from Colonial Times to the Present* (Amherst: University of Massachusetts Press, 2009), 8, 68.

9. David E. Nye, *Narratives and Spaces: Technology and the Construction of American Culture* (New York: Columbia University Press, 1997), 127.

10. *The Official Book of the Fair* (Chicago: Century of Progress, 1933), 7, 8; *A Century of Progress: Report of the President to the Board of Trustees, March 14, 1936* (Chicago: Century of Progress, 1936), 29, 32, 33–36. For an excellent overview of the COP, see Cheryl R. Ganz, *The 1933 Chicago World's Fair: A Century of Progress* (Urbana: University of Illinois Press, 2008).

11. *Official Book of the Fair*, 25; Rydell, *World of Fairs*, 92–114.

12. *Official Book of the Fair*, 8; Corie Lok, "Technology as Hope," *Technology Review*, April 2005, 88; Charles D. Stewart, "A Beam from Arcturus," *Atlantic Monthly*, March 1933, 332. Much of what Stewart wrote came from the *Official Book*; see Ganz, *1933 Chicago World's Fair*, ch. 2–4.

13. *Official Book of the Fair*, 27, 28; Rydell, *World of Fairs*, 102.

14. "The Century of Progress Exposition," *Science*, May 19, 1933, 464–465; J. Franklin Bell, "Applied Science and Industry at a Century of Progress Exposition," *Scientific Monthly*, March, 1933, 281–283; Dinsmore Alter, "The Century of Progress Meeting of the American Association for the Advancement of Science," *Scientific Monthly*, July 1933, 87, 88.

15. Carey Croneis, "The Earth Sciences at a Century of Progress," *Scientific Monthly*, April 1933, 383; Arthur B. Lamb, "A Century of Progress in Chemistry," *Science*, October 27, 1933, 371, 373, 376.

16. William Allen Pusey, foreword to Eben J. Carey, *Medical Science Exhibits: A Century of Progress* (Chicago: Century of Progress, 1936), xiii–xiv.

17. Carey, *Medical Science Exhibits*, 33–34.

18. Editorial, "Century of Progress in Medicine," *Hygenia* 11 (June 1933): 490; Carey, *Medical Science Exhibits*, 40; Thomas G. Hull, "A Century of Progress in Medicine," *Hygenia* 11 (December 1933): 1109–1112, 1144–1146.

19. Orvell, *Real Thing*, 168–197; Lincoln Kirstein, "A Century of Progress, 1833–1934," *The Nation*, June 20, 1934, 695, 697; "United States Department of Labor at the Century of Progress Exposition," *Monthly Labor Review* 37 (1933): 1086–1088.

20. "Introduction," Advisory Committee on Publication, Henry Crew, chairman, in Beard, *Century of Progress*, vii; Beard, "Idea of Progress," in Beard, *Century of Progress*, 3.

21. Beard, *Century of Progress*, 6, 15.

22. Louis Skidmore, "Planning the Exhibition Displays," *Architectural Record*, May 1933, 345; Nathaniel A. Owings, "Amusement Features of the Exposition,"

Architectural Record, May 1933, 355–362; Clarence W. Farrier, "The Gadgets: Shelters, Flags, Decoration," *Architectural Record*, May 1933, 363–365; G.A.B., "Science at the Century of Progress Exposition in 1934," *Scientific Monthly*, November 1934, 475–478.

23. "Is It Progress?" *Christian Century*, June 28, 1933, 838–839; Helen Cody Baker, "Century of Progress in Welfare," *Survey*, July 1933, 251–252.

24. Beard, *Century of Progress*, 86, tables 6, 7; "Fair Profits," *Business Week*, October 7, 1933, 11–12.

25. Matthew F. Bokovoy, *The San Diego World's Fairs and Southwestern Memory, 1880–1940* (Albuquerque: University of New Mexico Press, 2005), 163.

26. California Pacific Exposition, ch. 1, http://www.sandiegohistory.org/archives/amero/1935expo/ch1/; ch. 3, http://www.sandiegohistory.org/archives/amero/1935expo/ch3/ (accessed August 1, 2016).

27. "Message of Greeting by the President over the Telephone to the California Pacific International Exposition at San Diego, May 29, 1935," Franklin D. Roosevelt Library, http://www.fdrlibrary.marist.edu/_resources/images/msf/msf00804 (accessed August 1, 2016); California Pacific Exposition, ch. 4, http://www.sandiegohistory.org/archives/amero/1935expo/ch4/; ch. 5, http://www.sandiegohistory.org/archives/amero/1935expo/ch5/ (accessed August 1, 2016). The several speeches delivered by evangelist Aimee Semple McPherson were one of the more interesting features of the CPE. Her first visit on July 18, 1935, drew 20,000 listeners, who heard her challenge the faith in a golden tomorrow and advised them to return to the past and the religious conviction of days gone by. McPherson returned in September for a three-day traditional revival within the modernist revival that was the CPE. She once again admonished the people who had put their faith in sources other than God. Her sermons were an interesting contrast to the CPE world all around her, which promised salvation in the here and now with tangible benefits through a belief in the power of science to solve the problems of hunger, poverty, and disease. Modern society, she was aware, lessened the power of traditional faith as it answered the questions people regularly asked of their spiritual leaders in a manner that was both mysterious (how does radio work?) and practical (it works). See Arthur P. Chew, *Science Serving Agriculture* (Washington, DC: US Government Printing Office, 1936), ch. 4, 2–4.

28. Kenneth B. Ragsdale, *Centennial '36: The Year America Discovered Texas* (College Station: Texas A&M University Press, 1987), 97.

29. Ibid., 69, 94–97, 208–223 (quotation on 211), 233.

30. "Department of Labor Exhibit at Texas Centennial Exposition," *Monthly Labor Review* 43 (1936): 1123; Rydell et al.'s *Fair America* outlines the problems with the Texas Centennial concerning the role and participation of African Americans.

The Hall of Negro Life was torn down after the first year and replaced with a pavilion on Latin American life; see 88–89. FDR speech at the Cotton Bowl, Texas Centennial, June 12, 1936, http://www.fdrlibrary.marist.edu/_resources/images/msf/msf00896 (accessed August 1, 2016).

31. Ragsdale, *Centennial '36*, 255; see also xix, 39, 121, 291, 300.

32. Ibid., 301.

33. John Vacha, "Biggest Bash: Cleveland's Great Lakes Exposition," *Timeline* 13 (1996): 2–23. Vacha expanded this study in *Meet Me on Lake Erie, Dearie: Cleveland's Great Lakes Exposition, 1936–1937* (Kent, OH: Kent State University Press, 2010).

34. Letter, Mayor Harold Burton to E. G. Crawford, President, Cleveland Electric Illuminating Company, January 30, 1936; Speech for the "Come to Cleveland" Committee Speakers Bureau on the Cleveland Centennial Celebration, 1936, both in Harold Burton Papers, 1933–1941, Container 2, Folder 21, various letters, speeches, and pamphlets, Western Reserve Historical Society (hereafter WRHS); "Cleveland to Mark Hundredth Birthday," *New York Times*, June 21, 1936, 12; Franklin D. Roosevelt, "Informal Extemporaneous Remarks of the President," Cleveland Great Lakes Exposition, Cleveland, Ohio, August 14, 1936, ARC identifier 197583, item from Collection FDR-PPF: Papers as President, President's Personal File, 1933–1945, WRHS; "Cleveland Cheers Roosevelt at Show," *New York Times*, August 15, 1936, 4.

35. Roelif Loveland, "Steel Drama to Flare for Expo Throngs," *Cleveland Plain Dealer*, 1936, Burton papers, Container 3, Folder 8, newspaper articles, WRHS; "Cleveland Opens Lakes Exposition," *New York Times*, June 28, 1936, 30.

36. *Great Lakes Exposition Official Souvenir Guide, Cleveland 1936*, 1, 35; *Great Lakes Exposition Official Souvenir Guide, Cleveland 1937*, 31. Both found in Pamphlets C873 and C874, WRHS.

37. *Great Lakes Exposition Official Souvenir Guide, Cleveland 1936*, 22, 12; *Great Lakes Exposition Official Souvenir Guide, Cleveland 1937*, 19; *Souvenir of the 1936 Great Lakes Exposition* (Cleveland: Henry H. Hamm, 1936), 72 Photo Scenes, Pamphlets, S1536, WRHS; Vacha, "Biggest Bash," 2–23.

38. *Book of the Pageant: The Transportation Parade of the Years at the Great Lakes Exposition*, June 27–October 4, 1936, Cleveland, Ohio, Pamphlets, H1311, WRHS; *Souvenir Program, Pathways of Progress: The Pageant of Rochester*, Rochester Centennial Exhibition, August 11–September 9, 1934, http://www.libraryweb.org/ffi digitized/books/Souvenir_program_Pathways_of_Progress.pdf (accessed August 5, 2016).

39. Letter from Harold H. Burton to Grover Whalen, February 3, 1939; Letter from Grover Whalen to Harold Burton, January 25, 1939; "Statement at World's

Fair Luncheon, Waldorf Astoria Hotel, New York City, March 2, 1939, by Mayor Harold H. Burton, of Cleveland, typescript; Letter from William Gaston Rose to Burton, July 7, 1939, all in Burton Papers, Container 4, Folder 16, Letters, Speeches, World's Fair information, WRHS.

40. "100-Day Cleveland Fair," *New York Times*, June 29, 1936, XX2; "Cleveland's Fair On," *New York Times*, June 21, 1936, XX1; "World Fair Group Will Visit Texas," *New York Times*, August 2, 1936, N2.

41. Kevin Starr, *Endangered Dreams: The Great Depression in California* (New York: Oxford University Press, 1996), 353.

42. Richard Reinhardt, *Treasure Island: San Francisco's Exposition Years* (San Francisco: Scrimshaw, 1973), 7.

43. Ibid., 65–66, 82; Stanley Armstrong Hunter, *Temple of Religion and the Tower of Peace at the 1939 Golden Gate International Exposition* (San Francisco: Temple of Religion and Tower of Peace, 1940), 78; Honorable William Phillips, Under Secretary of State, *Address at the California-Pacific International Exposition*, May 30, 1935 (Washington, DC: US Government Printing Office, 1935), 1.

44. *Almanac for Thirty-Niners: Compiled by the Workers of the Federal Writers' Project of the Works Progress Administration in the City of San Francisco, with illustrations by the WPA Art Project in the City of San Francisco* (San Francisco: James Ladd Delkin, 1938).

45. Arthur Brown, Jr., "The Architectural Planning of the Exposition," *Architect and Engineer* 139 (February 1939): 20; "The San Francisco Fair," *Architectural Forum*, June 1939, 463–493; Patricia F. Carpenter and Paul Totah, eds., *The San Francisco Fair: Treasure Island, 1939–1940* (San Francisco: Scottwall, 1989), vii.

46. Eugen Neuhaus, *The Art of Treasure Island: First-Hand Impressions of the Architecture, Sculpture, Landscape, Design, Color Effects, Mural Decorations, Illumination, and Other Artistic Aspects of the Golden Gate International Exposition of 1939* (Berkeley: University of California Press, 1939), 15, 2, 19.

47. Rabbi Rudolph I. Coffee, foreword to Stanley Armstrong Hunger, *Temple of Religion*, xxiii–xxvii, Webb quoted on xxiv, Reinhardt quoted on xiii, xiv.

48. Tom Moriarity, "The Fair Closes," *California, Magazine of the Pacific*, November 1939, http://www.sfmuseum.org/hist5/ggie.html (accessed August 5, 2016).

49. Rydell, *World of Fairs*, 111–113; Sara Beth Levavy, "*Land of Liberty* in the World of Tomorrow," *Film History* 18 (2006): 440–458.

50. Sevan G. Terzian, "The 1939–1940 New York World's Fair and the Transformation of the American Science Extracurriculum," *Science Education* 93 (September 2009): 892–914; Warren I. Susman, "The People's Fair: Cultural Contradictions of a Consumer Society," in *Dawn of a New Day: The New York World's Fair, 1939–40*, ed. Helen A. Harrison (New York: New York University Press, 1980).

51. Peter J. Kuznick, "Losing the World of Tomorrow: The Battle of the Presentation of Science at the 1939 New York World's Fair," *American Quarterly* 46 (September 1994): 341–373; James Mauro, *Twilight at the World of Tomorrow: Genius, Madness, Murder, and the 1939 World's Fair on the Brink of War* (New York: Ballantine, 2010), 86–97, 117–130; Michael Robertson, "Cultural Hegemony Goes to the Fair: The Case of E. L. Doctorow's *World's Fair*," *American Studies* 33 (Spring 1992): 31–44 (and for an interesting analysis of Doctorow and his novel, see Nye, *Narratives and Spaces*, 93–112); George McAneny, "Introduction," in Gordon W. Gilkey, *Etchings: New York World's Fair—"Building the World of Tomorrow"* (New York: Charles Scribner's Sons, 1939), n.p.

52. Grover Whalen, "The World's Fair of New York," *L'Illustration*, July 1939, n.p.; Terry Smith, *Making the Modern*, 408, 409.

53. Gordon W. Gilkey, "The Ground Work, Plates 3, 4, 5 & 6," in Gilkey, *Etchings*, n.p. For an excellent photographic overview of the NYWF, see Larry Zim, Mel Lerner, and Herbert Rolfe, *The World of Tomorrow: The 1939 New York World's Fair* (New York: Harper & Son, 1988).

54. Wendt, *Science for the World of Tomorrow*, 272, 39, 297, 301.

55. Ibid., 128, 267, 271.

56. *Man and His Health: A Guide to Medical and Public Health Exhibits at the New York World's Fair 1939, Together with Information on the Conservation of Health and the Preservation of Life* (New York: Expositions Publications, 1939), 5, 92.

57. Ibid., 92, 28, 11.

58. Ibid., 12; Cogdell, *Eugenic Design*, 122.

59. *Man and His Health*, 73–74.

60. Gilkey, "Plate 41: Electricity," *Etchings*, n.p.; *Official Program, The New York World's Fair: The World of Tomorrow* (New York: Tichnor Brothers, 1939); Gilkey, "Plate 13: Theme Exhibit," *Etchings*, n.p.

61. Charles A. Johnson, *The Frontier Camp Meeting: Religion's Harvest Time* (Dallas: Southern Methodist University Press, 1955), 240; *Exhibition Techniques: A Summary of Exhibition Practice Based on Surveys Conducted at New York and San Francisco World's Fairs of 1939* (New York: New York Museum of Science and Industry, 1940), 1–18.

62. Ibid., 17–26, quotations on 20, 25.

63. Ibid., 38, 42, 52, 90; Gilkey, "Plate 35: The Drug Store," *Etchings*, n.p.

64. *Exhibition Techniques*, 59, 114.

65. David Gelernter, *1939: The Lost World of the Fair* (New York: Free Press, 1995), 339–375; Marco Duranti, "Utopia, Nostalgia and World War at the 1939–40 New York World's Fair," *Journal of Communication History* 41 (2006): 663–683. Duranti argues that the turn away from the utopian vision of the 1939 fair represents "the

failure . . . to resurrect a coherent narrative of progress in the face of renewed violence in Europe" (663), and that the utopian and nostalgic themes for the fair were "intentional acts of defiance, calculated to create an imaginative dreamscape where the traumatic consequences of technological progress could be defused" (683).

66. Cogdell, *Eugenic Design*, 203.

Chapter 4. A Woman's Place/A Family's Hearth

1. Maurine Shaw, "Modern Economy," *Better Homes and Gardens*, May 1937, 55. For excellent overviews of designers and their role, see Meikle, *Twentieth Century Limited*; J. Stewart Johnson, *American Modern, 1925–1940* (New York: Harry N. Abrams, 2000); Phyllis Ross, *Gilbert Rohde: Modern Design for Modern Living* (New Haven, CT: Yale University Press, 2009); Michael Adas, *Dominance by Design: Technological Imperatives and America's Civilizing Mission* (Cambridge, MA: Belknap Press of Harvard University Press, 2006); and of course the works by designers themselves, such as Loewy, Deskey, and Bel Geddes, who were avid self-promoters.

2. Steven Mintz and Susan Kellogg, *Domestic Revolutions: A Social History of American Family Life* (New York: Free Press, 1988), 110–125.

3. Elizabeth Burris-Meyer, *Decorating Livable Homes* (New York: Prentice-Hall, 1938), 342.

4. Katherine E. Ritchie, "Transformation in the Modern Manner," *Ladies' Home Journal*, February 1936, 116–118; Dorothy Draper, *Decorating Is Fun: How to Be Your Own Decorator* (New York: Doubleday, Doran, 1939), 7; Kristina Wilson, *Livable Modernism: Interior Decorating and Design during the Great Depression* (New Haven, CT: Yale University Press, 2004), 8.

5. Carolyn Haynes, "Women and Protestantism in Nineteenth-Century America," in *Perspectives on American Religion and Culture*, ed. Peter W. Williams (Malden, MA: Blackwell, 1999), 300–318; Lillie Devereuz Blake, *A Woman's Place Today* (New York: William Lowell, 1833); Mary Ryan, *Women in Public: Between Banners and Ballots, 1825–1880* (Baltimore, MD: Johns Hopkins University Press, 1990), 3–18, 58–94.

6. Pat Kirkham and Lynne Walker, "Women Designers in the USA, 1900–2000: Diversity and Difference," in *Women Designers in the USA, 1900–2000*, ed. Pat Kirkham (New York: Bard Graduate Center for the Study of the Decorative Arts, Yale University Press, 2000), 49–84; Susan Currell, *The March of Spare Time: The Problem and Promise of Leisure in the Great Depression* (Philadelphia: University of Pennsylvania Press, 2005), 125–39, explores the contested interiors modernity presented through advertising and gendered space; Janna Jones, "The Distance

from Home: The Domestication of Desire in Interior Design Manuals," *Journal of Social History* 31 (Winter 1997): 307.

7. Peter McNeil, "Designing Women: Gender, Sexuality, and the Interior Decorator, 1890–1940," *Art History* 17 (December 1994): 632; Adrian Forty, *Objects of Desire* (New York: Pantheon, 1986), 104; Candace Wheeler, "Interior Decoration as a Profession for Women," *The Outlook*, April 20, 1895, 649.

8. Haynes, "Women and Protestantism"; Blake, *Woman's Place Today*; Mary Ryan, *Women in Public*, 3–18, 58–94.

9. Megan Elias, "Model Mamas: The Domestic Partnership of Home Economics Pioneers Flora Rose and Martha Van Rensselaer," *Journal of the History of Sexuality* 15 (January 2006): 65–88.

10. Allen Tate and C. Ray Smith, *Interior Design in the 20th Century* (New York: Harper & Row, 1986), 333–334.

11. "Modernistic into Modern," *Arts and Decoration* 42 (November 1934): 10–12; Jennifer M. Downs, "'The New Modern Feeling': A Catalogue of the Collection," *Art Institute of Chicago Museum Studies* 27 (2001): 18–45, 105–108.

12. Monica Obniski, "Exhibiting Modernity through the Lens of Tradition in Gilbert Rohde's Design for Living Interior," *Journal of Design History* 20, no. 3 (2007): 227–242; Fisher quoted in Jennifer Scanlon, *Inarticulate Longings: The Ladies' Home Journal, Gender, and the Promises of Consumer Culture* (New York: Routledge, 1995), 33, 75; Lynd and Lynd, *Middletown in Transition*, 259–260; Kristina Wilson, *Livable Modernism*, 135; Tate and Smith, *Interior Design*, 294–306.

13. Currell, *March of Spare Time*, 101–122.

14. Kristina Wilson, *Livable Modernism*, 21–22; *Good Housekeeping* quotation from Cheryl Buckley, "Made in Patriarchy: Toward a Feminist Analysis of Women and Design," *Design Issues* 3 (Autumn 1986): 3–14; Pulos quotation from Dianne O. Pierce, "Design, Craft, and American Identity: Russel Wright's 'American Way' Project, 1940–2" (Master's thesis, Cooper-Hewitt, National Design Museum, Smithsonian Institution and Parsons, the New School for Design, 2010), 9.

15. Paul T. Frankl, *New Dimensions: The Decorative Arts Today in Words and Pictures* (New York: Brewer & Warren, 1928), 20.

16. Quoted in Pierce, "Design, Craft," 4.

17. Rohde quoted in Kristina Wilson, *Livable Modernism*, 11.

18. Ibid., 18; "Modern Magic in Glass," *Good Housekeeping*, September 1937, 56; quotation from Gilbert Seldes, "Introduction," in *10 Years of Industrial Design, Henry Dreyfuss, 1929–1939 New York* (New York: Pynson, 1939), n.p.

19. Shirley Ware, "Give Your Career Background," *Independent Woman* 19 (February 1940), 44.

20. Cheryl Robertson, "From Cult to Profession: Domestic Women in Search of Equality," in *The Material Culture of Gender/The Gender of Material Culture*, ed. Katherine Martinez and Kenneth L. Ames (Hanover, NH: The Winterthur Museum with the University Press of New England, 1997), 76.

21. Martha Delano, "Making Space for Modern Living," *Home and Garden*, May 1934, 50.

22. "Decorators Tell Just Who They Are," *New York Times*, June 19, 1935; Bridget May, "Nancy Vincent McClelland (1877–1959): Professionalizing Interior Decoration in the Early Twentieth Century," *Journal of Design History* 21, no. 1 (2008): 66 (quotation); Bobbye Tigerman, "'I Am Not a Decorator': Florence Knoll, the Knoll Planning Unit and the Making of the Modern Office," *Journal of Design History* 20, no. 1 (2007): 61–74; Kirkham, *Women Designers in the USA*, 62–64; Tate and Smith, *Interior Design*, 364–365; Elias, "'Model Mamas,'" 65.

23. Carleton Varney, *In the Pink: Dorothy Draper: America's Most Fabulous Decorator* (New York: Pointed Leaf, 2006), 27–30.

24. Derek Patmore, "Interior Decoration," *Journal of the Royal Society of Arts*, January 18, 1935, 209–221 (quotation on 210).

25. Alice Jackson and Bettina Jackson, *The Study of Interior Decoration* (New York: Doubleday, Doran, 1934), 1.

26. Ibid., 449, 450–451, 454–455.

27. John T. Greenan, *American Civilization Today: A Summary of Recent Social Trends* (New York: McGraw-Hill, 1934), 79.

28. Margaret Collins, "Careers, Limited," *Scribner's*, October 1937, 45; Sarah Comstock, "Marriage—or Career," *Good Housekeeping*, June 1932, 32–33, 156; "What Price the Career Mother," *Independent Woman*, February 1937, 42–43; Mary Ross, "New Careers for Daughters," *Parents' Magazine*, November 1931, 14–15, 63–65; "I Refused a Career," *Saturday Evening Post*, September 1931, 14–15, 73; Marian Castle, "Custom-Built Careers," *Independent Woman*, June 1935, 189, 202–204; William M. Marston, "The Cost of Careers," *Delineator*, June 1936, 7; Charlotte Muret, "Marriage as a Career," *Harper's*, August 1936, 249–257; "What Do the Women Think About Careers?" *Ladies' Home Journal*, November 1939, 12.

29. Frances D. McMullen, "New Jobs for Women," *North American Review*, August 1932, 134, 138; Robertson, "From Cult to Profession," 100–104.

30. "Decorative Arts in San Francisco," *American Magazine of Art*, June 1936, 395; "Modern Interiors: A Portfolio," *Arts and Decoration*, September 1933, 19.

31. Winnifred Fales, *What's New in Home Decorating* (New York: Dodd, Mead, 1936), 1, 3, 227. Review of Fales's book in *New York Times*, November 1, 1936.

32. Fales, *What's New*, 151–158, 86.

33. Elizabeth Lunbeck, *The Americanization of Narcissism* (Cambridge, MA: Harvard University Press, 2014), 143–153; Gladys Miller, *Decoratively Speaking: The Essentials and Principals of Interior Decoration* (New York: Doubleday, Doran, 1939), x, 270, 272, 278, 280, 295, 301, 312; Elizabeth Otey, "Modern Art Influence in Our Houses," *Good Housekeeping*, September 1935, 72; Sarah M. Lockwood, *Decoration: Past, Present and Future* (New York: Literary Guild, 1934), 90–91.

34. Thelma M. Burrows, *Successful Home Furnishing* (Peoria, IL: Manual Arts, 1938), 7, 23, 44.

35. Helen Koues, *How to Be Your Own Decorator* (New York: Tudor, 1939), 25, photo on 27.

36. Anna Hong Rutt, *Home Furnishing* (New York: John Wiley & Sons, 1935, 1944), 1, 5, 107.

37. Virginia Hamill, "Modern and Modernized," *Woman's Home Companion*, November 1938, 68; Rutt, *Home Furnishing*, 110, 115; Shaw, "Modern Economy," 55, 57–59.

38. Helen M. Daggett, *Interior Decorating: Leisure League Little Book #16* (New York: Leisure League of America, 1935), 5, 7, 8, 14, 16.

39. Ibid., 38, 48, 49, 17, 51.

40. Grace L. Pennock, "An Open-Minded Kitchen," *Ladies' Home Journal*, April 1938, 21, and advertisement on 22.

41. Burris-Meyer, *Decorating Livable Homes*, 16; Draper, *Decorating Is Fun*, 150–151. For an excellent discussion of the tug of war between male industrial kitchen designers and female consumers, see Shelley Nickles, "'Preserving Women': Refrigerator Design as Social Process in the 1930s," *Technology and Culture* 43 (October 2002): 693–727; Janet Busch, "Cooking Competition: Technology on the Domestic Market in the 1930s," *Technology and Culture* 24 (April 1983): 222–245; Eve Jochnowitz, "Feasting on the Future: Foods of the World of Tomorrow at the New York World's Fair of 1939–40," *Performance Research* 4 (Spring 1999): 110–120; quotation from "To-Morrow's Daughter," *Vogue*, February 1, 1939, 61; "Come to the World's Fair and Go Back a Woman of Tomorrow," Bonwit Teller advertisement, *Vogue*, February 1, 1939, 4–5.

42. Lydia Powel, *The Attractive Home: A Book of Good Ideas and Simple Rules for the Homemaker* (New York: Macmillan, 1939), 104, 106.

43. Ibid., 120, 5, 78, 79, 86.

44. Emily Post, *The Personality of a House: The Blue Book of Home Charm*, rev. ed. (New York: Funk & Wagnalls, 1939), 490, 491, 496, 497.

45. Gladys Miller, *Decoratively Speaking*, x, 270, 272, 278, 280, 295, 301, 312. On consumption, citizenship, and how it operated during the Depression era,

see Gary Cross, *An All-Consuming Century: Why Commercialism Won in Modern America* (New York: Columbia University Press, 2000); Kathleen G. Donohue, *Freedom from Want: American Liberalism and the Idea of the Consumer* (Baltimore, MD: Johns Hopkins University Press, 2004); Charles McGovern, "Consumption and Citizenship in the United States, 1900–1940," in *Getting and Spending: European and American Consumer Studies in the Twentieth Century*, ed. Susan Strasser, Charles McGovern, and Matthias Judt (New York: Cambridge University Press, 1998), 37.

46. Fales, *What's New*, 1, 3, 227, 151–158, 86 (emphasis added).

47. Ibid., 70, 67–68, 229.

48. Ibid., 87–88; Daniel T. Rodgers, *Atlantic Crossings: Social Politics in a Progressive Age* (Cambridge, MA: Harvard University Press, 1998), 395; "Tropical Modern in California," *House and Garden*, September 1940, 42–43; "Modern in Miami," *Country Life and the Sportsman*, September 1938, 56–61; Ruth Maloney, "Modern Moves into Colonial," *Better Homes and Gardens*, February 1940, 63; "Modern in California," *House Beautiful*, June 1940, 51; McMullen, "New Jobs for Women," 134. It is interesting that the Soviet Union came to view the modernization of the kitchen in the latter part of the 1950s and throughout the 1960s as key to the success of socialism. See Susan E. Reid, "The Khrushchev Kitchen: Domesticating the Scientific-Technological Revolution," *Journal of Contemporary History* 40 (Summer 2005): 289–316.

49. Obniski, "Exhibiting Modernity"; Ganz, *Chicago World's Fair*, 85–107. Ganz's chapter on fan dancer Sally Rand and her role on the midway in 1933 is an excellent discussion of the view and meaning women seemed to play at the 1933 event, which was replicated throughout the other fairs during the era. See 7–27. For an excellent discussion of the role and meaning of women at world's fairs in the early part of the twentieth century, see T. J. Boisseau and Abigail M. Markwyn, "World's Fairs in Feminist Historical Perspective," in *Gendering the Fair: Histories of Women and Gender at World's Fairs*, ed. T. J. Boisseau and Abigail M. Markwyn (Urbana: University of Illinois Press, 2010), 1–18.

50. "The Century of Progress Anticipates Homes of Tomorrow," *American Home*, June 1933, 18; Jan Rehnstrand, "New Home Ideas from the Century of Progress Exhibition," *School Arts* 33 (1933): 67–75; J. Harold Hawkins, "Trends in House Design at a Century of Progress," *Ladies' Home Journal*, June 1933, 26–29; *California Pacific International Exposition—Official Guide, Souvenir Program and Picture Book* (San Diego: G. F. Wolcott, 1935), 85.

51. Jochnowitz, "Feasting on the Future"; "Glass and Light in the Modern House," *Good Housekeeping*, May 1939, 151–158; "For Devotees of Modern," *House and Garden*, November 1940, 43.

52. Quotation from Rodgers, *Atlantic Crossings*, 395; "Tropical Modern in California," 42–43; "Modern in Miami," 56–61; Maloney, "Modern Moves into Colonial," 63; "Modern in California," 51; McMullen, "New Jobs for Women," 134 (see n. 46).

53. Janet M. Hooks, *Women's Occupations through Seven Decades* (Washington, DC: US Government Printing Office, 1947), 4–27, 156, 209–225; Grace Lees-Maffei, "Introduction: Professionalization as a Focus in Interior Design History," *Journal of Design History* 21, no. 1 (2008): 1–18; Penina Migdal Glazer and Miriam Slater, *Unequal Colleagues: The Entrance of Women into the Professions, 1890–1940* (New Brunswick, NJ: Rutgers University Press, 1987), 2–9; Julie Des Jardins, *The Madame Curie Complex: The Hidden History of Women in Science* (New York: Feminist Press, 2010), 15–20, 53–85.

54. Kirkham and Walker, "Women Designers," 49, 62.

55. Wendy Kaplan, "Women Designers and the Arts and Crafts Movement," in Kirkham, *Women Designers*, 86.

56. Edward S. Cooke, Jr., "Women Furniture Makers: From Decorative Designers to Studio Makers," in Kirkham, *Women Designers*, 295; Ella Howard and Eric Setliff, "'In a Man's World': Women Industrial Designers," in Kirkham, *Women Designers*, 269–289.

57. Julia Kirk Blackwelder, *Now Hiring: The Feminization of Work in the United States, 1900–1995* (College Station: Texas A&M University Press, 1997), 93–95; Beverly Russell, *Women of Design: Contemporary American Interiors* (New York: Rizzoli, 1980), 10; Margaret W. Rossiter, *Women Scientists in America: Struggles and Strategies to 1940* (Baltimore, MD: Johns Hopkins University Press, 1982), 313–316.

58. Howard and Setliff, "'In a Man's World.'"

59. Pat Kirkham and Penny Sparke, "'A Woman's Place . . . ?' Women Interior Designers, Part I: 1900–1950," in Kirkham, *Women Designers*, 305–316.

60. David A. Hanks and Anne Hoy, *American Streamlined Design: The World of Tomorrow* (Paris: Flammarion/The Liliane and David M. Stewart Program for Modern Design, The Lake St. Louis Historical Society, 2005), 249–264. See also Meikle, *Twentieth Century Limited*; J. Stewart Johnson, *American Modern*; Ross, *Gilbert Rohde*; Adas, *Dominance by Design*; Kristina Wilson, *Livable Modernism*. Perhaps because of this lacunae, Pat Kirkham edited *Women Designers in the USA, 1900–2000*, which outlines the contributions of women to American design.

61. Leslie Kanes Weisman, *Discrimination by Design: A Feminist Critique of the Man-Made Environment* (Urbana: University of Illinois Press, 1992), 2, 86. For women in architecture, see Alice T. Friedman, *Women and the Making of the Modern Home: A Social and Architectural History* (New York: Harry N. Abrams, 1998).

62. Christopher Reed, "Introduction," in *Not at Home: The Suppression of Domesticity in Modern Art and Architecture* (London: Thames & Hudson, 1996), 16.

63. Lisa Tiersten, "The Chic Interior and the Feminine Modern: Home Decorating as High Art in Turn-of-the-Century Paris," in Reed, *Not at Home*, 18.

64. Penny Sparke, "Elsie de Wolfe and Female Clients, 1905–15: Gender, Class and the Professional Interior Decorator," in *Women's Places: Architecture and Design, 1860–1960*, ed. Brenda Martin and Penny Sparke (New York: Routledge, 2003), 48. For more on this topic, see Peter Gabriel Filene, *Him/Her/Self: Sex Roles in Modern America* (Baltimore, MD: Johns Hopkins University Press, 1986); Robyn Muncy, *Creating a Female Dominion: American Reform, 1890–1935* (New York: Oxford University Press, 1991); Susan Fraiman, "Bad Girls of Good Housekeeping: Dominique Browning and Martha Stewart," *American Literary History* 23 (2011): 263; Jennifer Scanlon, *Inarticulate Longings: The* Ladies Home Journal, *Gender, and the Promises of Consumer Culture* (New York: Routledge, 1995), 169–228.

65. Florence B. Terhune, *Decorating for You* (New York: M. Barrows, 1944), 55, 54, 239.

66. Gordon Lippincott and Walter Margulies, "Design: Emphasis on Individuality," *Challenge*, October 1956, 23–27 (quotation on 26); Elaine Tyler May, "The Commodity Gap: Consumerism and the Modern Home," in Lawrence B. Glickman, ed., *Consumer Society in American History: A Reader* (Ithaca: Cornell University Press, 1999), 298–315; Per H. Hansen, "Networks, Narratives and New Markets: The Rise and Decline of Danish Modern Furniture Design, 1930–1970," *Business History Review* 80 (Autumn 2006): 468; Mintz and Kellogg, *Domestic Revolutions*, 133–149. It is interesting that the USSR came to view the modernization of the kitchen in the latter part of the 1950s and throughout the 1960s as key to the success of socialism. Through the application of science, reason, and technology, the kitchen and other domestic spaces would be transformed and thus would inspire socialism throughout the world. The Khrushchev regime put their faith in science to provide the answers to modernizing the Soviet home with women to be the primary benefactors. This same rationale dominated the pages of women's magazines and advice books during the Depression era, transferring much of the transformative power to the corporations and businesses that advertised household goods. The women advisors related how to apply the new science to the home, whether in the kitchen or the bedroom, while the advertisers and designers—both overwhelmingly male—explained why they needed them and where they could go to buy them. See Susan E. Reid, "The Khrushchev Kitchen: Domesticating the Scientific-Technological Revolution," *Journal of Contemporary History* 40 (Summer 2005): 289–316.

Chapter 5. Sounds for the Modern Age

1. "Street of Dreams," words by Sam Lewis, music by Victor Young, Miller Music Corporation, 1932 (renewed 1960); Alexander D. Richardson, "Thousands Turn to Music in the Hour of Needs," *Musician*, April 1933, 11. For a discussion of the tension between the vestiges of the past and the hope for the future, see Michael Kammen, *Mystic Chords of Memory* (New York: Vintage, 1991), 299–309.

2. Alastair Guinan, "Modern Mass Music," *Commonweal*, January 26, 1934, 353–354; LeRoy B. Campbell, "Hidden Meanings in Modern Music," *Musician*, June 1937, 105 (first quotation); LeRoy Campbell, "Music Study and Modern Youth," *Musician*, July 1939, 123 (second quotation).

3. Paul F. Lazarsfeld, *Radio and the Printed Page: An Introduction to the Study of Radio and Its Role in the Communication of Ideas* (New York: Duell, Sloan & Pearce, 1940), 15–44; Dickson Skinner, "Music Goes into Mass Production," *Harper's*, December 1, 1938, 484–489; Bruce Lenthall, "Critical Reception: Public Intellectuals Decry Depression-Era Radio, Mass Culture, and Modern America," in *Radio Reader: Essays in the Cultural History of Radio*, ed. Michele Hilmes and Jason Loviglio (New York: Routledge, 2002), 41–62; David Goodman, "Distracted Listening: On Not Making Sound Choices in the 1930s," in *Sound in the Age of Mechanical Reproduction*, ed. David Suisman and Susan Strasser (Philadelphia: University of Pennsylvania Press, 2012), 15–40; Barry Ulanoc, "The Jukes Take Over Swing," *American Mercury* 51 (1940): 172–177; Chris Rasmussen, "'The People's Orchestra': Jukeboxes as the Measure of Popular Musical Taste in the 1930s and 1940s," in Suisman and Strasser, *Sound in the Age of Mechanical Reproduction*, 181–198.

4. Bruce Lenthall, *Radio's America: The Great Depression and the Rise of Modern Mass Culture* (Chicago: University of Chicago Press, 2007); William H. Young and Nancy K. Young, *Music of the Great Depression* (Westport, CT: Greenwood, 2005), 1–31; Lundberg et al., 261–271 (quotations on 270); Lynd and Lynd, *Middletown in Transition*, 260–265; John A. Kouwenhoven, *The Arts in Modern American Civilization* (New York: Norton, 1948), 197–224.

5. Lewis Reid, "The Crooning Menace," *Musician*, April 1932, 16; Allison McCracken, "'God's Gift to Us Girls': Crooning, Gender, and the Re-Creation of American Popular Song, 1928–1933," *American Music* 17 (Winter 1999): 366, and her more comprehensive *Real Men Don't Sing: Crooning in American Culture* (Durham, NC: Duke University Press, 2015); Young and Young, *Music of the Great Depression*, 5–13.

6. "Soon," Ira and George Gershwin, 1935; "Chasing Shadows," Benny Davis and Abner Silver, 1935; "Life Is a Song," Joe Young and Fred Ahlert, 1935; "Once

in a While," Bud Green and Michael Edwards, 1937; "These Foolish Things," Holt Marvell and Jack Stachey/Harry Link, 1936; "That Old Feeling," Lew Brown and Sammy Fain, 1937; "Over the Rainbow," Yip Harburg and Harold Arlen, 1939; "East of the Sun," Brooks Bowman, 1935; "Heaven Can Wait," Eddie DeLange and Jimmy Van Huesen, 1939; "Wishing," B. G. DeSylva, 1939; "Pennies from Heaven," Johnny Burke and Arthur Johnson, 1937; "Alone," Arthur Freed and Nacio Herb Brown, 1936; "Lost," Phil Ohman, Johnny Mercer, and Mary Teetor, 1936; "Pocket Full of Dreams," Johnny Burke and Jimmy Monaco, 1938; "A Little Bit Independent," Edgar Leslie and Joe Burke, 1936.

7. Svetlana Boym, *The Future of Nostalgia* (New York: Basic Books, 2001), xv; Linda Hutcheon, "Irony, Nostalgia, and the Postmodern," in *Methods for the Study of Literature as Cultural Memory*, ed. Raymond Vervliet and Annamarie Estor (Amsterdam: Rodopi, 2000), 189–207; Clewell, *Mourning, Modernism, Postmodernism*, 3, 7.

8. Much of this has been discussed by Raymond Williams, *The Country and the City* (New York: Oxford University Press, 1973); Jameson, *Postmodernism*; and Jean-François Lyotard, *The Postmodern Condition: A Report on Knowledge* (Minneapolis: University of Minnesota Press, 1979), as well as others writing on modernism and postmodernity. See also Orvell, *Real Thing*; Malcolm Chase and Christopher Shaw, "The Dimensions of Nostalgia," in *The Imagined Past: History and Nostalgia*, ed. Malcolm Chase and Christopher Shaw (Manchester: Manchester University Press, 1989), 1–17.

9. Meikle, "Domesticating Modernity," 150.

10. Edward Comentale, "'Thought I Had Your Heart Forever' or the Modernity of Early Country Music," *Journal of Popular Music Studies* 20 (September 2008): 211–239; Dickson D. Bruce, Jr., *And They All Sang Hallelujah: Plain-Folk Camp-Meeting Religion, 1800–1845* (Knoxville: University of Kentucky Press, 1974), 96–121.

11. Peter Stanfield, *Horse Opera: The Strange History of the 1930s Singing Cowboy* (Urbana: University of Illinois Press, 2002), 102, 75. For an excellent biography, see Holly George-Warren, *Public Cowboy No. 1: The Life and Times of Gene Autry* (New York: Oxford University Press, 2007).

12. Kenneth J. Bindas, "Western Mystic: Bob Nolan and His Songs," *Western Historical Quarterly* 18 (October 1986): 439–456.

13. Elizabeth Outka, *Consuming Traditions: Modernity, Modernism, and the Commodified Authentic* (New York: Oxford University Press, 2009), 3–24; Beulah Charmley, "The American Cowboy Song: An Introduction to the Popular English and Scottish Ballad," *Education*, October 1935, 122; Avis D. Carlson, "Cowboy Ballads at Our Own Fireside: They Are as Wholly and Originally American as Cornbread,"

Better Homes and Gardens, November 1931, 23, 60; Alva Johnston, "Tenor on Horseback," *Saturday Evening Post*, September 1939, 18–19, 74–76.

14. Beth E. Levy, *Frontier Figures: American Music and the Mythology of the American West* (Berkeley: University of California Press, 2012); Virgil Thomson, "America's Musical Maturity: A Twentieth Century Story," *Yale Review* 51 (1961): 66–71; Roy Harris, "American Music Enters a New Phase," *Scribner's*, October 1934, 221.

15. Mikhail Bakhtin, *The Dialogic Imagination: Four Essays* (Austin: University of Texas Press, 1992); Mikhail Bakhtin, *Speech Genres and Other Late Essays* (Austin: University of Texas Press, 1986); "Life Is Just a Bowl of Cherries," Ray Henderson, Buddy DeSylva, and Lew Brown, 1931.

16. Simon Frith, *Performing Rites: On the Value of Popular Music* (Cambridge, MA: Harvard University Press, 1996), 158–170; Interview with Ossie Davis, conducted by Blackside, Inc., on August 29, 1992, for *The Great Depression*. Washington University Libraries, Film and Media Archive, Henry Hampton Collection.

17. Kenneth J. Bindas, *Swing, That Modern Sound: The Cultural Context of Swing Music in America, 1935–1947* (Jackson: University Press of Mississippi, 2001), 8; Carter quote from "Jazz versus Swing: Despite Altercation It's Still Syncopation," *Metronome*, April 1944, 23; Otis C. Ferguson, "The Spirit of Jazz," *New Republic*, December 30, 1936, 269–271; Wilder Hobson, "Swing High," *Vogue*, March 15, 1936, 112; Paul Whiteman, "This Thing Called Jazz," *Rotarian*, June 1939, 35.

18. "Orgy by Air," *Atlantic Monthly* 157 (1936): 384.

19. Dorothy Bergman, "Jazz, the Expression of the Age," *Musician*, September 1930, 12.

20. Frank Norris, "The Killer-Diller: The Life and Four-Four Time of Benny Goodman," *Saturday Evening Post*, May 7, 1938, 23, 7, 22.

21. William Roberts Tilford, "Swing! Swing! Swing! The Last Word in 'X Music,'" *Etude*, December 1937, 778.

22. Reed Dickerson, "Hot Music: Rediscovering Jazz," *Harper's Monthly*, April 1936, 570.

23. Cab Calloway, *The New Cab Calloway's Cat-ologue* (New York: Calloway, 1938); *Hepcats Jive Talk Dictionary*, http://www.dancestore.com/glossary-lindy-lingo.aspx (accessed August 5, 2016); Holman Harvey, "It's Swing," *Delineator*, November 1936, 10–11, 48–50; Lewis Bergman, "Swinging the Classics," *New York Times*, January 14, 1940; Gustav Klemm, "The Jargon of Jazz," *Etude*, August 1934, 455–456.

24. "Stompin at the Savoy," words by Andy Razaf, music by Benny Goodman, Chick Webb, and Edgar Sampson, 1936; "It Don't Mean a Thing (If It Ain't Got That Swing)," words by Irving Mills, music by Duke Ellington, 1932; "Night & Day," Cole Porter, 1932; "I'm in a Dancing Mood," words by Maurice Sigler and Al

Goodheart, music by Al Hoffman, 1936; "Let's Dance," words by Fanny Baldridge, music by Greg Stone and Joseph Bonime, 1935; "Minnie the Moocher," Cab Calloway, Clarence Gaskill, and Irving Mills, 1931; Betty Boop cartoon, http://youtube/c11mnZUM6bQ (accessed August 5, 2016); "'Tain't What You Do," Trummy Young and Sy Oliver, 1939.

25. "When It's Sleepy Time Down South," Leon Rene, Otis Rene, and Clarence Muse, 1931; "Throw Another Log on the Fire," Charles Tobias, Jack Scholl, and Murray Mencher, 1933; "Thanks for the Memory," Leo Robin and Ralph Rainger, 1937; "Star Dust," words by Mitchell Parish, music by Hoagy Carmichael, 1930; "Yesterdays," words by Otto Harbach, music by Jerome Kern, recorded by Leo Reisman, 1933; "In a Shanty in Old Shanty Town," Joe Young, Jack Little, and Ira Schuster, 1932; "The Old Spinning Wheel," Billy Hill, 1934.

26. "Stormy Weather," words by Ted Koehler, music by Harold Arlen, 1933; "These Foolish Things," words by Holt Marvell, music by Jack Strachey and Harry Link, 1936; "Sophisticated Lady," words by Irving Mills and Mitchell Parish, music by Duke Ellington, 1933; "Boulevard of Broken Dreams," Jan Garber, 1934.

27. "Wrap Your Troubles in Dreams," words by Ted Koehler and Billy Moll, music by Gus Arnheim, 1931; "Street of Dreams," words by Sam Lewis, music by Victor Young, 1932; "This Is No Dream," Tommy Dorsey, Benny Davis, and Ted Shapiro, 1939; "The Glory of Love," Billy Hill, 1936; "Brother, Can You Spare a Dime," words by Yip Harburg, music by Jay Gorney, 1932; "Daydreaming," Johnny Mercer and Harry Warren, 1938; "In the Middle of a Dream," Tommy Dorsey, Einar Swan, and Al Stillman, 1939; "I've Got a Pocketful of Dreams," words by John Burke, music by James Monaco, 1938; "With My Eyes Wide Open I'm Dreaming," Harry Revel and Mack Gordon, 1934; "Isn't It Romantic," Lorenz Hart and Richard Rodgers, 1932; "Beyond the Blue Horizon," words by Leo Robin, music by Richard Whiting and W. Harling, 1930.

28. "Wishing," B. G. DeSylva, 1939; "I'll Never Be the Same," words by Gus Kahn, music by Matt Malneck and Frank Signorelli, 1932; "Over the Rainbow," words by Yip Harburg, music by Harold Arlen, 1939; "Happy Days Are Here Again," words by Jack Yellin, music by Milton Ager, 1929; "It's a Wonderful World," Harold Adamson, Jan Javitt, and Johnny Watson, 1939; "New Sun in the Sky," Howard Dietz and Arthur Schwartz.

29. Doron K. Antrim, "How to Write a Song Hit," *American Mercury* 50 (1940): 49–53, outlines the reality of songwriting as a business and the intricacies of creating, selling, and distributing one's work.

30. Lundberg et al., *Leisure*, 270; Howard Hanson, "Machine Music a Challenge to the Profession," *Musician*, March 1, 1930, 20; "Great Musical Revival Result of

the Force of Radio," *Etude*, February 1, 1938, 72; Pitts Sanborn, "There's Music in the Air," *Scholastic*, January 11, 1936, 11–12.

31. For a detailed discussion of the impact and utilization of the radio and record among jazz and swing musicians, see Bindas, *Swing*, esp. ch. 2, 20–38; Mark Katz, *Capturing Sound: How Technology Has Changed Music* (Berkeley: University of California Press, 2004), 80–93; Leadbelly quoted in Benjamin Filene, *Romancing the Folk: Public Memory and American Roots Music* (Chapel Hill: University of North Carolina Press, 2000), 721.

32. Doron K. Antrim, "Radio Rescues the Musical Amateur," *Rotarian*, January 1938, 23–24; J. B. Stetson, "Local Radio Stations Aid Teachers," *Musician*, October 1932, 15; Joseph E. Maddy, "Bandmastering by Radio," *School Life*, September 1931, 8–9; "50 Chickens for a Piano," *School Life*, April 1933, 145, 152; "Amateur Musicians Coming to the Front," *Musician*, May 1933, 6; Charles W. Ferguson, "Music Is My Hobby," *Reader's Digest*, February 1936, 105–108.

33. John Dickinson, "Music Recreation and Radio," *Etude*, September 1934, 517, 545 (quotation); "Wisconsin Tests Value of Radio in the Classroom: A Report by the Research Committee," *School Life*, February 1931, 104–105; Shelly Cooper, "Marguerite V. Hood and Music Education Radio Broadcasts in Rural Montana (1937–39)," *Journal of Research in Music Education* 53 (Winter 2005): 1–13; Walter Damrosch, "Music and the Radio," *Annals of the American Academy of Political and Social Science* 177 (January 1935): 91–93.

34. Mary L. Tenery, "What Radio Offers Music Teachers," *Musician*, February 1937, 26–27 (quotation on 26).

35. Quotation from "How Singers for Radio Are Made in Studio," *Popular Mechanics*, January 1935, 70; Frederick Warren, "A Special Technic for Singing in Broadcast Studios," *Musician*, December 1932, 13; James P. Kraft, *Stage to Studio: Musicians and the Sound Revolution, 1890–1950* (Baltimore, MD: Johns Hopkins University Press, 1996), 59–87; Susan Schmidt Horning, *Chasing Sound: Technology, Culture, and the Art of Studio Recording from Edison to the LP* (Baltimore, MD: Johns Hopkins University Press, 2013), 32–55.

36. Leopold Stokowski, "New Vistas in Radio," *Atlantic Monthly*, January 1935, 2, 6.

37. R. Raven-Hart, "Composing for Radio," *Musical Quarterly* 16 (January 1930): 133–139; R. Raven-Hart, "Radio and a New Theory of Tone-Quality," *Musical Quarterly* 17 (July 1931): 380–388; quotation from "Radio Music of the Future," *Popular Mechanics*, November 1937, 692.

38. Lee Pattison to Harry Hopkins, text of speech, 1935, in Lee Pattison Papers, Box 1, #23, Claremont Graduate School, Claremont, CA; Nikolai Sokoloff, *The*

Federal Music Project (Washington, DC: U.S. Government Printing Office, 1936), frontispiece. For an overview of the FMP's activities, see Kenneth J. Bindas, *All of This Music Belongs to the Nation: The WPA's Federal Music Project and American Society, 1935–1939* (Knoxville: University of Tennessee Press, 1995).

39. Gilbert Green to Harle Jarvis, "Narrative Report: San Mateo, California, February, 1936," WPA files, 211.1 Record Group 69, Box 13, 1936 California Narrative Reports, National Archives; Bindas, *All of This Music*, 35–46, 105–116.

40. Nikolai Sokoloff, "America's Vast New Musical Awakening," *Etude*, April 1937, 221; Bindas, *All of This Music*, 17–34, 47–70; Grofé quotation from Frances Boardman, "American Music Culture Dawn Is Seen," *Universal Weekly* (St. Paul, Minnesota), July 31, 1938, WPA files 211.1, Record Group 69, Box 66, National Archives.

41. Kenneth J. Bindas, "A Society without Soul: The Fear of Modernism in the 1937 Opera *The Romance of Robot*," *Journal of American Culture* 17 (Spring 1994): 71–77.

42. "Electrical Music," *Popular Mechanics*, January 1934, 42; "Music of the Future Now a Reality," *Popular Mechanics*, January 1936, 20–22; "Radio Music Turns to Color in Your Home," *Popular Mechanics*, October 1931, 534–535.

43. C. E. Seashore, "Psychology in Music: The Role of the Experimental Psychologist in the Science and Art of Music," *Musical Quarterly* 16 (April 1930): 229–237; "Jazz Enters the Laboratory for Psychological Study," *Science News*, July 1, 1939, 12–13; Michael Erdelyi, "The Relation between 'Radio Plugs' and Sheet Sales of Popular Music," *Journal of Applied Psychology* 24 (December 1940): 702.

44. Interview with Maya Angelou, conducted by Blackside, Inc., on April 11, 1992, for *The Great Depression*, Washington University Libraries, Film and Media Archive, Henry Hampton Collection; Edward Podolsky, "Some Unusual Effects of Music," *Musician*, September 1939, 155; Earl Dardes, "Music! How Its Strains Inspire Us," *Musician*, September 1936, 136–137.

45. Bill C. Malone, *Don't Get Above Your Raisin': Country Music and the Southern Working Class* (Urbana: University of Illinois Press, 2002), 24, 8; Katherine Meizel, "A Singing Citizenry: Popular Music and Civil Religion in America," *Journal of the Scientific Study of Religion* 45 (December 2006): 497–503.

46. Gordon Lynch, "The Role of Popular Music in the Construction of Alternative Spiritual Identities and Ideologies," *Journal for the Scientific Study of Religion* 45 (December 2006): 481–488; Eduardo de la Fuente, "Prophet and Priest, Ascetic and Mystic: Towards a Cultural Sociology of the Twentieth Century Composer," in *Philosophical and Cultural Theories of Music*, ed. Eduardo de la Fuente and Peter Murphy (Boston: Brill, 2010), 102.

EPILOGUE. NEW DIRECTIONS AND CHALLENGES

1. "Nothing Left: The Long, Slow Surrender of American Liberals," *Harper's Magazine*, March 2014, 28–35.

2. Kenneth J. Bindas, "Neon in the Desert: Robert Sherwood's *The Petrified Forest* (1936) and the Return of Hope," *Journal of Popular Film and Television* 27 (Spring 1999): 21–31.

3. See, for example, Roland Marchand, *Advertising the American Dream: Making Way for Modernity, 1920–1940* (Berkeley: University of California Press, 1985); Katherine J. Parkin, *Food Is Love: Advertising and Gender Roles in Modern America* (Philadelphia: University of Pennsylvania Press, 2006); Charles McGovern, *Sold American: Consumption and Citizenship, 1890–1945* (Chapel Hill: University of North Carolina Press, 2006); Gary S. Cross and Robert N. Proctor, *Packaged Pleasures: How Technology and Marketing Revolutionized Desire* (Chicago: University of Chicago Press, 2014); Cross, *All-Consuming Century*; William L. Bird, Jr., *"Better Living": Advertising, Media, and the New Vocabulary of Business Leadership, 1935–1955* (Evanston, IL: Northwestern University Press, 1999); Cynthia B. Meyers, *A Word from Our Sponsor: Admen, Advertising, and the Golden Age of Radio* (New York: Fordham University Press, 2014); Lenthall, *Radio's America*; Susan Smulyan, *Selling Radio: The Commercialization of American Broadcasting, 1920–1934* (Washington, DC: Smithsonian Institution Press, 1994); David Goodman, *Radio's Civic Ambition: American Broadcasting and Democracy in the 1930s* (New York: Oxford University Press, 2011); Andrew Bergman, *We're in the Money: Depression America and Its Films* (New York: New York University Press, 1971); Sarah Berry, *Screen Style: Fashion and Femininity in 1930s Hollywood* (Minneapolis: University of Minnesota Press, 2000); Currell, *March of Spare Time*; Sharon Ann Musher, *Democratic Art: The New Deal's Influence on American Culture* (Chicago: University of Chicago Press, 2015).

4. Daniel Bell, *The Cultural Contradiction of Capitalism* (New York: Basic Books, 1976), 20.

5. Wendy L. Wall, *Inventing the "American Way": The Politics of Consensus from the New Deal to the Civil Rights Movement* (New York: Oxford University Press, 2008), 5, 34–35.

6. Genter, *Late Modernism*, 7.

7. Richard M. Abrams, *America Transformed: Sixty Years of Revolutionary Change, 1941–2001* (New York: Cambridge University Press, 2006), ix.

8. Ibid., xv.

9. Matthew D. Tribbe, *No Requiem for the Space Age: The Apollo Moon Landings and American Culture* (New York: Oxford University Press, 2014), 160.

10. Daniel T. Rodgers, *Age of Fracture* (Cambridge, MA: Harvard University Press, 2011), 7, 18.

11. Tom Wolfe, "The Me Decade and the Third Great Awakening," in *Mauve Gloves & Madmen, Clutter & Vine* (New York: Farrar, Straus & Giroux, 1976), 126–170 (quotations on 163, 135).

12. Jefferson Cowie, *Stayin' Alive: The 1970s and the Last Days of the Working Class* (New York: New Press, 2012), 18. See also Jefferson Cowie, "We Can't Go Home Again: Why the New Deal Won't Be Renewed," *New Labor Forum* 20 (Winter 2011): 10–14, where he suggests that "had it not been for the Great Depression, it is probable that American liberalism would not have taken its modern form; we would have been left with the chaotic brilliance of progressivism without cohesive liberal creed" (14).

13. Rodgers, *Age of Fracture*, 98. For an excellent survey of this sea change, see Michael Schaller, *Right Turn: American Life in the Reagan-Bush Era, 1980–1992* (New York: Oxford University Press, 2007).

14. Johnstone, *Religion in Society*, 1–20, 35–52.

BIBLIOGRAPHY

Abrams, Richard M. *America Transformed: Sixty Years of Revolutionary Change, 1941–2001*. New York: Cambridge University Press, 2006.

Adas, Michael. *Dominance by Design: Technological Imperatives and America's Civilizing Mission*. Cambridge, MA: Belknap Press of Harvard University Press, 2006.

Administrative and Program Operation of the National Youth Administration, June 26, 1935–January 1, 1937. Washington, DC: US Government Printing Office, 1937.

"AHR Roundtable: Historians and the Question of 'Modernity.'" *American Historical Review* 116 (June 2011): 631–751.

Akin, William E. *Technocracy and the American Dream: The Technocrat Movement, 1900–1941*. Berkeley: University of California Press, 1977.

Allen, Glen Scott. *Master Mechanics and Wicked Wizards: Images of the American Scientist as Hero and Villain from Colonial Times to the Present*. Amherst: University of Massachusetts Press, 2009.

Almanac for Thirty-Niners: Compiled by the Workers of the Federal Writers' Project of the Works Progress Administration in the City of San Francisco, with Illustrations by the WPA Art Project in the City of San Francisco. San Francisco: James Ladd Delkin, 1938.

Alter, Dinsmore. "The Century of Progress Meeting of the American Association for the Advancement of Science." *Scientific Monthly*, July 1933, 87–91.

"Amateur Musicians Coming to the Front." *Musician*, May 1933, 6.

Annual Report of the Civilian Conservation Corps: Fiscal Year Ended June 30, 1938. Washington, DC: Government Printing Office, 1938.

Annual Report of the Director of the Civilian Conservation Corps, Fiscal Year Ended June 30, 1941. Washington, DC: Government Printing Office, 1941.

"Another Challenge to Modernism." *Literary Digest*, September 18, 1934, 26.

Antrim, Doron K. "How to Write a Song Hit." *American Mercury*, May 1940, 49–53.

———. "Radio Rescues the Musical Amateur." *Rotarian*, January 1938, 23–24.

Aubrey, Edwin Ewart. "What Is Modernism." *Journal of Religion* 15 (October 1935): 426–447.

Babson, Roger W. *How to Increase Church Attendance*. New York: Fleming H. Revell, 1936.

———. *A Revival Is Coming*. New York: Fleming H. Revell, 1936.

Baker, Helen Cody. "Century of Progress in Welfare." *Survey*, July 1933, 251–252.

Baker, Richard, Sr. "The Forest Camps of America." *Contemporary Review*, June 1935, 715–720.

Bakhtin, Mikhail. *The Dialogic Imagination: Four Essays*. Austin: University of Texas Press, 1992.

———. *Speech Genres and Other Late Essays*. Austin: University of Texas Press, 1986.

Beard, Charles, ed. *A Century of Progress*. Chicago: Harper & Brothers, 1933.

Bell, Daniel. *The Cultural Contradiction of Capitalism*. New York: Basic Books, 1976.

Bell, J. Franklin. "Applied Science and Industry at a Century of Progress Exposition." *Scientific Monthly*, March 1933, 281–283.

Bellah, Robert. "Civil Religion in America." *Daedalus* 96 (Winter 1967): 1–21.

Benite, Zvi Ben-Dor. "Modernity: The Sphinx and the Historian." *American Historical Review* 116, no. 3 (June 2011): 638–652.

Bergman, Andrew. *We're in the Money: Depression America and Its Films*. New York: New York University Press, 1971.

Bergman, Dorothy. "Jazz, the Expression of the Age." *Musician*, September 1930, 12.

Berle, Adolph, and Gardiner Means. *The Modern Corporation and Private Property*. New York: Macmillan, 1932.

Berman, Marshall. *All That Is Solid Melts into Air: The Experience of Modernity*. London: Verso, 1982.

Berry, Sarah. *Screen Style: Fashion and Femininity in 1930s Hollywood*. Minneapolis: University of Minnesota Press, 2000.

Bhambra, Gurminder K. "Historical Sociology, Modernity, and Postcolonial Critique." *American Historical Review* 116, no. 3 (June 2011): 653–662.

Billington, Monroe, and Cal Clark. "Clergy Reaction to the New Deal: A Comparative Study." *Historian* 48 (August 1986): 509–524.

Bindas, Kenneth J. *All of This Music Belongs to the Nation: The WPA's Federal Music Project and American Society, 1935–1939*. Knoxville: University of Tennessee Press, 1995.

———, ed. *The Civilian Conservation Corps and the Construction of the Virginia Kendall Reserve, 1933–1939*. Kent, OH: Kent State University Press, 2013.

———. "Neon in the Desert: Robert Sherwood's *The Petrified Forest* (1936) and the Return of Hope." *Journal of Popular Film and Television* 27 (Spring 1999): 21–31.

———. *Remembering the Great Depression in the Rural South*. Gainesville: University Press of Florida, 2007.

———. "A Society without Soul: The Fear of Modernism in the 1937 Opera *The Romance of Robot*." *Journal of American Culture* 17 (Spring 1994): 71–77.

———. *Swing, That Modern Sound: The Cultural Context of Swing Music in America, 1935–1947*. Jackson: University Press of Mississippi, 2001.

———. "Western Mystic: Bob Nolan and His Songs." *Western Historical Quarterly* 18 (October 1986): 439–456.

Bird, William L., Jr. *"Better Living": Advertising, Media, and the New Vocabulary of Business Leadership, 1935–1955*. Evanston, IL: Northwestern University Press, 1999.

Blackwelder, Julia Kirk. *Now Hiring: The Feminization of Work in the United States, 1900–1995*. College Station: Texas A&M University Press, 1997.

Blake, Lillie Devereuz. *A Woman's Place Today*. New York: William Lowell, 1933.

Boisseau, T. J., and Abigail M. Markwyn. "World's Fairs in Feminist Historical Perspective." In *Gendering the Fair: Histories of Women and Gender at World's Fairs*, edited by T. J. Boisseau and Abigail M. Markwyn. Urbana: University of Illinois Press, 2010. 1–16.

Bokovoy, Matthew F. *The San Diego World's Fairs and Southwestern Memory, 1880–1940*. Albuquerque: University of New Mexico Press, 2005.

Bonomi, Patricia U. *Under the Cope of Heaven: Religion, Society, and Politics in Colonial America*. Rev. ed. New York: Oxford University Press, 2003.

Bosley, Harold. "Is Liberal Protestantism a Religion?" *Christian Century*, June 1936, 898–900.

Boym, Svetlana. *The Future of Nostalgia*. New York: Basic Books, 2001.

Brandimarte, Cynthia, with Angela Reed. *Texas State Parks and the CCC: The Legacy of the Civilian Conservation Corps*. College Station: Texas A&M University Press, 2013.

Brinkley, Alan. *The End of Reform*. New York: Vintage, 1995.

Brooks, Cleanth, Jr. "The Christianity of Modernism." *American Review*, February 1936, 435–446.

Brown, Arthur, Jr. "The Architectural Planning of the Exposition." *Architect and Engineer* 139 (February 1939): 20.

Buckley, Cheryl. "Made in Patriarchy: Toward a Feminist Analysis of Women and Design." *Design Issues* 3 (Autumn 1986): 3–14.

Burnham, John C., ed. *Science in America: Historical Selections*. New York: Holt, Rinehart & Winston, 1971.

Burris-Meyer, Elizabeth. *Decorating Livable Homes*. New York: Prentice Hall, 1938.

Burrows, Thelma M. *Successful Home Furnishing*. Peoria, IL: Manual Arts, 1938.

Busch, Janet. "Cooking Competition: Technology on the Domestic Market in the 1930s." *Technology and Culture* 24 (April 1983): 222–245.

California Pacific International Exposition—Official Guide, Souvenir Program and Picture Book. San Diego: G. F. Wolcott, 1935.

Calloway, Cab. *The New Cab Calloway's Cat-ologue*. New York: Calloway, 1938.

Campbell, LeRoy B. "Hidden Meanings in Modern Music." *Musician*, June 1937, 105.

———. "Music Study and Modern Youth." *Musician*, July 1939, 123.

Carey, Eben J. *Medical Science Exhibits: A Century of Progress*. Chicago: Century of Progress, 1936.

Carlson, Avis D. "Cowboy Ballads at Our Own Fireside: They Are as Wholly and Originally American as Cornbread." *Better Homes and Gardens*, November 1931, 23.

Carpenter, Joel A. "Fundamentalist Institutions and the Rise of Evangelical Protestantism, 1929–1942." *Church History*, March 1980, 62–75.

Carpenter, Patricia F., and Paul Totah, eds. *The San Francisco Fair: Treasure Island, 1939–1940*. San Francisco: Scottwall, 1989.

Castle, Marian. "Custom-Built Careers." *Independent Woman*, June 1935, 189, 202–204.

The CCC at Work: A Story of 2,500,000 Young Men. Washington, DC: FSA/CCC, 1941.

CCC in Ohio. Columbus, OH: Federal Writers' Project Publication, 1938.

"The Century of Progress Anticipates Homes of Tomorrow." *American Home*, June 1933, 18–19.

"The Century of Progress Exposition." *Science*, May 19, 1933, 464–465.

"Century of Progress in Medicine." *Hygenia*, June 1933, 488–491.

A Century of Progress: Report of the President to the Board of Trustees, March 14, 1936. Chicago: Century of Progress, 1936.

Chakrabarty, Dipesh. "The Muddle of Modernity." *American Historical Review* 116, no. 3 (June 2011): 663–675.

Chappell, David L. *A Stone of Hope: Prophetic Religion and the Death of Jim Crow*. Chapel Hill: University of North Carolina Press, 2004.

Charmley, Beulah. "The American Cowboy Song: An Introduction to the Popular English and Scottish Ballad." *Education*, October 1935, 119–122.

Chase, Malcolm, and Christopher Shaw, eds. *The Imagined Past: History and Nostalgia*. Manchester: Manchester University Press, 1989.

Chase, Stuart. *Men and Machines*. New York: Macmillan, 1929.

———. *A New Deal*. New York: Macmillan, 1932.

———. *Technocracy: An Interpretation*. New York: John Day, 1933.

Chertoff, Gerson B. *Development of Interest in Social Problems, Evaluation Studies Report #2*. Columbus: National Youth Administration in Ohio, 1937.

Chew, Arthur P. *Science Serving Agriculture*. Washington, DC: US Government Printing Office, 1936.

Clewell, Tammy. *Mourning, Modernism, Postmodernism*. New York: Palgrave Macmillan, 2009.

Cogdell, Christina. *Eugenic Design: Streamlining America in the 1930s*. Philadelphia: University of Pennsylvania Press, 2004.

Cohen, Lizbeth. *Making a New Deal: Industrial Workers in Chicago, 1919–1939*. New York: Cambridge University Press, 1990.

Cohen, Stanley. *The Tree Army: A Pictorial History of the Civilian Conservation Corps, 1933–1942*. Missoula, MT: Pictorial Histories, 1980.

Cole, Olen. *The African American Experience in the Civilian Conservation Corps*. Tallahassee: University Press of Florida, 1999.

Collins, Margaret. "Careers, Limited." *Scribner's*, October 1937, 45.

Comentale, Edward. "'Thought I Had Your Heart Forever' or the Modernity of Early Country Music." *Journal of Popular Music Studies* 20 (September 2008): 211–239.

Comstock, Sarah. "Marriage—or Career." *Good Housekeeping*, June 1932, 32–33, 156.

Cooke, Edward S., Jr. "Women Furniture Makers: From Decorative Designers to Studio Makers." In Kirkham, *Women Designers*, 291–304.

Cooper, Shelly. "Marguerite V. Hood and Music Education Radio Broadcasts in Rural Montana (1937–39)." *Journal of Research in Music Education* 53 (Winter 2005): 1–13.

Corbett, Mary Jane. "Youth in Relief Families: A Social Survey." MA thesis, Ohio State University, 1936.

Corbett, Mary Jane, and Donald J. McNassor. *The Morale of Youth Workers: A Report on the Development of Morale of 1000 Youth Employed on Work Projects of the National Youth Administration in Ohio*, Division of Research in Program Evaluation, Report #3, January 15, 1938. Columbus, OH: National Youth Administration, 1938.

Cowie, Jefferson. *Stayin' Alive: The 1970s and the Last Days of the Working Class*. New York: New Press, 2012.

———. "We Can't Go Home Again: Why the New Deal Won't Be Renewed." *New Labor Forum* 20 (Winter 2011): 10–14.

Cowley, Malcolm. *The Dream of the Golden Mountains*. New York: Viking, 1980.

Croneis, Carey. "The Earth Sciences at a Century of Progress." *Scientific Monthly*, April 1933, 380–384.

Cross, Gary. *An All-Consuming Century: Why Commercialism Won in Modern America*. New York: Columbia University Press, 2000.

Cross, Gary S., and Robert N. Proctor. *Packaged Pleasures: How Technology and Marketing Revolutionized Desire*. Chicago: University of Chicago Press, 2014.

Crunden, Robert M. *American Salons: Encounters with European Modernism, 1885–1917*. New York: Oxford University Press, 1993.

Currell, Susan. *The March of Spare Time: The Problem and Promise of Leisure in the Great Depression*. Philadelphia: University of Pennsylvania Press, 2005.

Cutler, Phoebe. *The Public Landscape of the New Deal*. New Haven, CT: Yale University Press, 1985.

Daggett, Helen M. *Interior Decorating: Leisure League Little Book #16*. New York: Leisure League of America, 1935.

Damrosch, Walter. "Music and the Radio." *Annals of the American Academy of Political and Social Science* 177 (January 1935): 91–93.

Dardes, Earl. "Music! How Its Strains Inspire Us." *Musician*, September 1936, 136–137.

Davenport, Walter. "Thy Woods and Templed Hills." *Collier's*, September 9, 1933, 10–12.

"Decorative Arts in San Francisco." *American Magazine of Art*, June 1936, 395–398.

de la Fuente, Eduardo. "Prophet and Priest, Ascetic and Mystic: Towards a Cultural Sociology of the Twentieth Century Composer." In *Philosophical and Cultural Theories of Music*, edited by Eduardo de la Fuente and Peter Murphy. Boston: Brill, 2010. 87–106.

Delano, Martha. "Making Space for Modern Living." *Home and Garden*, May 1934, 50.

Denning, Michael. *The Cultural Front: The Laboring of American Culture in the Twentieth Century*. New York: Verso, 1996.

"Department of Labor Exhibit at Texas Centennial Exposition." *Monthly Labor Review* 43 (1936): 1123.

Des Jardins, Julie. *The Madame Curie Complex: The Hidden History of Women in Science*. New York: Feminist Press, 2010.

Dewey, John. *Art as Experience*. New York: Milton, Balch, 1934.

———. "Authority and Resistance to Social Change." *School and Society*, October 10, 1936, 457–466.

———. *A Common Faith*. New Haven, CT: Yale University Press, 1934.

———. "Education and New Social Ideals." Radio broadcast over WEVD, January 14, 1936, published in *Vital Speeches*, February 24, 1936, 327–328.

———. "Education, the Foundation for Social Organization." *Journal of the National Education Association* 25 (December 1936): 274.

———. "A God of the God." *Christian Century*, February 8, 1933, 12193–12196.

———. "Intelligence and Power." *New Republic*, April 25, 1934, 306–307.

———. *Liberalism and Social Action*. New York: Pedigree, 1935.

———. "The Liberation of Modern Religion." *Yale Review* 23 (June 1934): 751–770.

Dickerson, Reed. "Hot Music: Rediscovering Jazz." *Harper's Monthly*, April 1936, 567–574.

Dickinson, John. "Music Recreation and Radio." *Etude*, September 1934, 517.

Donohue, Kathleen G. *Freedom from Want: American Liberalism and the Idea of the Consumer*. Baltimore, MD: Johns Hopkins University Press, 2004.

Douglas, Lloyd Cassel. "Hearts in Tune." In *Music and Religion*, edited by Stanley Armstrong Hunter. New York: Abingdon, 1930.

Downs, Jennifer M. "'The New Modern Feeling': A Catalogue of the Collection." *Art Institute of Chicago Museum Studies* 27 (2001): 18–45, 105–108.

Draper, Dorothy. *Decorating Is Fun: How to Be Your Own Decorator*. New York: Doubleday, Doran, 1939.

"Dr. Fosdick Shifts the Emphasis." *Christian Century*, November 20, 1935, 1480–1482.

Duranti, Marco. "Utopia, Nostalgia and World War at the 1939–40 New York World's Fair." *Journal of Communication History* 41 (2006): 663–683.

Exhibition Techniques: A Summary of Exhibition Practice Based on Surveys Conducted at New York and San Francisco World's Fairs of 1939. New York: New York Museum of Science and Industry, 1940.

Eysteinsson, Ástráedhur. *The Concept of Modernism*. Ithaca, NY: Cornell University Press, 1990.

Fales, Winnifred. *What's New in Home Decorating*. New York: Dodd, Mead, 1936.

Feigenbutz, Elizabeth Louise. "Service Rating in the National Youth Administration of Ohio." MA thesis, Ohio State University, 1941.

Filene, Benjamin. *Romancing the Folk: Public Memory and American Roots Music*. Chapel Hill: University of North Carolina Press, 2000.

Filene, Edward. *Successful Living in This Machine Age*. New York: Simon & Schuster, 1931.

Filene, Peter Gabriel. *Him/Her/Self: Sex Roles in Modern America*. Baltimore, MD: Johns Hopkins University Press, 1986.

Final Report of the National Youth Administration, Fiscal Years 1936–1943. Washington, DC: US Government Printing Office, 1944.

Final Report on the WPA Program, 1935–1943. Washington, DC: US Government Printing Office, 1946.

Ford, Henry. "Machinery, the New Messiah." *Forum*, March 1928, 359–364.

"For Devotees of Modern." *House and Garden*, November 1940, 43.

Forman, Paul. "The Primacy of Science in Modernity, or Technology in Postmodernity, and the Ideology in the History of Technology." *History and Technology* 23 (May/June 2007): 1–152.

Forty, Adrian. *Objects of Desire*. New York: Pantheon, 1986.

Fosdick, Harry Emerson. "Beyond Modernism: A Sermon." *Christian Century*, December 4, 1935, 1549–1552.

Fraiman, Susan. "Bad Girls of Good Housekeeping: Dominique Browning and Martha Stewart." *American Literary History* 23 (2011): 263.

Frankl, Paul T. *New Dimensions: The Decorative Arts Today in Words and Pictures*. New York: Brewer & Warren, 1928.

Friedman, Alice T. *Women and the Making of the Modern Home: A Social and Architectural History*. New York: Harry N. Abrams, 1998.

Friedman, Susan Stanford. "Definitional Excursions: The Meanings of *Modern/Modernity/Modernism*," *Modernism/modernity* 8, no. 3 (2001): 493–513.

Frith, Simon. *Performing Rites: On the Value of Popular Music*. Cambridge, MA: Harvard University Press, 1996.

G. A. B. "Science at the Century of Progress Exposition in 1934." *Scientific Monthly*, November 1934, 475–478.

Ganz, Cheryl R. *The 1933 Chicago World's Fair: A Century of Progress*. Urbana: University of Illinois Press, 2008.

Gay, Peter. *Modernism: The Lure of Heresy from Baudelaire to Beckett and Beyond*. New York: Norton, 2008.

Gelernter, David. *1939: The Lost World of the Fair*. New York: Free Press, 1995.

Genter, Robert. *Late Modernism: Art, Culture, and Politics in Cold War America*. Philadelphia: University of Pennsylvania Press, 2010.

George-Warren, Holly. *Public Cowboy No. 1: The Life and Times of Gene Autry*. New York: Oxford University Press, 2007.

Gilbert, Dan. *Our Retreat from Modernism*. San Diego: Danielle, 1939.

Gilkey, Gordon W. "The Ground Work, Plates 3, 4, 5 & 6," in *Etchings: New York World's Fair—"Building the World of Tomorrow,"* etchings and text by Gordon W. Gilkey. New York: Charles Scribner's Sons, 1939.

"Glass and Light in the Modern House." *Good Housekeeping*, May 1939, 151–158.

Glazer, Penina Migdal, and Miriam Slater. *Unequal Colleagues: The Entrance of Women into the Professions, 1890–1940*. New Brunswick, NJ: Rutgers University Press, 1987.

Glover, Katherine (conversation with John Dewey). "Tomorrow May Be Too Late." *Good Housekeeping*, March 1934, 20–21, 222–225.

Gluck, Carol. "The End of Elsewhere: Writing Modernity Now." *American Historical Review* 116, no. 3 (June 2011): 676–687.

Good, Albert H. *Park and Recreation Structures*. New York: Princeton Architectural Press, 1999; a reprint of the 1938 edition published by the US Department of the Interior, National Park Service.

Goodman, David. "Distracted Listening: On Not Making Sound Choices in the 1930s." In *Sound in the Age of Mechanical Reproduction*, edited by David Suisman and Susan Strasser. Philadelphia: University of Pennsylvania Press, 2012. 15–46.

———. *Radio's Civic Ambition: American Broadcasting and Democracy in the 1930s*. New York: Oxford University Press, 2011.

"Great Musical Revival Result of the Force of Radio." *Etude*, February 1, 1938, 72.

Greenan, John T. *American Civilization Today: A Summary of Recent Social Trends*. New York: McGraw-Hill, 1934.

Greene, Alison Collis. "The End of 'The Protestant Era.'" *Church History*, September 2011, 600–610.

Grieve, Victoria. *The Federal Art Project and the Creation of Middlebrow Culture*. Urbana: University of Illinois Press, 2009.

Guinan, Alastair. "Modern Mass Music." *Commonweal*, January 26, 1934, 353–354.

Gutman, Marta. "Race, Place, and Play: Robert Moses and the WPA Swimming Pools in New York City." *Journal of the Society of Architectural Historians* 67 (December 2008): 532–553.

Halbwach, Maurice. *On Collective Memory*. Edited and translated by Lewis A. Coser. Chicago: University of Chicago Press, 1992.

Hall, Stuart. "Cultural Studies: Two Paradigms." In *Media, Culture, and Society: A Critical Reader*, edited by Richard Collins et al. London: Sage, 1986. 33–48.

Hamill, Virginia. "Modern and Modernized." *Woman's Home Companion*, November 1938, 68–69.

Handy, Robert T. "The American Religious Depression, 1925–1935." In *Religion in American History*, edited by Jon Butler and Harry S. Stout. New York: Oxford University Press, 1998. 371–383.

Hankins, Barry. *The Second Great Awakening and the Transcendentalists*. Westport, CT: Greenwood, 2004.

Hanks, David A., and Anne Hoy. *American Streamlined Design: The World of Tomorrow*. Paris: Flammarion/The Liliane and David M. Stewart Program for Modern Design, The Lake St. Louis Historical Society, 2005.

Hansen, Per H. "Networks, Narratives and New Markets: The Rise and Decline of Danish Modern Furniture Design, 1930–1970." *Business History Review* 80 (Autumn 2006): 449–483.

Hanson, Howard. "Machine Music a Challenge to the Profession." *Musician*, March 1, 1930, 10.

Harris, Roy. "American Music Enters a New Phase." *Scribner's*, October 1934, 218–221.

Harvey, Holman. "It's Swing." *Delineator*, November 1936, 10–11, 48–50.

Hawkins, J. Harold. "Trends in House Design at a Century of Progress." *Ladies' Home Journal*, June 1933, 26–29.

Haynes, Carolyn. "Women and Protestantism in Nineteenth-Century America." In *Perspectives on American Religion and Culture*, edited by Peter W. Williams. Malden, MA: Blackwell, 1999. 300–318.

Hayward, Percy R. *The Dream Power of Youth: Young People Today and the Religion of Jesus*. New York: Harper & Brothers, 1930.

Heineman, Kenneth J. *A Catholic New Deal: Religion and Reform in Depression Pittsburgh*. University Park: Pennsylvania State University Press, 1999.

Hobson, Wilder. "Swing High." *Vogue*, March 15, 1936, 90–91, 112, 114.

Holland, Kenneth, and Frank Ernest Hill. *Youth in the CCC*. New York: Arno, 1942, 1974.

Hollinger, David A. "The Knower and the Artificer." *American Quarterly* 39, no. 1 (Spring 1987): 37–55.

Hooks, Janet M. *Women's Occupations through Seven Decades*. Washington, DC: US Government Printing Office, 1947.

Hoover, Herbert. *American Individualism*. New York: Doubleday, Page, 1922.

Hopkins, June. "The American Way to Welfare: Harry Hopkins and New Deal Work Relief." In *The New Deal and Public Policy*, edited by Byron W. Daynes, William D. Pederson, and Michael P. Riccards. New York: St. Martin's, 1998. 215–244.

Horning, Susan Schmidt. *Chasing Sound: Technology, Culture, and the Art of Studio Recording from Edison to the LP*. Baltimore, MD: Johns Hopkins University Press, 2013.

Howard, Ella, and Eric Setliff. "'In a Man's World': Women Industrial Designers." In Kirkham, *Women Designers*, 269–289.

"How Singers for Radio Are Made in Studio." *Popular Mechanics*, January 1935, 70.

Hull, Thomas G. "A Century of Progress in Medicine." *Hygenia*, December 1933, 1109–1112, 1144–1146.

Hunter, James Davison. *American Evangelicalism: Conservative Religion and the Problem of Modernity*. New Brunswick, NJ: Rutgers University Press, 1983.

Hunter, Stanley Armstrong. *Temple of Religion and the Tower of Peace at the 1939 Golden Gate International Exposition*. San Francisco: Temple of Religion and Tower of Peace, 1940.

Hutcheon, Linda. "Irony, Nostalgia, and the Postmodern." In *Methods for the Study of Literature as Cultural Memory*, edited by Raymond Vervliet and Annemarie Estor. Amsterdam: Rodopi, 2000. 189–207.

Hutchison, William R. *The Modernist Impulse in American Protestantism*. Cambridge, MA: Harvard University Press, 1976.

Huyssen, Andreas. *After the Great Divide: Modernism, Mass Culture, and Postmodernism.* Bloomington: Indiana University Press, 1986.

"I Refused a Career." *Saturday Evening Post*, September 1931, 14–15, 73.

Jackson, Alice, and Bettina Jackson. *The Study of Interior Decoration.* New York: Doubleday, Doran, 1934.

Jackson, Brinkerhoff. "Modernism in Architecture." *Sewanee Review* 44 (April–June 1936): 179–187.

Jackson, Jerma A. *Singing in My Soul: Black Gospel Music in a Secular Age.* Chapel Hill: University of North Carolina Press, 2004.

Jadock, Darrell. "Introduction I: The Modernist Crisis." In *Catholicism Contending with Modernity: Roman Catholic Modernism and Anti-Modernism in Historical Context*, edited by Darrell Jadock. New York: Cambridge University Press, 2000. 1–19.

Jameson, Fredric. *Postmodernism, or, The Cultural Logic of Late Capitalism.* Durham, NC: Duke University Press, 1991.

"Jazz Enters the Laboratory for Psychological Study." *Science News*, July 1, 1939, 12–13.

"Jazz versus Swing: Despite Altercation It's Still Syncopation." *Metronome*, April 1944, 23.

Jochnowitz, Eve. "Feasting on the Future: Foods of the World of Tomorrow at the New York World's Fair of 1939–40." *Performance Research* 4 (Spring 1999): 110–120.

Johnson, J. Stewart. *American Modern, 1925–1940.* New York: Harry N. Abrams, 2000.

Johnson, Palmer O., and Oswald L. Harvey. *The National Youth Administration.* Washington, DC: US Government Printing Office, 1938.

Johnston, Alva. "Tenor on Horseback." *Saturday Evening Post*, September 1939, 18–19, 74–76.

Johnstone, Ronald L. *Religion in Society: A Sociology of Religion.* Englewood Cliffs, NJ: Prentice Hall, 1992.

Jolley, Harley E. *"That Magnificent Army of Youth and Peace": The Civilian Conservation Corps in North Carolina, 1933–1942.* Raleigh: Office of Archives and History, 2007.

Jones, Janna. "The Distance from Home: The Domestication of Desire in Interior Design Manuals." *Journal of Social History* 31 (Winter 1997): 307–326.

Kammen, Michael. *Mystic Chords of Memory.* New York: Vintage, 1991.

Kaplan, Wendy. "Women Designers and the Arts and Crafts Movement." In Kirkham, *Women Designers*, 85–99.

Katz, Mark. *Capturing Sound: How Technology Has Changed Music.* Berkeley: University of California Press, 2004.

Kennedy, David M. *Freedom from Fear: The American People in Depression and War, 1929–1945*. New York: Oxford University Press, 1984.

Kevles, Daniel J. "Physicists and the Revolt against Science in the 1930s." *Physics Today* 31 (February 1978): 23–30.

Kidd, Thomas S. *The Great Awakening: The Roots of Evangelical Christianity in Colonial America*. New Haven, CT: Yale University Press, 2007.

Kincheloe, Samuel C. *Research Memorandum on Religion in the Depression, Bulletin #33*. New York: Social Science Research Council, 1937.

Kirkham, Pat, ed. *Women Designers in the USA, 1900–2000*. New Haven, CT: Yale University Press, 2000.

Kirkham, Pat, and Penny Sparke. "'A Woman's Place . . . ?' Women Interior Designers, Part I: 1900–1950." In Kirkham, *Women Designers*, 305–316.

Kirkham, Pat, and Lynne Walker. "Women Designers in the USA, 1900–2000: Diversity and Difference." In Kirkham, *Women Designers*, 49–84.

Kirstein, Lincoln. "A Century of Progress, 1833–1934." *The Nation*, June 20, 1934, 695–697.

Klemm, Gustav. "The Jargon of Jazz." *Etude*, August 1934, 455–456.

Koues, Helen. *How to Be Your Own Decorator*. New York: Tudor, 1939.

Kouwenhoven, John A. *The Arts in Modern American Civilization*. New York: Norton, 1948.

Kraft, James P. *Stage to Studio: Musicians and the Sound Revolution, 1890–1950*. Baltimore, MD: Johns Hopkins University Press, 1996.

Kuznick, Peter J. "Losing the World of Tomorrow: The Battle of the Presentation of Science at the 1939 New York World's Fair." *American Quarterly* 46 (September 1994): 341–373.

Lamb, Arthur B. "A Century of Progress in Chemistry." *Science*, October 27, 1933, 371–376.

Lazarsfeld, Paul F. *Radio and the Printed Page: An Introduction to the Study of Radio and Its Role in the Communication of Ideas*. New York: Duell, Sloan & Pearce, 1940.

Lears, Jackson. *Rebirth of a Nation: The Making of Modern America, 1877–1920*. New York: Harper Collins, 2009.

Lees-Maffei, Grace. "Introduction: Professionalization as a Focus in Interior Design History." *Journal of Design History* 21, no. 1 (2008): 1–18.

Lenthall, Bruce. "Critical Reception: Public Intellectuals Decry Depression-Era Radio, Mass Culture, and Modern America." In *Radio Reader: Essays in the Cultural History of Radio*, edited by Michele Hilmes and Jason Loviglio. New York: Routledge, 2002. 41–62.

———. *Radio's America: The Great Depression and the Rise of Modern Mass Culture*. Chicago: University of Chicago Press, 2007.

Leuchtenberg, William E. *Franklin D. Roosevelt and the New Deal*. New York: Harper & Row, 1963.

Levavy, Sara Beth. "*Land of Liberty* in the World of Tomorrow." *Film History* 18 (2006): 440–458.

Levy, Beth E. *Frontier Figures: American Music and the Mythology of the American West*. Berkeley: University of California Press, 2012.

Levy, William. "The Ohio NYA Enriched Work Experience Program." PhD diss., Ohio State University, 1945.

Lindley, Betty, and Ernest K. Lindley. *A New Deal for Youth: The Story of the National Youth Administration*. New York: Viking, 1938.

Lindsay, Mary Rodgers. *Youth Gets Its Chance: A Study of NYA Workers in New York City*. New York: National Youth Administration, 1938.

Lippincott, Gordon, and Walter Margulies. "Design: Emphasis on Individuality." *Challenge*, October 1956, 23–27.

Lockwood, Sarah M. *Decoration: Past, Present and Future*. New York: Literary Guild, 1934.

Lok, Corie. "Technology as Hope." *Technology Review*, April 2005, 88.

Lorwin, Lewis L. *Youth Work Program: Problems and Policies*. Washington, DC: American Council on Education, 1941.

Lunbeck, Elizabeth. *The Americanization of Narcissism*. Cambridge, MA: Harvard University Press, 2014.

Lundberg, George A., Mirra Komarovsky, and Mary Alice McInerny. *Leisure: A Suburban Study*. New York: Columbia University Press, 1934.

Lynch, Gordon. "The Role of Popular Music in the Construction of Alternative Spiritual Identities and Ideologies." *Journal for the Scientific Study of Religion* 45 (December 2006): 481–488.

Lynd, Robert S., and Helen Merrell Lynd. *Middletown in Transition: A Study in Cultural Conflicts*. New York: Harcourt, Brace & World, 1937.

Lyotard, Jean-François. *The Postmodern Condition: A Report on Knowledge*. Minneapolis: University of Minnesota Press, 1979.

Mack, Dwayne. "'May the Work I've Done Speak for Me': African American Civilian Corps Enrollees in Montana, 1933–1934." *Western Journal of Black Studies* 27 (2003): 236–245.

Maddy, Joseph E. "Bandmastering by Radio." *School Life*, September 1931, 8–9.

Maher, Neil M. *Nature's New Deal: The Civilian Conservation Corps and the Roots of the American Environmental Movement*. New York: Oxford University Press, 2008.

Malone, Bill C. *Don't Get above Your Raisin': Country Music and the Southern Working Class*. Urbana: University of Illinois Press, 2002.

Maloney, Ruth. "Modern Moves into Colonial." *Better Homes and Gardens*, February 1940, 63.

Man and His Health: A Guide to Medical and Public Health Exhibits at the New York World's Fair 1939, Together with Information on the Conservation of Health and the Preservation of Life. New York: Expositions Publications, 1939.

A Manual for Instructors in the Civilian Conservation Corps Camps. Washington, DC: US Government Printing Office, 1935.

Marchand, Roland. *Advertising the American Dream: Making Way for Modernity, 1920–1940*. Berkeley: University of California Press, 1985.

Marston, William M. "The Cost of Careers." *Delineator*, June 1936, 7.

Martin, Brenda, and Penny Sparke, eds. *Women's Places: Architecture and Design, 1860–1960*. New York: Routledge, 2003.

Marty, Martin E. *Modern American Religion*. Vol. 2. Chicago: University of Chicago Press, 1991.

Mathews, Shailer. "Unrepentant Liberalism." *American Scholar*, July 1938, 296–308.

Mauro, James. *Twilight at the World of Tomorrow: Genius, Madness, Murder, and the 1939 World's Fair on the Brink of War*. New York: Ballantine, 2010.

May, Bridget. "Nancy Vincent McClelland (1877–1959): Professionalizing Interior Decoration in the Early Twentieth Century." *Journal of Design History* 21, no. 1 (2008): 59–74.

May, Elaine Tyler. "The Commodity Gap: Consumerism and the Modern Home." In *Consumer Society in American History: A Reader*, edited by Lawrence B. Glickman. Ithaca, NY: Cornell University Press, 1999. 298–315.

McClelland, Linda Flint. *Building the National Parks: Historic Landscape Design and Construction*. Baltimore, MD: Johns Hopkins University Press, 1998.

McCracken, Allison. "'God's Gift to Us Girls': Crooning, Gender, and the Re-Creation of American Popular Song, 1928–1933." *American Music* 17 (Winter 1999): 365–395.

———. *Real Men Don't Sing: Crooning in American Culture*. Durham, NC: Duke University Press, 2015.

McDannell, Colleen. *Picturing Faith: Photography and the Great Depression*. New Haven, CT: Yale University Press, 2004.

McElvaine, Robert S. *The Great Depression, America, 1929–1941*. New York: Random House, 1984.

McGovern, Charles. "Consumption and Citizenship in the United States, 1900–1940." In *Getting and Spending: European and American Consumer Studies in the Twen-*

tieth Century, edited by Susan Strasser, Charles McGovern, and Matthias Judt. New York: Cambridge University Press, 1998. 37–58.
———. *Sold American: Consumption and Citizenship, 1890–1945*. Chapel Hill: University of North Carolina Press, 2006.
McNeil, Peter. "Designing Women: Gender, Sexuality, and the Interior Decorator, 1890–1940." *Art History* 17 (December 1994): 631–656.
Meikle, Jeffrey L. *American Plastic: A Cultural History*. New Brunswick, NJ: Rutgers University Press, 1995.
———. "Domesticating Modernity: Ambivalence and Appropriation, 1920–40." In *Designing Modernity: The Arts of Reform and Persuasion, 1885–1945*, edited by Wendy Kaplan. New York: Thames & Hudson, 1995. 143–167.
———. *Twentieth Century Limited: Industrial Design in America, 1925–1939*. Philadelphia: Temple University Press, 1979.
Meizel, Katherine. "A Singing Citizenry: Popular Music and Civil Religion in America." *Journal of the Scientific Study of Religion* 45 (December 2006): 497–503.
Meyers, Cynthia B. *A Word from Our Sponsor: Admen, Advertising, and the Golden Age of Radio*. New York: Fordham University Press, 2014.
Mielnik, Tara Mitchell. *New Deal, New Landscape: The Civilian Conservation Corps and South Carolina's State Parks*. Columbia: University of South Carolina Press, 2011.
Miller, Donald L. *Mumford: A Life*. New York: Weidenfeld & Nicolson, 1989.
Miller, Gladys. *Decoratively Speaking: The Essentials and Principals of Interior Decoration*. New York: Doubleday, Doran, 1939.
Mintz, Steven, and Susan Kellogg. *Domestic Revolutions: A Social History of American Family Life*. New York: Free Press, 1988.
"Modern in California." *House Beautiful*, June 1940, 51.
"Modern in Miami." *Country Life and the Sportsman*, September 1938, 56–61.
"Modern Interiors: A Portfolio." *Arts and Decoration*, September 1933, 19.
"Modernistic into Modern." *Arts and Decoration*, November 1934, 10–12.
"Modern Magic in Glass." *Good Housekeeping*, September 1937, 56–57.
Mumford, Lewis. "An Appraisal of Lewis Mumford's *Technics and Civilization*." *Daedalus* 88 (Summer 1959): 527–536.
———. *Technics and Civilization*. New York: Harcourt, Brace, 1934.
Muncy, Robyn. *Creating a Female Dominion: American Reform, 1890–1935*. New York: Oxford University Press, 1991.
Muret, Charlotte. "Marriage as a Career." *Harper's*, August 1936, 249–257.
Musher, Sharon Ann. *Democratic Art: The New Deal's Influence on American Culture*. Chicago: University of Chicago Press, 2015.
"Music of the Future Now a Reality." *Popular Mechanics*, January 1936, 20–22.

Naremore, James, and Patrick Brantlinger, eds. *Modernity and Mass Culture*. Bloomington: Indiana University Press, 1991.

Neuhaus, Eugen. *The Art of Treasure Island: First-Hand Impressions of the Architecture, Sculpture, Landscape, Design, Color Effects, Mural Decorations, Illumination, and Other Artistic Aspects of the Golden Gate International Exposition of 1939*. Berkeley: University of California Press, 1939.

"The New Modernism." *Christian Century*, March 4, 1936, 351–353.

Nickles, Shelley. "'Preserving Women': Refrigerator Design as Social Process in the 1930s." *Technology and Culture* 43 (October 2002): 693–727.

Niebuhr, Reinhold. "The Church and Political Action." *Christian Century*, August 1, 1934, 992–994.

———. *The Essential Reinhold Niebuhr: Selected Essays and Addresses*. Edited by Robert McAfee Brown. New Haven, CT: Yale University Press, 1986.

———. "The Fellowship of Socialist Christians." *World Tomorrow*, June 14, 1934, 297–298.

———. "Modern Utopias." *Scribner's*, September 1936, 142–145.

———. "Our Romantic Radicals." *Christian Century*, April 10, 1935, 474–476.

———. *Reflections on the End of an Era*. New York: Charles Scribner's Sons, 1934.

———. "When Will Christians Stop Fooling Themselves." *Christian Century*, May 16, 1934, 658–660.

"Niebuhr Questions the Vitality of the Protestant Religion." *Newsweek*, April 29, 1933, 28.

Norris, Frank. "The Killer-Diller: The Life and Four-Four Time of Benny Goodman." *Saturday Evening Post*, May 7, 1938, 22.

"Nothing Left: The Long, Slow Surrender of American Liberals." *Harper's*, March 2014, 28–35.

Nye, David E. *Narratives and Spaces: Technology and the Construction of American Culture*. New York: Columbia University Press, 1997.

Obniski, Monica. "Exhibiting Modernity through the Lens of Tradition in Gilbert Rohde's Design for Living Interior." *Journal of Design History* 20, no. 3 (2007): 227–242.

Off-Campus Projects in Ohio Colleges and Universities. Columbus: National Youth Administration in Ohio, 1937.

The Official Book of the Fair. Chicago: Century of Progress, 1933.

Official Program, The New York World's Fair: The World of Tomorrow. New York: Tichnor Brothers, 1939.

Oliver, Alfred C., and Harold M. Dudley, eds. *New America: The Spirit of the Civilian Conservation Corps*. New York: Longmans, Green, 1937.

"Orgy by Air." *Atlantic Monthly*, March 1936, 384–387.

Orr, Horace E. "Liberalism and Youth." *Christian Century*, August 15, 1934, 1044–1045.

Orvell, Miles. *The Real Thing: Imitation and Authenticity in American Culture, 1880–1940*. Chapel Hill: University of North Carolina Press, 1989.

Otey, Elizabeth. "Modern Art Influence in Our Houses." *Good Housekeeping*, September 1935, 72–73.

Outka, Elizabeth. *Consuming Traditions: Modernity, Modernism, and the Commodified Authentic*. New York: Oxford University Press, 2009.

Owings, Nathaniel A. "Amusement Features of the Exposition." *Architectural Record*, May 1933, 355–362.

Oxley, Howard W. "Enrollees Become Better Citizens." *School Life*, March 1937, 215–216.

———. "Inducting CCC Enrollees into Citizenship." *School Life*, April 1938, 286.

Paige, John C. *The Civilian Conservation Corps and the National Park Service, 1933–1945: An Administrative History*, National Park Service, US Department of the Interior study. Washington, DC: Government Printing Office, 1985.

Parkin, Katherine J. *Food Is Love: Advertising and Gender Roles in Modern America*. Philadelphia: University of Pennsylvania Press, 2006.

Pasquill, Robert, Jr. *The Civilian Conservation Corps in Alabama, 1933–1942: A Great and Lasting Good*. Tuscaloosa: University of Alabama Press, 2008.

Patmore, Derek. "Interior Decoration." *Journal of the Royal Society of Arts*, January 18, 1935, 209–221.

Patterson, Ernest Minor. "Economic Adjustment in a Machine Age." *Proceedings of the American Philosophical Society* 70 (1931): 263–273.

Pells, Richard. *Modernist America: Art, Music, Movies, and the Globalization of American Culture*. New Haven, CT: Yale University Press, 2011.

———. *Radical Visions and American Dreams: Culture and Social Thought in the Depression Years*. Middletown, CT: Wesleyan Press, 1973.

Pennock, Grace L. "An Open-Minded Kitchen." *Ladies' Home Journal*, April 1938, 56.

Phillips, Sarah T. *This Land, This Nation: Conservation, Rural America, and the New Deal*. New York: Cambridge University Press, 2007.

Phillips, William. Under Secretary of State. *Address at the California-Pacific International Exposition*, May 30, 1935. Washington, DC: US Government Printing Office, 1935.

Pierce, Dianne O. "Design, Craft, and American Identity: Russel Wright's 'American Way' Project, 1940–2." Master's thesis, Cooper-Hewitt, National Design

Museum, Smithsonian Institution, and Parsons, the New School for Design, 2010.

Podolsky, Edward. "Some Unusual Effects of Music." *Musician*, September 1939, 155.

Post, Emily. *The Personality of a House: The Blue Book of Home Charm*. Rev. ed. New York: Funk & Wagnalls, 1939.

Powel, Lydia. *The Attractive Home: A Book of Good Ideas and Simple Rules for the Homemaker*. New York: Macmillan, 1939.

Pupin, Michael. *Romance of the Machine*. New York: Charles Scribner's Sons, 1930.

The Purpose and Progress of the National Youth Administration in Ohio. Columbus, OH: National Youth Administration, 1936.

Rabinovitz, Lauren. *Electric Dreamland: Amusement Parks, Movies, and American Modernity*. New York: Columbia University Press, 2012.

"Radio Music of the Future." *Popular Mechanics*, November 1937, 692.

"Radio Music Turns to Color in Your Home." *Popular Mechanics*, October 1931, 534–535.

Ragsdale, Kenneth B. *Centennial '36: The Year America Discovered Texas*. College Station: Texas A&M University Press, 1987.

Randall, John Herman. *Our Changing Civilization*. New York: Frederick Stokes, 1929.

Rasmussen, Chris. "'The People's Orchestra': Jukeboxes as the Measure of Popular Musical Taste in the 1930s and 1940s." In Suisman and Strasser, *Sound in the Age of Mechanical Reproduction*, 181–198.

Raven-Hart, R. "Composing for Radio." *Musical Quarterly* 16 (January 1930): 133–139.

———. "Radio and a New Theory of Tone-Quality." *Musical Quarterly* 17 (July 1931): 380–388.

Reed, Christopher, ed. *Not at Home: The Suppression of Domesticity in Modern Art and Architecture*. London: Thames & Hudson, 1996.

Reforestation by the CCC. Washington, DC: US Government Printing Office, 1941.

Rehnstrand, Jan. "New Home Ideas from the Century of Progress Exhibition." *School Arts* 33 (1933): 67–75.

Reid, Lewis. "The Crooning Menace." *Musician*, April 1932, 16.

Reid, Susan E. "The Khrushchev Kitchen: Domesticating the Scientific-Technological Revolution." *Journal of Contemporary History* 40 (Summer 2005): 289–316.

Reiman, Richard A. *The New Deal and American Youth*. Athens: University of Georgia Press, 1992.

Reinhardt, Richard. *Treasure Island: San Francisco's Exposition Years*. San Francisco: Scrimshaw, 1973.

Ribuffo, Leo P. *The Old Christian Right: The Protestant Far Right from the Great Depression to the Cold War*. Philadelphia: Temple University Press, 1983.

Richards, George. *Beyond Fundamentalism and Modernism: The Gospel of God*. New York: C. Scribners's Sons, 1934.

Richardson, Alexander D. "Thousands Turn to Music in the Hour of Needs." *Musician*, April 1933, 11.

Ritchie, Katherine E. "Transformation in the Modern Manner." *Ladies' Home Journal*, February 1936, 116–118.

Robertson, Cheryl. "From Cult to Profession: Domestic Women in Search of Equality." In *The Material Culture of Gender/The Gender of Material Culture*, edited by Katherine Martinez and Kenneth L. Ames. Hanover, NH: The Winterthur Museum with the University Press of New England, 1997.

Robertson, Michael. "Cultural Hegemony Goes to the Fair: The Case of E. L. Doctorow's *World's Fair*." *American Studies* 33 (Spring 1992): 31–44.

Rodgers, Daniel T. *Age of Fracture*. Cambridge, MA: Harvard University Press, 2011.

———. *Atlantic Crossings: Social Politics in a Progressive Age*. Cambridge, MA: Harvard University Press, 1998.

Rogers, Walter. *The Professional Practice of Landscape Architecture: A Complete Guide*. New York: Wiley, 1997.

Roosevelt, Franklin D. "As the President Sees It." In Oliver and Dudley, *New America*, 1–8.

———. *My Friends: Twenty-Eight History Making Speeches by Franklin Delano Roosevelt*. Edited by Edward H. Kavinoky and Julian Park. Buffalo, NY: Foster & Stewart, 1945.

———. *On Our Way*. New York: John Day, 1934.

———. *The Public Papers and Addresses of Franklin D. Roosevelt*. Vol. 2 and 5, New York: Random House, 1938; vol. 6, New York: Macmillan, 1941.

Roseman, Mark. "National Socialism and the End of Modernity." *American Historical Review* 116, no. 3 (June 2011): 688–701.

Ross, Dorothy. "American Modernities, Past and Present." *American Historical Review* 116, no. 3 (June 2011): 702–714.

Ross, Mary. "New Careers for Daughters." *Parents' Magazine*, November 1931, 14–15, 63–65.

Ross, Phyllis. *Gilbert Rohde: Modern Design for Modern Living*. New Haven, CT: Yale University Press, 2009.

Rossiter, Margaret W. *Women Scientists in America: Struggles and Strategies to 1940*. Baltimore, MD: Johns Hopkins University Press, 1982.

Russell, Beverly. *Women of Design: Contemporary American Interiors*. New York: Rizzoli, 1980.

Rutt, Anna Hong. *Home Furnishing*. New York: John Wiley & Sons, 1935, 1944.

Ryan, Alan. *John Dewey and the High Tide of American Liberalism*. New York: Norton, 1995.

Ryan, Mary. *Women in Public: Between Banners and Ballots, 1825–1880*. Baltimore, MD: Johns Hopkins University Press, 1990.

Rydell, Robert W. "Introduction: Making America (More) Modern: America's Depression-Era World's Fairs." In *Designing Tomorrow: America's World's Fairs of the 1930s*, edited by Robert W. Rydell and Laura Burd Schiavo. New Haven, CT: Yale University Press, 2010.

———. *World of Fairs: The Century of Progress Expositions*. Chicago: University of Chicago Press, 1993.

Rydell, Robert W., John E. Findling, and Kimberly D. Pelle, eds. *Fair America: World's Fairs in the United States*. Washington, DC: Smithsonian Institution Press, 2000.

Saler, Michael. "Modernity and Enchantment: A Historiographic Review." *American Historical Review* 111, no. 3 (June 2006): 692–716.

Sanborn, Pitts. "There's Music in the Air." *Scholastic*, January 11, 1936, 11–12.

Sandoz, Ellis. *Republicanism, Religion, and the Soul of America*. Columbia: University of Missouri Press, 2006.

"The San Francisco Fair." *Architectural Forum*, June 1939, 463–493.

Saunders, Kenneth. "What Is the Modern Mind?" *Saturday Review of Literature*, August 22, 1931, 65–67.

Scanlon, Jennifer. *Inarticulate Longings: The* Ladies Home Journal, *Gender, and the Promises of Consumer Culture*. New York: Routledge, 1995.

Schaller, Michael. *Right Turn: American Life in the Reagan-Bush Era, 1980–1992*. New York: Oxford University Press, 2007.

Schlesinger, Arthur M., Jr. *The Coming of the New Deal*. Boston: Houghton Mifflin, 1959.

———. *The Politics of Upheaval*. Boston: Houghton Mifflin, 1960.

Schultze, Quentin J. "Evangelical Radio and the Rise of the Electronic Church, 1921–1948." *Journal of Broadcasting and Electronic Media* 32 (Summer 1988): 289–306.

Scrattish, Nick. *Historic Resource Study: Cuyahoga Valley National Recreation Area*. Denver, CO: US Department of the Interior, National Park Service, 1985.

Seashore, C. E. "Psychology in Music: The Role of the Experimental Psychologist in the Science and Art of Music." *Musical Quarterly* 16 (April 1930): 229–237.

Seldes, Gilbert. *10 Years of Industrial Design, Henry Dreyfuss, 1929–1939 New York*. New York: Pynson, 1939.

Sessions, Elden B. "Educational Work of the Civilian Conservation Corps Camps in Ohio." Unpublished PhD diss., Ohio State University, 1937.

Shaw, Maurine. "Modern Economy." *Better Homes and Gardens*, May 1937, 55–60, 155.

Sinclair, Donna, and Richard McClure, eds. "No Goldbricking Here: Oral Histories of the CCC in the Columbia National Forest, 1933–1942." Heritage Program, Gifford Pinchot National Forest and History Department, Portland State University, August 2003. http://www.ccrh.org/oral/ccc%20book_all.pdf (accessed August 5, 2016).

Singal, Daniel J. "Film, Popular Entertainment, and the Melting Pot through the Lens of Modernist Culture." *Modern Intellectual History* 10 (2013): 489–501.

———. "Towards a Definition of American Modernism." *American Quarterly* 39, no. 1 (Spring 1987): 7–26.

Skidmore, Louis. "Planning the Exhibition Displays." *Architectural Record*, May 1933, 345.

Skinner, Dickson. "Music Goes into Mass Production." *Harper's*, December 1, 1938, 484–489.

Smail, Daniel Lord, and Andrew Shryock. "AHR Forum: History and the 'Pre,'" *American Historical Review* 118 (June 2013): 709–737.

Smith, Terry. *Making the Modern: Industry, Art, and Design in America*. Chicago: University of Chicago Press, 1993.

Smulyan, Susan. *Selling Radio: The Commercialization of American Broadcasting, 1920–1934*. Washington, DC: Smithsonian Institution Press, 1994.

Sokoloff, Nikolai. "America's Vast New Musical Awakening." *Etude*, April 1937, 221–222.

———. *The Federal Music Project*. Washington, DC: US Government Printing Office, 1936.

Souvenir of the 1936 Great Lakes Exposition. Cleveland, OH: Henry H. Hamm, 1936.

Sparke, Penny. "Elsie de Wolfe and Female Clients, 1905–15: Gender, Class and the Professional Interior Decorator." In Martin and Sparke, *Women's Places*, 47–68.

Stanfield, Peter. *Horse Opera: The Strange History of the 1930s Singing Cowboy*. Urbana: University of Illinois Press, 2002.

Starr, Kevin. *Endangered Dreams: The Great Depression in California*. New York: Oxford University Press, 1996.

Stetson, J. B. "Local Radio Stations Aid Teachers." *Musician*, October 1932, 15.

Stewart, Charles D. "A Beam from Arcturus." *Atlantic Monthly*, March 1933, 331–336.

Stewart, Herbert Leslie. *Modernism, Past and Present*. London: John Murray, 1932.

Stokowski, Leopold. "New Vistas in Radio." *Atlantic Monthly*, January 1935, 1–16.

Susman, Warren. "The People's Fair: Cultural Contradictions of a Consumer Society." In *Culture as History: The Transformation of American Society in the Twentieth Century*. New York: Pantheon, 1984.

Sutton, Matthew Avery. *American Apocalypse: A History of Modern Evangelicalism*. Cambridge, MA: Harvard University Press, 2014.

———. "Was FDR the Antichrist? The Birth of Fundamentalist Antiliberalism in a Global Age." *Journal of American History* 98 (March 2012): 1052–1074.

Suzik, Jeffrey Ryan. "Building Better Men: The CCC Boy and the Changing Social Ideal of Manliness." *Men and Masculinity* 2 (October 1999): 152–179.

Symes, Carol. "When We Talk about Modernity." *American Historical Review* 116, no. 3 (June 2011): 715–726.

Tate, Allen, and C. Ray Smith. *Interior Design in the 20th Century*. New York: Harper & Row, 1986.

Taylor, Nick. *American-Made: The Enduring Legacy of the WPA: When FDR Put the Nation to Work*. New York: Bantam, 2008.

"Technology as Hope." *Technology Review*, April 2005, 88.

Tenery, Mary L. "What Radio Offers Music Teachers." *Musician*, February 1937, 26–27.

The Tenth Youth. Washington, DC: US Government Printing Office, 1940.

Terhune, Florence B. *Decorating for You*. New York: M. Barrows, 1944.

Terzian, Sevan G. "The 1939–1940 New York World's Fair and the Transformation of the American Science Extracurriculum." *Science Education* 93 (September 2009): 892–914.

Thomas, Lynn M. "Modernity's Failings, Political Claims, and Intermediate Concepts." *American Historical Review* 116, no. 3 (June 2011): 727–740.

Thomson, Virgil. "America's Musical Maturity: A Twentieth Century Story." *Yale Review* 51 (1961): 66–71.

Tichi, Cecilia. *Shifting Gears: Technology, Literature, Culture*. Chapel Hill: University of North Carolina Press, 1987.

Tiersten, Lisa. "The Chic Interior and the Feminine Modern: Home Decorating as High Art in Turn-of-the-Century Paris." In Reed, *Not at Home*, 18–32.

Tigerman, Bobbye. "'I Am Not a Decorator': Florence Knoll, the Knoll Planning Unit and the Making of the Modern Office." *Journal of Design History* 20, no. 1 (2007): 61–74.

Tilford, William Roberts. "Swing! Swing! Swing! The Last Word in 'X Music.'" *Etude*, December 1937, 778.

"Tomorrow's Daughter." *Vogue*, February 1, 1939, 60.

Tribbe, Matthew D. *No Requiem for the Space Age: The Apollo Moon Landings and American Culture*. New York: Oxford University Press, 2014.

Trice, Allison N., and Charles H. Robertson. *Bible vs. Modernism: A Compendium of Sundry Critical Hypotheses and Their Refutation*. Nashville, TN: Rock City, 1935.

"Tropical Modern in California." *House and Garden*, September 1940, 42–43.

Ulanoc, Barry. "The Jukes Take Over Swing." *American Mercury* 51 (1940): 172–177.

"United States Department of Labor at the Century of Progress Exposition." *Monthly Labor Review* 37 (1933): 1086–1088.

Vacha, John. "Biggest Bash: Cleveland's Great Lakes Exposition." *Timeline* 13 (1996): 2–23.

———. *Meet Me on Lake Erie, Dearie: Cleveland's Great Lakes Exposition, 1936–1937*. Kent, OH: Kent State University Press, 2010.

Van Dusen, Henry P. "The Sickness of Liberal Religion." *World Tomorrow*, August 1931, 256–259.

Varney, Carleton. *In the Pink: Dorothy Draper: America's Most Fabulous Decorator*. New York: Pointed Leaf, 2006.

Virginia Kendall Reserve State Park Historic District, National Register of Historical Places Registration Form, US Department of the Interior, prepared by Jeffrey Winstel. National Park Service, 1995.

Walker, Helen M. *The CCC through the Eyes of 272 Boys: A Summary of a Group Study of the Reactions of 272 Cleveland Boys to Their Experience in the Civilian Conservation Corps*. Cleveland, OH: Western Reserve University Press, 1938.

Wall, Wendy L. *Inventing the "American Way": The Politics of Consensus from the New Deal to the Civil Rights Movement*. New York: Oxford University Press, 2008.

Walsh, William Thomas. "What Does 'Modern' Mean?" *Catholic World*, November 1930, 129–135.

"The Waning Belief in Heaven and Hell." *Literary Digest*, March 3, 1934, 20.

Ware, Shirley. "Give Your Career Background." *Independent Woman*, February 1940, 44–45.

Warren, Frederick. "A Special Technic for Singing in Broadcast Studios." *Musician*, December 1932, 13.

Weisman, Leslie Kanes. *Discrimination by Design: A Feminist Critique of the Man-Made Environment*. Urbana: University of Illinois Press, 1992.

Wendt, Gerald. *Science for the World of Tomorrow*. New York: Norton, 1939.

Wenger, Beth. "Synagogues and the 'Spiritual Depression' in the 1930s." In *Perspectives on American Religion and Culture*, edited by Peter W. Williams. New York: Blackwell, 1999. 124–139.

Whalen, Grover. "The World's Fair of New York." *L'Illustration*, July 1939, n.p.
"What Do the Women Think about Careers?" *Ladies' Home Journal*, November 1939, 12.
"What Price the Career Mother." *Independent Woman*, February 1937, 42–43.
Wheeler, Candace. "Interior Decoration as a Profession for Women." *Outlook*, April 9, 1899, 559.
Whiteman, Paul. "This Thing Called Jazz." *Rotarian*, June 1939, 34–36.
Wieman, Henry Nelson. "John Dewey's *Common Faith*." *Christian Century*, November 14, 1934, 1450–1452.
Wilk, Christopher, ed. *Modernism: Designing a New World, 1914–1939*. London: V&A Publishing, 2006.
Williams, Peter W. *America's Religions: From Their Origins to the Twenty-First Century*. Urbana: University of Illinois Press, 1990, 2008.
Williams, Raymond. *The Country and the City*. New York: Oxford University Press, 1973.
Williams, Rosalind. "Lewis Mumford's *Technics and Civilization*." *Technology and Culture* 43 (January 2002): 139–149.
Wills, Garry. *Head and Heart: American Christianities*. New York: Penguin, 2007.
Wilson, Bryan. "Secularization: The Inherited Model." In *The Sacred in a Secular Age: Toward Revisionism in the Scientific Study of Religion*, edited by Philip E. Hammond. Berkeley: University of California Press, 1985. 9–20.
Wilson, James. "Community, Civility, and Citizenship: Theatre and Indoctrination in the Civilian Conservation Corps of the 1930s." *Theatre History Studies* 23 (June 2003): 77–94.
Wilson, Kristina. *Livable Modernism: Interior Decorating and Design during the Great Depression*. New Haven, CT: Yale University Press, 2004.
Wilson, Richard Guy, Dianne H. Pilgrim, and Dickran Tashjian. *The Machine Age in America*. New York: Brooklyn Museum in association with Harry N. Abrams, 1986.
Winslow, W. Thacher. *Youth: A World Problem: A Study in World Perspective of Youth Conditions, Movements and Programs*. Washington, DC: US Government Printing Office, 1937.
Wirth, Conrad. *Civilian Conservation Corps Program of the United States Department of the Interior*, March 1933 to June 30, 1943, A report to Harold L. Ickes, Secretary of the Interior. Washington, DC: US Government Printing Office, January 1944.
"Wisconsin Tests Value of Radio in the Classroom: A Report by the Research Committee." *School Life*, February 1931, 104–105.
Wolfe, Tom. "The Me Decade and the Third Great Awakening." In *Mauve Gloves & Madmen, Clutter & Vine*. New York: Farrar, Straus & Giroux, 1976.

Wolin, Richard. "Modernity: The Peregrinations of a Contested Historiographical Concept." *American Historical Review* 116, no. 3 (June 2011): 741–751.

Workers' Handbook, WPA. Washington, DC: US Government Printing Office, 1936.

Young, William H., and Nancy K. Young. *Music of the Great Depression.* Westport, CT: Greenwood, 2005.

Zema, Demetrius. *The Thoughtlessness of Modern Thought: Concerning the Ideas of Civilization, Culture, Science, and Progress.* Fordham University Conferences, Fall Session, 1933. New York: Fordham University Press, 1934.

Zim, Larry, Mel Lerner, and Herbert Rolfe. *The World of Tomorrow: The 1939 New York World's Fair.* New York: Harper & Row, 1988.

INDEX

www.ingramcontent.com/pod-product-compliance
Ingram Content Group UK Ltd.
Pitfield, Milton Keynes, MK11 3LW, UK
UKHW041853031026
15587UKWH00006B/1206/J

9 780700 624003